THE DUALLY DIAGNOSED

A THERAPIST'S GUIDE TO HELPING THE SUBSTANCE ABUSING, PSYCHOLOGICALLY DISTURBED PATIENT

THE DUALLY DIAGNOSED

A THERAPIST'S GUIDE TO HELPING THE SUBSTANCE ABUSING, PSYCHOLOGICALLY DISTURBED PATIENT

THE DUALLY DIAGNOSED

A THERAPIST'S GUIDE TO HELPING THE SUBSTANCE ABUSING, PSYCHOLOGICALLY DISTURBED PATIENT

by

DENNIS C. ORTMAN, PH.D.

Jason Aronson Inc.
Northvale, New Jersey
London

Director of Editorial Production: Robert D. Hack

This book was set in 10 pt. Galliard by Alpha Graphics of Pittsfield, New Hampshire and printed and bound by Book-mart Press of North Bergen, New Jersey.

Library of Congress Cataloging-in-Publication Data

Ortman, Dennis C.
    The dually diagnosed : a therapist's guide to helping the substance abusing, psychologically disturbed patient / by Dennis C. Ortman.
        p. cm.
    Includes bibliographical references and index.
    ISBN 1-56821-770-6 (alk. paper)
    1. Dual diagnosis—Treatment. I. Title.
    [DNLM: 1. Substance Dependence—therapy. 2. Diagnosis, Dual (Psychiatry) 3. Mental Disorders—therapy. 4. Psychotherapy—methods. WM 270 077d 1997]
    RC564.68.O775 1997
    DNLM/DLC
    for Library of Congress   96-29280

Printed in the United States of America on acid-free paper. For information and catalog write to Jason Aronson Inc., 230 Livingston Street, Northvale, New Jersey 07647. Or visit our website: http://www.aronson.com

In Memory of
Jane Skorina,
Dolores Nieratka,
and
Bernard Mikol,
both teachers
and inspirers

CONTENTS

Part III: Inpatient Treatment

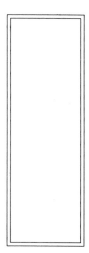

PREFACE

My own clinical experience gave birth to this study on the treatment of dually diagnosed patients. I remember vividly my frustration in working with one particular patient who made me aware of my need to explore this issue, although at the time, I did not label her a dual diagnosis patient.

Carol, a young woman in her thirties, came to the University Clinic at the recommendation of another therapist because her insurance benefits had expired. She had been seeing a psychiatrist for two years because of difficulties she experienced during her divorce and the initiation of a malpractice suit against a physician. In the first session, she said she was unsure about what she was looking for in therapy and described a series of relationships with older men with whom she became involved sexually. After a period of time, each of these relationships ended with her being rejected. She said that she felt lonely and depressed and did not understand why all of these relationships failed. In subsequent sessions, she related a troubled childhood. Her father had abandoned the family when she was an infant. Her mother had difficulty raising her six children alone and was hospitalized for depression for over a year. During her hospitalization, her children lived in various foster homes.

In the second session, Carol admitted using marijuana. She claimed she had smoked off and on since adolescence and that now she was experiencing so much stress, she smoked to relax. She de-

scribed going into the bathroom when she felt depressed and light-
ing up a joint. She would put a towel under the door to keep the smoke
from going into her apartment and alerting her three young children.

Carol reported that her previous therapist, who was psychodynamic in orientation, regularly interpreted to her that her drug use
was merely a symptom of other problems. I too interpreted her drug
use as a manifestation of an underlying conflict that, I believed, once
resolved, would result in a decreased need to smoke and eventually
end in abstinence. In light of her deprived childhood, I suspected that
her drug use was a way of covering up painful affects and of seeking
oral gratification. During our sessions, I invited her to free associate
and attempted to respond empathically and interpret her conflicts,
just as I had been taught to do. I did not inquire specifically about
her drug use, but explored its meaning when she brought up the issue.

One day, about four months into the treatment, she revealed that
she had come to several sessions "stoned." I was shocked that I did
not recognize it; however, I had at times noticed that her thinking
seemed confused and that I had had a difficult time following her
reports during the sessions. She seemed to contradict herself repeatedly. She said that using drugs before sessions helped her to relax and
speak more freely, as I had requested. I wondered how effective my
work had been with her up to that point and knew that, for the treatment to progress, I had to address more directly her use of marijuana.

I consulted with my supervisor about how to work with this patient, and he encouraged me to continue interpreting to her her drug
use as a means of avoiding painful affects. He admitted that in nearly
forty years of clinical work he had not treated an addicted person. He
said that while working in a hospital setting for several years he referred patients with substance abuse problems to the medical staff.
In his private practice, he said, people with drug problems simply did
not come to him for treatment. The reason, he believed, was that his
therapeutic method did not produce quick results and that those who
abuse drugs want instant gratification and avoid therapists who work
psychoanalytically, as he did.

I realized I was facing a therapeutic dilemma and had several
options. First, I could continue to treat Carol's depression with the
therapeutic methods I had been taught in my clinical psychology

program, which focused on interpreting the dynamics of her conflicts. Yet, I was not convinced that her drug use would disappear, since she continued to use drugs after more than two years of treatment with her previous therapist. Secondly, I could continue to treat her depression and refer her to someone else to address her drug problem. However, it seemed to me that that would fragment the treatment. Thirdly, I could refuse to see her until she became drug free and refer her to a substance abuse specialist. If I made the referral, I was not sure she would follow through, and the opportunity to help her would be lost. Finally, I could attempt to address both her psychiatric and substance use disorders in therapy. Because I was trained in a clinical psychology program that offered only one elective substance abuse course, this last option meant that I would have to learn about substance abuse treatment on my own. I would then have to alter my usual therapeutic approach and attempt to integrate two very different treatment methods, the one for treating addictions and the other for treating psychological problems. I chose this last option and undertook the personal investigations that have resulted in this book.

I began by trying to read as much as I could about the treatment of patients with both substance abuse and psychiatric problems, but discovered that nearly all the literature was concerned with the treatment of the mentally ill substance abuser, usually in an inpatient or intensive outpatient setting. There was practically nothing in print that focused on treating the less severely impaired dually diagnosed client normally found in the outpatient setting. I decided to undertake my own study of how experienced outpatient therapists treat their dually diagnosed patients. Not surprisingly, I could find very few therapists who claimed extensive experience in working with this population. Fortunately, those I found were pleased to share their experiences and insights, describing what they do with these patients and why they do it. The result of this inquiry was my dissertation, entitled *An Exploratory Study: How Therapists Treat Patients with Coexisting Substance Use and Psychiatric Disorders in Outpatient Individual Therapy.*

I have written this book as a contribution to the continuing dialogue on how to treat these dually diagnosed patients who present themselves in outpatient settings, a topic that has been significantly neglected in the literature. However, with the present cost-saving restrictions mandated by managed care, a greater emphasis is now being placed on the treatment of these patients, even the more seriously ill, in the outpatient setting. Clinicians are encountering an increasing number and a broader spectrum of these difficult patients. Many may feel ill-prepared to address the needs of these patients because their training has focused on the treatment of either the psychiatric or the substance abuse problem, but not on the integrated treatment of both disorders.

The Dually Diagnosed is intended to be a practical book—a sort of treatment guide for therapists. It is divided into three parts. In Part I, the introduction, some basic notions and a summary of the literature are presented. Chapter 1 sketches out the dual diagnosis problem and the continuing dialogue toward a solution. The second chapter describes the type of patients found in the outpatient setting and the therapeutic dilemmas they pose. The third chapter presents different views on the interaction of the disorders along with their implications for treatment. Chapter 4 focuses on how and why therapists must modify their therapeutic techniques in treating this population.

In Part II, each chapter addresses a specific clinical decision-making issue regarding the treatment of the dually diagnosed, and presents ideas and practical approaches for addressing the issue. Each of Chapters 5 through 15 responds to an urgent clinical question. Which disorder needs to be addressed first, and why? How do you assess for both the substance use and psychiatric disorders and overcome the many complications involved in the interaction of the disorders? How do you address the patient's denial regarding his drug use and mental illness? How do you determine if the patient needs to be referred to another setting or another specialist and what criteria can be used to make this decision? What is the value of prescription medication for this population? What are the advantages, limits, and strategies for involving the dually diagnosed in twelve step programs? How insistent should the therapist be about abstinence? How should the therapist respond to relapses? How and to what extent do you involve the family in treatment? Is it ever necessary to terminate treatment with the resistant client and under what circumstances may this occur? How do you measure success in working with this population?

The final section, Part III, is devoted to the treatment of the dually diagnosed in an inpatient setting. How the inpatient and outpatient settings relate to each other in the treatment of the dually diagnosed is also discussed. The book concludes with an Epilogue which reviews the sixteen treatment principles elaborated throughout the text.

In preparing and writing this book, I have followed the advice of no less an astute observer of human nature than Sigmund Freud (1914) who recommended: "I learnt to restrain speculative tendencies and to follow the unforgotten advice of my master, Charcot: To look at the same thing again and again until they themselves begin to speak." First of all, I listened to my patients, who told me in many persistent ways what help they needed from me. They told me of their pain in struggling with emotional and mental problems, with drugs and alcohol, and how treatment relieved this pain. Secondly, I listened to my colleagues, who described to me in detail their experiences in working with their dual diagnosis patients and their strategies and techniques developed through many years of trial and error. I paid close attention to those who have listened attentively and perceptively to their patients and reflected deeply on what they learned. Finally, I became a student of the increasing number of clinicians and researchers who have written about their work with the dually diagnosed. In this book, I have attempted to integrate the insights I have gained in my own clinical work and in listening attentively to the experience of others. I offer these reflections as a contribution to the ongoing dialogue among clinicians about how best to treat this increasingly large and underserved patient population.

My expectation is that this book will be useful to therapists who work in both the mental health and substance abuse fields. Even though I am writing from the perspective of a psychologist employed in the mental health field, I believe these treatment principles, strategies, and techniques are applicable to treating dual diagnosis patients in any setting and can be helpful for both addiction and non-addiction professionals, and for the training of clinicians in the addiction and mental health fields. Psychiatrists, social workers, nurses, psychologists, counselors, and substance abuse specialists increasingly encounter patients in their work settings who present with either a mental health or substance abuse problem, but in reality have a comorbid condition. These clinicians may welcome the insights and suggestions offered in this book.

I also have a larger hope for this book. The clarion call to treat the dually diagnosed has gone out to professionals in both the mental health and substance abuse fields. Professionals in these fields have worked in isolation, treating either the substance use or psychiatric disorder of their patients. Yet the ever mounting number of treatment failures of these patients, who are now coming to be identified as dually diagnosed, has caused clinicians to rethink their treatment models. These clinicians are learning that to work effectively with these patients they must address both disorders in an integrated fashion; they are becoming painfully aware of their lack of training to do so. In the quest to become better clinicians, they are looking for guidance from fellow professionals in other service fields. The call to treat the dual diagnosis patient has begun to crack the walls that have separated the various specialties. Professionals in both the substance abuse and mental health treatment communities are beginning to talk with one another and work together to find ways of treating more effectively these difficult patients. My hope is that this book will help further the dialogue among these professionals so that the dual diagnosis patients we encounter will be better served.

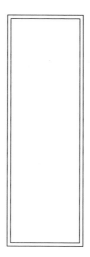

ACKNOWLEDGMENTS

Although this book is attributed to a single author, who bears full responsibility for its content, it is the fruit of a cooperative effort. The work could not have been accomplished without the encouragement, support, and insights of many people.

First of all, I am indebted to those who first stimulated my interest in researching the treatment of the dually diagnosed and guided my initial study: Drs. Bernard Green, John Franklin, Dolores Nieratka, and Gerald Wehmer. They offered me invaluable advice, challenged me to clarify my thinking, and encouraged me to persevere in my work.

I am also grateful to my therapist colleagues who generously shared their time and insights. Drs. Judith Kovach, Jane Skorina, Michael Abramsky, Terrance Filter, Howard Moore, Barry Mintzes, John Franklin, Clifford Furgison, and Mitchell Solomon have worked for many years with the dually diagnosed and succeeded in creating innovative treatment models by integrating approaches from the mental health and substance abuse fields. Not only did they unhesitatingly share their wisdom, but they modelled what it means to be a wise and compassionate therapist with this most challenging patient.

I would like to thank Bob Hack, my production editor, and the staff of Jason Aronson for their helpful suggestions and guidance through the publishing process.

Most of all, I want to thank my family who sacrificed without complaint while I was preoccupied with completing this work. Nicole, Jackie, and David patiently accepted my many retreats to the computer room. My wife, Fran, as always, was my greatest support and most insightful critic through the several drafts of this study. Without her steadfast love, I would not have been able to complete this project.

I

BASIC NOTIONS

THE ONGOING DIALOGUE: INTRODUCTION

THE DUAL DIAGNOSIS PROBLEM

In the last decade, there have been reports of an ongoing crisis in the mental health care service field where a new population of problem patients is emerging: those with coexisting psychiatric and substance use disorders. Clinicians in the mental health field feel competent to address the psychiatric problems of these clients, but are at a loss as to how to deal with the addiction problems. Therapists in the substance abuse field confront the addiction, but are reluctant to address the psychiatric difficulties. Tragically, those with a dual diagnosis are shuttled between various service agencies that each address a portion of their problem, resulting in a sort of "Ping-Pong" therapy. Or worse, these difficult patients are ignored and deemed untreatable. Those clinicians with the courage to address both issues in the clients they serve proceed by trial and error, since no coherent and empirically validated treatment model exists for these patients.

Prevalence of the Dually Diagnosed

The experience of therapists in practically every clinical setting as well as the reports of an increasing number of researchers testify to the prevalence of individuals with coexisting substance use and psychiatric disorders. As early as the 1970s, researchers such as Bert Pepper and colleagues (1981) and Leona Bachrach (1982) identified a group of patients that they called "young adult chronic patients." This group of patients, members of the "baby boom" generation born between 1946 and 1961, represents a particular challenge to health service systems, they claimed. The patients they described were predominantly male, frequently schizophrenic, noncompliant with treatment, aggressive, impulsive, and clinically diverse. A complicating factor in both their illness and treatment was the fact that a large percentage of them were also substance abusers. These "problem patients," who had severe difficulties in social functioning and a high rate of recidivism, were recognized by clinicians as flooding the mental health services system. Bachrach (1982) proposed that the confluence of two primary forces, deinstitutionalization policies and demographic factors, has resulted in the increase of their numbers. Previously, most individuals with chronic mental disorders were admitted to state hospitals where they remained for life. Today, these patients are served by many different agencies within the community and are stabilized by psychotropic medication. From a demographic standpoint, those of the "baby boom" generation are nearly a third of the nation's population. This large group of potential patients is exceedingly mobile and floods the various service agencies. Furthermore, this population was exposed to the drug culture of the 1960s, and many experimented with different types of drugs. Drug use is more acceptable to them than to those of an older generation, and consequently, there is a higher rate of substance abuse in this age group.

The groundbreaking work of these researchers has opened the door to further investigations into a newly recognized group of individuals now labeled "dually diagnosed" patients, that is, those with a coexisting psychiatric and substance use disorder. Several studies highlight the magnitude of the dual diagnosis problem. The literature review of Way and McCormick (1990) discovered that the reported prevalence rates of the mentally ill who abuse substances ranges from 7% to over 60%. The most comprehensive investigation to date of the prevalence of mental illness and substance use disorders in the United States is that of the National Institute of Mental Health's Epidemiologic Catchment Area Study (Regier et al. 1990). In this research project, 20,291 subjects in five cities were interviewed from 1980 to 1984. The results indicated that lifetime prevalence rates for psychiatric disorders alone were 22.5%, for alcohol use disorders, 13.5%, and for other drug use disorders, 6.1%. Twenty-nine percent of those who have ever had a mental disorder have also had a diagnosable alcohol and/or drug abuse problem during their lives, an odds ratio 2.7 times higher than the general population. Fifty-three percent of those who have ever had a substance use disorder have also had one or more psychiatric disorders, an odds ratio 4.5 times higher than the general population. Among patients with a treatment history in a specialty mental health or addictive disorder program, based on a six-month prevalence rate, the researchers found the comorbidity of alcohol use disorders and mental illness was 56%. For other drugs, the comorbidity rate was 64.4%. The lifetime prevalence rate for a dual diagnosis among those in institutional settings is more than twice that found in the community at large. Mental hospitals have the highest rate (82.2%), followed by prisons (82.0%) and nursing homes (65.5%). When looking at the lifetime prevalence rate of substance use disorders with specific psychiatric diagnoses, the researchers found that those with schizophrenia had a lifetime comorbidity of 47%, with antisocial personality disorder (83.6%), with any anxiety disorder (23.7%), with panic disorders (35.8%), with obsessive compulsive disorders (32.8%), with affective disorders (32.0%), and with bipolar disorders (60.7%).

Zimberg (1993) believes these prevalence rates are probably an underestimation of the numbers of the dually diagnosed because of the high degree of denial of alcoholism and drug abuse. The study relied on the self-reports of those interviewed. There were no data from significant others, and no urine drug screens were done. Furthermore, symptoms such as hallucinations, depression, delirium, and anxiety, which are often associated with substance abuse, were not rated positive (for a comorbid psychiatric condition) if found only in the presence of alcohol or other drug disorders.

A more recent large scale National Comorbidity Study of over 8,000 adults in noninstitutional settings (Kessler et al. 1994) reported that nearly 50% of those interviewed had at least one lifetime psychiatric disorder, and almost 30% reported a disorder within the past year. Furthermore, more than half of all lifetime disorders occurred in the 14% of the population that had a history of three or more comorbid conditions. Although the rates of coexisting substance use and psychiatric disorders were not specified in the study, the researchers observed that the most common psychiatric disorders were major depression and alcohol dependence. Consistent with other studies in the literature, these researchers found that women had elevated rates of affective and anxiety disorders, that men had elevated rates of substance use disorders and antisocial personality disorder, and that most disorders declined with age and higher socioeconomic status. In a further analysis of the data concerning drug use and dependence (excluding alcohol), Warner et al. (1995) reported that 51 percent of the respondents used an illegal drug at some time in their lives, and 15.4% admitted doing so in the past 12 months. Of those interviewed, 7.5% had been drug dependent at some time in their lives, and 1.8% had been dependent in the past 12 months. These figures indicate clearly the magnitude of the dual diagnosis population in this country.

In a recent workshop, Pepper reported an interesting fact regarding the shifting settings in which the dually diagnosed are found. Since the early 1970s, there has been a 700% increase in jail and prison cells nationwide. Whereas in 1972 there were 196,000 cells, today there are approximately 1.4 million. At the same time, in the past 30 years, the population of psychiatric institutions has been reduced from 550,000 to 100,000. An estimated 80% of those in the prison population can be diagnosed as having a personality disorder and/or mental illness, most commonly antisocial personality, schizophrenia, and bipolar disorders. An estimated 92% of these individuals also have substance abuse problems. Clearly, the largest congregation of the dually diagnosed today reside in correctional institutions, rather than mental health facilities.

Some Treatment Difficulties

However, the sheer numbers alone of the dually diagnosed does not constitute the problem. Several factors contribute to making the dual diagnosis patient difficult to treat. First of all, because of the complicated interactions of substance use and psychiatric disorders, these patients are more vulnerable to relapsing into their illnesses, making them a particularly unstable group. Bouts of drinking or drug use inevitably lead to an exacerbation of psychiatric symptoms, and the return of disturbing emotional or mental problems often progresses into a relapse to substance use for self-medication. Several studies portray the unstable characteristics of this population. For example, in a study comparing substance abusing and non-substance-abusing psychiatric patients, Kay and colleagues (1989) reported that the substance abusers tended to be more suicidal, homicidal, destructive, and irresponsible than controls. In their study of 187 chronic mentally ill patients living in the community, Drake and Wallach (1989) identified features that distinguished dual diagnosis patients. The mentally ill substance abusers are less able to care for themselves, more vulnerable to homelessness, less compliant with medications, more vulnerable to rehospitalization, and more difficult to diagnose than non-abusing patients. They often come to emergency rooms for service and do not follow through with treatment. Bachrach (1982) noted that the dually diagnosed are problem patients who are socially unresponsive, hostile, demanding, manipulative, and socially acting out individuals.

Secondly, caregivers have particular difficulties in treating these clients. Practitioners are trained either in the mental health field to work with patients suffering from psychiatric disorders or in the substance abuse field to work with alcoholics or addicts. Most clinicians feel incompetent to diagnose or treat both disorders in these patients. Furthermore, the dual diagnosis patient tends to evoke negative countertransference reactions in therapists. Therapists may react to these often hostile, demanding, manipulative, and acting out clients with a negative and rejecting attitude. Also, these patients are particularly difficult to diagnose accurately because the use of the substance may disguise and mimic other psychopathologies, and conversely, psychiatric symptoms may hide a drug problem. The true nature of the disorders takes time to manifest itself. These patients need to be carefully assessed for both substance use and psychiatric disorders and observed over a period of time. Unfortunately, the caregiver may not have the needed time to make an accurate diagnosis within the constraints of time limited therapy mandated by our present managed care system. There are also difficulties in medicating these patients. Any prescribed medication may cause complications because of the drug interactions between psychotropics and street drugs and alcohol and the tendency of these patients to abuse medications. These patients are also notoriously noncompliant in taking their medications, preferring to self-medicate themselves with their drug of choice.

Contrasting Treatment Models

Thirdly, one of the greatest difficulties in treating this population is not merely the lack of tested treatment models, but the history of antagonism and competition between those who work in the mental health and substance abuse fields. Separate cultures, traditions, philosophies, views of the etiology and relationship of the disorders, and administrative systems have developed in the different fields of service. As a result, there have been few cooperative efforts to develop effective strategies for addressing both disorders and integrated treatment models. Laura Schmidt (1991) interviewed therapists in eighteen alcohol and mental health residential agencies to understand their treatment philosophies. She discovered differences in etiological models, therapeutic techniques, and roles of treatment providers and clients in the two different types of services. She found that alcoholism treatment providers considered alcoholism to be a primary disease in which psychological symptoms were consequences of the underlying chemical dependency. In contrast, mental health therapists treated substance abuse as a symptom of an underlying mental disorder. Alcoholism therapists held abstinence to be the primary goal of treatment and used techniques to confront the client's denial system. Mental health therapists aimed at psychological health, tolerated controlled drinking, and used more supportive techniques. The substance abuse specialists insisted on a greater degree of client motivation during the screening than the psychotherapists. Alcoholism therapists, who were often recovering addicts, shared their experiences with their clients and clearly identified with them. Mental health members tended to have academic degrees, assume an expert role with their clients, and maintain a professional distance. Furthermore, others have observed that addiction therapists are suspicious of the use of any mood- or mind-altering drugs, while mental health professionals recognize the need for prescribing medications for many psychiatric disorders.

Different treatment models predominate in the fields of substance abuse and mental health. Brower and colleagues (1989) note that several basic models of chemical dependency are used by substance abuse clinicians. They classify these chemical dependency treatment models as moral, learning, disease, self-medication, and social. These authors further suggest that those in the addiction field are most influenced by the disease recovery model that has grown out of the experience with Alcoholics Anonymous (AA Service Center 1976). According to this model, substance abuse is a primary, chronic, progressive, and fatal disease that follows identifiable stages (Jellinek 1952, 1960). There is no known cure for the disease. It can only be arrested by complete abstinence. Other psychiatric symptoms are viewed as consequences of the addiction disease process and can be addressed only after abstinence has been achieved. The major treatment strategy is to maintain abstinence by identifying oneself as an addict, admitting one's powerlessness over substances, learning new behaviors to substitute for drug use, and developing a nondrinking social network.

In the mental health field, there are many treatment models such as the psychoanalytic, cognitive, social learning, and behavioral models, which arise from different assumptions about human nature. Clinicians, in general, subscribe to the biopsychosocial model of psychiatric disorders, which attempts to integrate the insights of the above models (Engel 1977, Evans and Sullivan 1990). According to this integrative model, various psychiatric disorders have different combinations of biological, psychological, and social factors that contribute to their etiology and progression. An adequate assessment of an individual for treatment requires that all these factors be considered. The fundamental treatment strategy is to address in a combined and comprehensive fashion the factors that contribute to the disease process. Substance abuse is often viewed, from this perspective, as an attempt by the patient to medicate himself from the discomfort caused by the psychiatric disturbance (Bell and Khantzian 1991). Consistent with this model, clinicians may also emphasize biological, psychological, or social factors in their treatment approaches according to their preferred therapeutic philosophies.

In summary, the dual diagnosis problem consists of:

1. The increasing number of people with coexisting substance use and psychiatric disorders;
2. The vulnerability of these patients to relapse into both disorders;
3. The difficulties caregivers have in treating them; and
4. The lack of adequate integrated treatment models addressing both disorders.

As a result of these complications, those with coexisting substance use and psychiatric disorders remain inadequately treated or untreated altogether. The most severe cases frequently end up in prison or homeless on the streets, outside the reaches of our health care systems.

THE DIALOGUE TOWARD A SOLUTION

Defining the Population

The growing volume of literature on the treatment of dually disordered patients is often confusing and contradictory, in part because of the lack of consensus on the definition of "dual diagnosis." The term "dual diagnosis" refers most generally to any person with two diagnosed disorders. In the common usage among mental health professionals, it refers to anyone with multiple diagnosable conditions. Using the multiaxial system of the *DSM-IV*, these patients may have several Axis I diagnoses or multiple diagnoses across several different Axes. In the recent past, this term was applied particularly to individuals who were mentally retarded and suffered a psychiatric disorder. Today, the term refers typically to those who have coexisting substance use and psychiatric disorders. As is frequently the case, these individuals may abuse several different substances and have more than one psychiatric diagnosis and still be classified as dually diagnosed.

Clinicians and researchers agree that the dual diagnosis population is heterogeneous and difficult to define. In their review of the literature, Ridgely and colleagues (1986) note the problem of defining this population and the impact of the varieties of definitions on research and treatment. Osher (1989) provides a useful classification of dually diagnosed patients. He distinguishes three subgroups that can be visually represented by the overlapping of two circles. One circle represents psychiatric disorders, the other, substance use disorders. One group consists of patients with a primary psychiatric diagnosis, whose symptoms are exacerbated by the use of psychoactive drugs. A second group includes those with a primary substance use disorder, which is causally related to the psychiatric disturbance. Some observers call this group the "chemically abusing mentally ill" (CAMI) or "mentally ill chemical abusers" (MICA), if the psychiatric disorder is severe. The third group, represented in the area of overlap of the two circles, is composed of those with two separate illnesses, which have different etiologies and exacerbate each other.

The definition of dual diagnosis is complicated by the fact that *substance use disorder* and *psychiatric disorder* are not univocal terms and are each variously defined. Each can be represented on a continuum of increasing severity of dysfunction. According to one researcher (Richards 1993), the levels of the addictive processes range in increasing severity from the rational use of substances to controlled appropriate use to insidious dependence to one-trial dependence to substance abuse to symptomatic dependence to compulsive accelerating addiction to psychotic addiction. Definitions of substance use disorders vary from distinctions based on the presence or absence of physiological dependence to constructs relying on legal, social, occupational, or psychological problems to definitions based on the quantity, frequency, or intensity of use (Rounsaville et al. 1986). The description and definition of problematic drug use is further complicated by there being different classes of drugs: stimulants, sedative-hypnotics, narcotic-analgesics, hallucinogens, and psychiatric medications. Each class of drugs produces different effects in individuals who use them in idiosyncratic patterns. For example, some use their drugs of choice daily, while others binge episodically; the routes of administration also vary. Increasingly today, people abuse several different kinds of drugs simultaneously.

Mental illness is an analogous term, referring to a broad range of symptoms and dysfunction. According to one formulation, the severity of psychopathology ranges from stress and adjustment reactions to neurotic to narcissistic to borderline to psychotic to florid psychotic (Richards 1993). Definitions of psychopathology are variously defined by categorically based disease concepts, dimensionally based trait constructs, or clinically derived formulations (Meyer 1986). Furthermore, as with polysubstance abusers, individuals may be suffering from several psychiatric disorders simultaneously.

In its most general conceptualization as the comorbidity of psychiatric and substance use disorders, dual diagnosis can refer to almost innumerable combinations of both disorders with varying degrees of severity. For example, a schizophrenic who abuses cocaine regularly and a person suffering from dysthymia and infrequent binge drinking are both classified as dual diagnosis patients.

An overview of the dual diagnosis treatment literature reveals a bias towards considering the true dual diagnosis patient as the one who suffers both a serious mental illness and a full-blown addiction. As a consequence, practically all the treatment models described by these clinicians and researchers focus on the inpatient treatment and followup of this most difficult patient. Furthermore, it appears that a majority of those who write about treating dual diagnosis patients are physicians/psychiatrists whose experience is primarily working with these most disturbed patients.

I prefer to define the dual diagnosis patient in the more general sense of anyone who has a coexisting substance use and psychiatric disorder, regardless of the severity of either disorder. Admittedly, there are identifiable subgroups within this population that have different treatment needs, as will be described later. It is a disservice to the less seriously disturbed substance abuser to not recognize his unique treatment needs. More connects than separates that large group of individuals who both suffer emotional/mental problems and abuse substances. As the two disorders progress, no matter the initial severity, they will interact and exacerbate each other. Consequently, both disorders must be treated in an integrated manner for a full recovery of the whole person.

A Case Example

The following vignette illustrates the necessity of addressing both disorders for the treatment to progress.

A 43-year-old divorced woman, Rita, was referred to me by another therapist. This therapist had been treating her for a longstanding depression for a year and felt that the treatment had reached a standstill. Rita was one of twelve children and had grown up in a household in which both parents drank heavily. She had always felt ignored as a child and continued to feel like an outsider in her family. She had had two unsuccessful marriages to alcoholic men and was engaged to a man who drank heavily. I inquired about her own drinking and drug use and discovered that she had two or three drinks every day to relax. Sometimes she drank to intoxication with her fiance. Her previous therapist had neglected to inquire about her drinking. Because Rita had complained so vociferously about how much trouble the drinking of others had caused her, it had never occurred to her therapist that Rita might have a drinking problem herself. I proceeded to make a contract with Rita not to drink while in treatment. I also educated her about how the drinking would interfere with the treatment and deepen her depression. As the treatment progressed, we discussed how she was using alcohol to cope with disturbing feelings. She began to talk more freely about her painful feelings of abandonment, her unmet needs in relationships, and her tendency to withdraw in anger from others to protect herself. Once she had stopped drinking, her paralyzing depression began to lift, and she began to confront her problems honestly.

Some Emerging Treatment Models

As mentioned above, the majority of the writings about the treatment of the dually diagnosed concerns the severely mentally ill in inpatient settings. In the literature, several clinicians describe their programs, reflect on what they have learned, and suggest principles of programming for dual diagnosis treatment. For example, Ridgely and colleagues (1987) surveyed and visited eleven dual diagnosis programs to discern the critical components of treatment programming. They identified common problems and efforts in the process of engagement, assessment, concomitant treatment, the measurement of outcome, and service system changes. Minkoff (1989, 1992) describes an integrated treatment model that he helped develop at the Caulfield Center, a psychiatric unit near Boston. He proposes that the addiction model for substance abuse and the biopsychosocial model for mental illness have parallel concepts of illness and recovery that lend themselves to forming an integrated model of treatment for dual diagnosis patients. He distinguishes two phases of treatment that require different therapeutic efforts: a phase of acute stabilization and a phase of ongoing stabilization and rehabilitation. Osher and Kofoed (1989) agree with Minkoff that an integration of models is necessary and that different phases of treatment with different therapeutic tasks must be identified; however, these authors distinguish phases of engagement, persuasion, active treatment, and relapse prevention.

Much less is written about the treatment of dual diagnosis clients in outpatient settings. Even the few studies that have been conducted are concerned with the treatment of the severely mentally ill. Hanson and colleagues (1990) describe an abstinence-oriented day treatment program designed to address the specific needs of a dually disordered population with serious mental illness. They report that this group is able to be actively engaged with a supportive, low-demand treatment that addresses both disorders. An examination of the six-month and one-year treatment statuses of 118 patient participants revealed that a significant number responded favorably to a treatment matched to their needs; favorable outcome was correlated with the degree of active participation. Experience with an outpatient pilot program for the dually diagnosed with severe psychiatric illnesses taught Kofoed and his colleagues (1986) that a unified team approach treating both disorders under one roof is superior to concurrent treatment of each disorder in separate settings. Although many patients dropped out of the program, treatment retention was associated with reduced hospital utilization.

Individual Therapy with Substance Abusers

In the outpatient setting, individual therapy is typically the treatment of choice. However, there has been a long-standing controversy in the substance abuse field regarding the effectiveness of individual therapy with alcoholics and addicts. Patients in programs dominated by the twelve step approach are often told to postpone therapy for a year. This recommendation is based on the negative experiences of many recovering persons with conventionally trained mental health therapists, who tend to ignore the substance abuse problem and increase anxiety by exploring sensitive issues, which leads to an increase in drug use. However, Chad Emrick (1982) reviewed studies from 1952 to 1981 in which some form of psychologically oriented treatment of alcohol abuse was evaluated and concluded that such treatment is effective in improving client's drinking behavior. Treated patients tend to be more abstinent, drink less frequently, and drink with fewer resulting problems. No one specific therapeutic approach was found to be consistently more effective than any other.

Several more recent studies evaluated the effectiveness of individual therapy with this population. In a study conducted at the Philadelphia Veterans Administration Medical Center, a group of researchers investigated the effects of psychotherapy on methadone-maintained opiate addicts. One hundred-and-ten subjects were divided into three treatment groups. One group received drug counseling alone; another, counseling plus supportive-expressive psychotherapy; and a third group received both counseling and cognitive behavioral therapy. These researchers found that all three groups showed significant improvement, but that those patients who received the additional psychotherapies showed greater improvement with less use of medication (Woody et al. 1983). In contrast, a study conducted at the New Haven Methadone Maintenance Program to evaluate the effectiveness of short-term interpersonal psychotherapy for opiate addicts found no significant difference in outcome between groups treated with weekly individual psychotherapy and with monthly low-contact treatment. Several problems surfaced. The patients in both groups were difficult to engage in treatment, dropped out early, and quickly returned to drug use (Rounsaville et al. 1983). However, Carroll and colleagues (1991) compared the effectiveness of relapse prevention and interpersonal psychotherapy with cocaine abusers and found that all the treated subjects showed significant improvement in maintaining abstinence. Among more severe users, subjects who received relapse prevention treatment were significantly more likely to achieve abstinence than those who did not.

Modification of Techniques

Therapists recognize that in doing psychotherapy with addicted individuals they must alter their usual therapeutic techniques. Traditional therapeutic models and techniques appear to be inadequate with this population. Several authors describe, from their own experience, the modifications that need to be made. For example, Baranackie and colleagues (1992) examined the techniques used by eight cognitive-behavioral therapists during the treatment of opiate-dependent patients. The researchers were surprised to find that, contrary to some standardized treatment for working with this population, behavioral techniques were rarely used during the early phase of treatment and remained at a low level throughout treatment. These authors surmise that the denial and mistrust of these patients prevented the effective use of standard techniques.

Working from a psychoanalytic perspective, Wurmser (1984) cautions that clinicians must be "mainly therapists and neither policemen nor guards," and must employ tact, benevolence, and understanding rather than confrontation and intrusion. He observes a similar pathological dynamic in both severe neurosis and compulsive drug use and alters his therapeutic techniques accordingly. Wurmser (1987) recommends that a combination of methods be employed in treating the drug abuser. The vertical approach of analysis must be complemented by a horizontal, behavioral approach in which the therapist makes suggestions to his patient and recommends participation in Alcoholics Anonymous and the use of Antabuse and antidepressants.

Also working from a psychoanalytic perspective, Resnick and Resnick (1984) recommend that in the treatment of cocaine addicts the first goal must be to stop all use of cocaine. The use of self-help groups and medication is encouraged. Cognitive-behavioral methods are used, including contingency contracts, regular urinalysis, and cognitive relabeling. Through psychoanalytic exploration, the therapist also helps the patient recognize how cocaine use is an attempt to soothe the despair and rage from early developmental deprivations.

Khantzian (1980, 1981, 1985a, 1986) suggests that in the initial stages of treatment the therapist must assume multiple roles, similar to a primary care physician who attends to many of his patients' needs. He must concern himself with the issues of safety, stabilization, and control, making arrangements for medical care and supporting pharmacological treatments and involvement in twelve step programs. The therapist needs to keep the focus on the control of drinking without demanding abstinence prematurely and without accepting uncontrolled drinking. Khantzian observes that the addict's difficulties with affect regulation and modulation require increased therapist activity in helping the patient label and tolerate his feelings. He further notes that excessive passivity, neutrality, and reliance on uncovering techniques on the part of the therapist are inappropriate for these patients.

Treatment in Stages

In recent years, there has emerged a consensus that the psycho-therapeutic treatment of chemically dependent persons occurs in stages, with different goals and techniques appropriate for each stage. Kaufman and Reoux (1988), Kaufman and McNaul (1992), Millman (1986), and Zimberg (1985) identify three stages, while Brown (1985) and Zweben (1986) specify at least four. In the initial stage of treatment, all the authors agree that helping the patient achieve and maintain sobriety is the main therapeutic goal. The therapist needs to be active, supportive, and directive, and provide structure for the patient. The development of a treatment contract, detoxification, education regarding the effects of drug use, participation in a twelve step program, and family involvement in therapy are important features of this initial phase. The use of Antabuse and periodic urinalysis are treatment options. Millman (1986) and Zimberg (1985) point out the difficulty of establishing a therapeutic alliance with the addicted person because of denial and of significant transference and countertransference issues.

In the middle phase of treatment, the authors agree that the focus on alcohol and drug use must be continued to help the patient maintain sobriety. The basic work at this stage is to help the patient accept his identity as a recovering person, develop a support network, and identify the circumstances and internal states that trigger drug use. Millman (1986) suggests that it is important to help the patient understand the relationship of the psychoactive drug effects with his or her own personality pattern.

In the final stage of treatment, these authors contend that traditional psychotherapeutic techniques can be more readily used. Once sobriety has been well established, insight-oriented therapy can be beneficial for the addict. In the early stages of recovery, these authors suggest, uncovering therapy may arouse too much anxiety in the patient and lead to a return to drinking or drug use. In this final stage, therapeutic efforts can be directed to exploring interpersonal conflicts, underlying developmental issues, and traumatic events. Nevertheless, the therapist needs to exercise caution so that these explorations do not lead to a relapse and must continually monitor the patient for a return to drug use.

Psychotherapy for the Dually Diagnosed

The recent evidence of substantial psychopathology coexisting with addictions has heightened the awareness of the utility of psychotherapy for the addicted population. In a followup evaluation of the data from the above mentioned Philadelphia Veterans Administration Study, Woody and colleagues (1984) divided the 110 subjects into groups according to the degree of severity of psychiatric illness. They found that the high severity patients made little progress with counseling alone, but made considerable progress with added psychotherapy. In describing her model for the treatment of substance abusers, Zweben (1986) cautions that there are several exceptions to the guideline of postponing therapeutic work on other issues until abstinence is solidly achieved. Some serious psychiatric disorders are so intertwined with the chemical abuse that it is unlikely that the abuse cycle can be broken without initiating concurrent treatment of the psychiatric disorder.

Kaufman (1989) offers some suggestions for the psychotherapy of dually diagnosed patients. He follows the same therapy-in-stages approach he recommended for substance abusers (1988, 1992, 1994), but suggests that dual diagnosis patients require many specialized techniques. The careful assessment of psychopathology with specific attention to determining whether the signs and symptoms of mental illness are primary or secondary is critical. Detoxification and the passage of time are needed to make this assessment accurately. Maintaining abstinence is even more important for this group than for the single-diagnosed substance abuser because of the complications caused by the use of drugs and alcohol. Because of the mental illness, the ability to maintain abstinence may be limited. Therefore, Kaufman (1989) recommends that the demand for total abstinence may have to evolve gradually through the treatment. During early recovery, the therapist should not confront the defenses too rapidly or remove them prematurely. Instead, these defenses should be redirected and supported to help maintain abstinence and continued treatment. During the early phase of treatment, psychotherapy should be supportive for the most part. Psychodynamic insight-oriented therapy can be used, nevertheless, to help resolve conflicts that may interfere with participation in twelve step programs. In the advanced stage of recovery, more traditional reconstructive psychotherapy can be done, particularly with nonpsychotic patients.

It should be obvious that, at this point in the clinical and academic community's reflection on the treatment of the dual diagnosis patient, there is little consensus on anything but the barest outline of an integrated treatment model. While there is some serious discussion about how the mentally ill substance abuser should be treated in an inpatient setting, there is virtual silence on what clinicians in the context of outpatient therapy do or should do to treat their dually diagnosed clients. While there are numerous recommendations on how to treat persons having either a substance use or a psychiatric disorder in the context of individual therapy, there are few guidelines on how to treat individuals suffering from both disorders.

2

A SELF-SELECTION PROCESS: THE OUTPATIENT SETTING

The dually diagnosed appear in several different settings where they are treated or, more likely, half treated, according to the specialization of the facility. Depending upon the acuteness and severity of their disorders, individuals are referred to facilities with varying levels of restrictiveness and intensity of treatment. Those diagnosed with psychiatric disorders are treated in inpatient units if their condition is most severe, in day hospital programs if less severe, and in outpatient settings if their condition is stabilized. Similarly, those diagnosed with substance-use disorders are treated in different settings according to the severity of their problem, whether inpatient, intensive outpatient, or outpatient. In this chapter, a picture of the dual diagnosis patients encountered in the outpatient mental health setting and some suggestions regarding specific therapeutic tasks with various groups of the dually diagnosed are presented.

It should be noted that today several factors place a heavier treatment burden on the outpatient setting than in the past. First of all, with the prevailing philosophy of deinstitutionalization, mental health professionals believe that patients should be mainstreamed into the community as quickly as possible. Inpatient services are needed for the stabilization of acute symptoms, while the burden of ongoing rehabilitation and recovery falls on the shoulders of outpatient clinicians. Secondly, the advances in psychotropic medications in recent years make it possible for many chronic patients to function in society, thus reducing the need for so many hospitals. Thirdly, in conjunction with these trends, the number of psychiatric hospital beds has been reduced by over 500 percent in the last 30 years to about 100,000 beds. Finally, the contemporary managed care environment has put a premium on cost effectiveness. As a result, greater restrictions have been placed on hospital admissions, and the length of stay of patients has been reduced significantly. As a cost containment measure, patients who were formerly treated in inpatient services for extended periods of time are now being more quickly discharged to the outpatient services.

THE MANY FACES OF THE DUAL DIAGNOSIS PATIENT

The dually diagnosed are a heterogeneous population. However, different groups of these patients tend to come to different settings for treatment. There are numerous studies that describe the type of dual diagnosis patient found in inpatient settings, generally those patients with a severe mental illness. In contrast, there is relative silence about the sort of dual diagnosis patient who comes for outpatient treatment.

The Substance Abusing Client

There are no scientific studies that I could find of the types of dual diagnosis patients who present themselves in the outpatient setting. However, there are many investigations about the personality characteristics of substance abusers encountered in that setting. While not advocating the existence of an addictive personality, several authors suggest that there are some traits commonly found in this population. For example, Khantzian et al. (1990) observe that substance abusers demonstrate vulnerabilities and disturbances in four areas: affect regulation, relationship problems, self-care failures, and self-esteem deficits. According to them, addicts typically either feel their distress as persistent and unbearable or they do not experience any feeling at all. Difficulties in affect modulation are manifested in affective lability and associated depression marked by shame and guilt. Many addicts exhibit conflicts regarding intimacy, fearing closeness, yet intolerant of rejection and other disappointments in relationships. As a protective measure, they may develop a facade of self-sufficiency and deny their dependency needs. Problems with narcissism are also in evidence. Addicts often have a fragile sense of self-esteem, which becomes evident in exaggerated preoccupations with power, performance, and achievement, and in exaggerated needs for acceptance and approval. Finally, because of their frequent association with dangerous circumstances and their tolerance of the negative consequences of drug use, addicts are often considered to harbor conscious and unconscious self-destructive motives. These authors suggest that these destructive tendencies are more likely to be rooted in deficiencies in the capacity for self-care.

In his review of the literature regarding the alcoholic personality, Flores (1988) suggests that while there is little evidence for a prealcoholic personality, there is ample evidence for shared post-alcoholic characteristics that may result from the ravages of the addiction process. Minnesota Multiphasic Personality Inventory profiles consistently identify alcoholics as immature, self-centered, impulsive, unreliable, lacking frustration tolerance, superficially sociable, and frequently having difficulties with societal mores and authority figures. Alcoholics also appear to exhibit significant conflicts around their dependency needs; they fear losing control, yet have an external locus of control. These characteristics make the substance abuser an uncongenial patient for many clinicians.

One of the therapists interviewed in my study admitted that he had to confront his negative attitudes and stereotype regarding substance abusers in order to be able to treat them effectively. Because of some of their characteristics, he did not believe that substance abusers were good candidates for psychotherapy. He confessed:

> I had a stereotype of the substance abusing person. Whatever their intellect or their interest might be, that ultimately they really were not interested in looking at their internal world. They were guarded, rigid, externalizing individuals. . . . My assumptions about an alcoholic had been that they would be suffering from severe inhibition of affects, denial of depressive feelings, infantile character structures, abusive family background, a poor candidate for any insight oriented psychotherapy. . . . They usually weren't too nice to their kids or their spouses. They were rude, inconsiderate,

and had lots of negative personal qualities. In theory, I was committed to finding the likable core inside everybody. That really put
me to the test. I tended to really shy away from anybody whose
primary problem was alcohol.

The small group of substance abusers this therapist had met
seemed to possess these negative qualities. They were personality-
disordered alcoholics. Then he met a lady and several other recovering alcoholics who shattered that stereotype: "Working with this
woman, I realized that she was not only insightful; she was wonder-
fully creative, expressive, fascinated with the internal workings of her
life and mind and her relationships with her friends."

I have also met several insightful, articulate, and sensitive substance abusers in recovery. For example, Bill, a 30-year-old recovering alcoholic, came to see me because he was lonely and depressed
after the breakup of a homosexual relationship. He had been sober
for two years and had participated in an outpatient substance abuse
program. He had started drinking and smoking marijuana when he
was 16 and had been consuming six to eight beers daily when he
decided to quit. Bill thought that all his problems were related to his
drinking. When he found that he was still depressed even after two
years of sobriety, he decided to seek treatment at a mental health clinic.
During the sessions, he displayed an extraordinary sensitivity and
insightfulness regarding his abusive childhood and the effects it had
on his development. He realized that he had been depressed since his
early teens, when he realized his homosexual inclinations. Bill spoke
articulately about his feelings of rejection by his parents and peers and
about how he used alcohol and marijuana to cover up the pain. He
related how, while in college, he attempted suicide, suffered a psychotic break, and was hospitalized. After a series of unhappy relationships, he began the slow road to recovery that has resulted in the
confident acceptance of his sexuality.

The Dual Diagnosis Patient

Since there are no reports of the kinds of dual diagnosis patients
found in outpatient settings, I asked several clinicians who have
worked for many years in private practice to describe their dually

diagnosed caseload. They estimated that about 25 percent of their clients have problems that are significantly affected by their drug or alcohol use. These clinicians reported that their clients present themselves because of personal, marital, family, and work problems. They suffer a variety of neurotic disorders and some characterological problems. Few are chronic psychotic patients. Most suffer depression, anxiety disorders, or adjustment reactions, and several are victims of sexual abuse. Among the dually diagnosed in this outpatient population, by far the most abused substance is alcohol. Some abuse marijuana or prescription drugs. A few abuse or use cocaine recreationally. Practically no heroin or crack cocaine users are treated in their private practices. In the private outpatient setting, the most common dual diagnosis is undoubtedly alcohol abuse or dependence and depression and/or anxiety.

My experience in a publicly funded Community Mental Health clinic suggests that a larger portion of the clients suffer coexisting substance use and psychiatric disorders, approximately a third to a half. A larger percentage than in private practice have chronic and severe mental problems associated with their substance abuse. Furthermore, more heroin and crack users and polysubstance abusers present themselves for treatment in that setting.

One therapist, who works in a private practice and has treated dual diagnosis patients for over 16 years, described the personality characteristics of his current caseload of 16 dually diagnosed patients:

> I guess the thing that jumps out at me about this group of patients is the fact that most clinicians would probably characterize them as narcissistic personalities or with some type of borderline features. There's a number in the group who have had frank thought disorder symptoms at times, at least six or eight of them. They probably are characterized by somewhat less capacity to verbalize affects than the average private practice outpatient. They have less tolerance of anxiety than the average outpatient. They probably have a somewhat higher incidence of trauma and a hypersensitivity to painful affects. They also seem to have a profound association with shame dynamics, lots of self-abasement, self-humiliating, embarrassing, and shameful affects. Some tend to be impulsive. In a few of the cases, there is rage and a propensity to violence, although this is not typical.

This experienced clinician further observed that abusing substances tends to make people look alike in the end:

> Dual diagnosis patients start more different than they end. The longer somebody has a substance abuse disorder, the more like other patients with substance abuse disorders they become. It doesn't matter what the personality dynamics are or what the etiology of the psychopathology. Ultimately, they tend to converge and end up the same way, though they start from diverse paths to the disorder.

The reason for the similarity of presentation of most substance abusers over time is that they increasingly organize their lives around the acquisition and use of their substance of choice. The pursuit of the drug becomes the organizing principle of their lives as they move further into the addiction process.

Another noteworthy characteristic of the dual diagnosis patient is an externalizing tendency that makes them difficult to treat. One clinician, who has ten years of experience working with these patients, remarked:

> I think it has to do with the fact that people who use a substance have a kind of external orientation to the location of problems and are avoidant of thinking about themselves as the source of their own problems. They may know it at some level, but they don't want to think about it. I think it's intrinsic to the nature of the addiction process that it gradually promotes that externalized way of thinking and feeling like the problem isn't me; it's somebody else, or something else, or it's the nature of the world.

Chronic Patients

With the reduction of inpatient hospital beds and the restrictions placed on inpatient treatment by managed care companies, more and more chronic patients with severe mental disturbances and substance abuse are encountered in outpatient settings.

Joe, a 40-year-old man, sought treatment at our outpatient clinic after being discharged from the hospital. This had been Joe's tenth hospitalization in the past 15 years. He had a difficult childhood in which he was physically abused repeatedly by an alcoholic father. His mother had a steady stream of lovers and eventually divorced Joe's father when Joe was 12 years old. He began drinking as a teenager and became intoxicated two or three times a month. At the same time, he was introduced to marijuana, which he claims immediately became his drug of choice. Joe had several brief employments and injured his back in an auto accident when he was 20. Since that time, he has been on prescription pain killers and unable to sustain employment. Joe describes himself as always being depressed and angry, picking fights frequently as a child and young man. In fact, he has been arrested five times for assault and battery. He said he does not trust people and frequently thinks people are plotting to harm him. He has also attempted suicide three times by overdosing on medication. Joe's first hospitalization was prompted by his first suicide attempt at age 25.

Through the years and numerous hospitalizations, Joe has been diagnosed as suffering from paranoid schizophrenia, bipolar disorder, major depression, and post-traumatic stress disorder. He has been prescribed several different psychotropic medications at one time or another: Thorazine, Mellaril, Lithium, Klonopin, Zoloft, Tegretol, and Depakote. Joe has never been consistently compliant in taking these medications because he said he does not like the way they make him feel. He said he prefers to smoke marijuana, which he claims is more effective in relaxing him and controlling his mood swings. He never remained in treatment longer than a few months and frequently misses therapy sessions. In all his years of treatment, both inpatient and outpatient, he claims no one ever addressed his use of marijuana.

An increasing number of people today, like Joe, are abusing marijuana. Many first became acquainted with the drug during the 1960s as part of the countercultural movement. Unfortunately, the marijuana used today is ten to twenty times stronger than that of three decades ago, and the effects are that much more potent. Research shows that 3 percent of heavy marijuana users today develop schizophrenic symptoms that do not remit with abstinence. Joe exhibits many of the characteristics of the dually diagnosed that make them difficult patients to treat:

1. Confusing symptoms make an accurate diagnosis difficult; often the substance abuse problem remains undiagnosed and untreated;
2. Tendency to act out with suicidal and assaultive behavior;
3. Poor social functioning and job instability;
4. Noncompliance with medication;
5. Frequency of hospitalizations; and
6. Difficulty in being engaged in treatment.

Models of Dual Diagnosis

I believe that there are essentially three different models of dual diagnosis. The most common is dual diagnosis with substance abuse and depression and/or anxiety. Research (e.g., Schuckit 1986) is indicating that there may be a genetic predisposition, an underlying vulnerability, to both substance abuse and depression. Patients with this type of dual diagnosis generally present themselves in outpatient settings. However, if they suffer a major affective disorder, such as a major depressive or manic episode, and become suicidal or out of control, they may be hospitalized.

The second and rarest dual diagnosis is one that involves substance abuse and some sort of underlying thought disorder, such as schizophrenia or a paranoid delusional disorder, where the substance abuse is masking and mimicking the psychosis. These are often the chronic patients who are hospitalized when they have acute psychotic episodes and then discharged to outpatient services. These are also the mentally ill substance abusers most difficult to engage in treatment and, although the most rare dual diagnosis, the most written about in the literature.

The third model is substance abuse and an underlying character disorder in which the drug use often facilitates acting out behaviors. These patients may present themselves in either inpatient or outpatient settings and are often difficult to treat because their maladaptive behaviors are ego syntonic. The literature (e.g., Kaufman 1994) identifies antisocial, borderline, and narcissistic personality disorders as most common in this group, although a vast array of personality features is also encountered.

THERAPEUTIC TASKS WITHIN THE OUTPATIENT SETTING
Stages of Treatment

The recovery process for the dually diagnosed has been divided into specific phases: (1) acute stabilization, (2) engagement, (3) prolonged stabilization, and (4) rehabilitation/recovery (Minkoff 1989). The various treatment settings provide the environment for accomplishing specific therapeutic tasks within this ongoing and lifelong process of recovery. For those in acute crisis, the inpatient setting provides a safe haven, stabilization, and an initial engagement in recovery for the disorders. Patients are stabilized on medication, given an initial diagnosis, and detoxed if necessary. The outpatient setting aims at accomplishing the latter tasks of prolonged stabilization and rehabilitation/recovery. It should be noted that only a small minority of the dually diagnosed end up in inpatient services because of the severity of their psychiatric or addictive symptoms. However, nearly all who seek treatment appear in outpatient settings at one time or another.

In today's managed care environment, as mentioned above, the relative emphasis on the treatment settings has been altered. Previously, treatment was often initiated on the inpatient unit and maintained on the outpatient. Patients could be readily admitted to hospitals for long stays beyond the initial stabilization of symptoms. Sufficient time was given for an adequate diagnosis, for an engagement in treatment, and for the beginning of long-term rehabilitation. In contrast, today only the most severely and acutely disturbed are authorized admission into hospitals and those for brief stays, sometimes lasting only a few days. An initial assessment and treatment plan must be done quickly, often within the first 24 hours of the stay. Once the most severe symptoms are stabilized and the patient is no longer deemed a danger to himself or others, the individual is discharged. Normally, a followup appointment is made with an outpatient therapist upon discharge. With this shift of emphasis, a greater therapeutic burden is placed upon the outpatient services to initiate treatment, engage the patient, and sustain an ongoing recovery program. The task of motivating the patient and providing a bridge to outpatient services thus becomes crucial for inpatient programs.

The Outpatient Setting: Potential and Limits

Clinicians recognize that the outpatient setting has both potential and limitations. It is effective for people who are motivated to change, and often the therapist helps them realize their need to change. As one experienced therapist stated:

> People come for help because something is interfering with their lives, with their pleasure, relationships, or job. Nobody comes into treatment wanting to change; they just want to feel better. As therapists, we say, "Things will get better, and we will help you. But you will have to take some responsibility for it."

Initially, people may even feel that treatment is imposed upon them and be resistant to participation in therapy. Unless the therapist can engage the patient and transform the motivation from an externalized pressure to a willing participation, the treatment will probably not progress. Outpatient treatment will not work with people who are in all-out denial and refuse to admit that they have either a substance abuse or psychiatric problem.

Not only is motivation for change essential for successful outpatient treatment, but patients must be able to contain their acting out behaviors. They must have both the will and internal resources to participate actively in the therapeutic process. They cannot be so cognitively impaired from alcohol and drug use or disturbed because of the severity of their thought disorder that they cannot be engaged in therapy. For example, if someone is actively hallucinating and unable to care for himself, he is not a good candidate for outpatient treatment. If someone cannot control his impulse to drink or use drugs, he is not a good candidate. If someone is profoundly depressed and suicidal or is impulsive and assaultative, he will not benefit from therapy until he is stabilized.

Because of the relatively unstructured nature of the outpatient setting and the expectations and resources of both therapists and clients, an implicit self-selection process occurs for patients engaged in outpatient treatment. Clients come who are functional in the world, have internal resources, and have supportive relationships. In the private practice setting, most of the patients are employed, have insurance benefits, and have a relatively stable social network. In the publicly funded clinics, the patients generally have either internal resources or someone who helps structure their lives and assures that they have the support necessary to sustain a treatment.

Four Typical Scenarios

In the mental health outpatient setting, there are four typical situations in which clinicians encounter dual diagnosis patients. In each of these situations, the therapeutic task is somewhat different. The first common situation occurs when someone who has been in recovery for his substance abuse comes to the therapist for treatment of his mental health problems. After someone begins a life of sobriety, it is not uncommon for other problems and disturbing feelings that were covered up with alcohol or drugs to come to the surface. Some patients become disillusioned when their newly found sobriety does not resolve all their problems, so they turn to mental health specialists. Others experience themselves as "dry drunks" who manifest all the behaviors of a substance abuser without drug use and do not find relief from this state in traditional substance abuse treatment.

Many of these clients participate actively in Alcoholics Anonymous or Narcotics Anonymous groups. Some may have been going to meetings for only a short time and are looking for any means available to improve their lives. Although in the past, therapy has had a bad reputation among twelve step members, attitudes are now changing. AA members may refer others in recovery to therapists whom they have experienced as sensitive to and understanding of substance abuse issues.

Another common source of referrals of dually diagnosed patients who are already in the early stages of recovery is from substance abuse treatment agencies. After completing chemical dependency programs and achieving sobriety, these patients discover that they are still depressed or anxious and face other nondrug-related problems. Their drug counselors refer them to therapists who can help them with their mental health issues.

The second common scenario occurs when clients come to be treated for some psychiatric disorder, while not acknowledging any substance abuse problem. Those people come to mental health professionals long before they go to substance abuse counselors for their problems. Often they come in the early stages of alcoholism, not

understanding that their abuse of substances is part of the other problem they are experiencing. They come for marital problems or because
they feel stressed out, depressed, and anxious. They come because they
are experiencing conflicts at home or at work and do not know how
to manage their overwhelming feelings. They come because they feel
empty, have no direction in life, and have suicidal thoughts. They come
because they remember their incest now that Oprah and Roseanne
talk about it, and that it is all right to talk about it, not understanding
that they also have a substance abuse problem. In general, people come
to see therapists with a specific mental health problem that concerns
them. In the course of discussing their problems, it becomes clear to
the therapist that they also have a problem with alcohol or drugs.

While many of these patients come on their own for help, some
are referred by other therapists who are unaware of how their patient's
substance use might be interfering with treatment. One therapist, who
has developed an expertise for working with victims of incest and also
with the dually diagnosed, commented:

> I have had people referred to me by other psychologists and social
> workers who say, "Therapy isn't working, and I'm sure it's because
> this person has been sexually abused." They'll come in, and I'll
> ask them about their use of substances and find out there's a good
> likelihood that this person is addicted. The previous therapist will
> never have asked these questions. It's not often that a person comes
> staggering into your office, and it's obvious they are intoxicated.
> Most people are smart enough not to do that. So if you don't ask
> the questions, you probably won't get the answers.

The third situation, in which someone comes to the therapist for
help only with a substance abuse problem, occurs much less frequently
than the other cases. Generally, people who want help for their drug
problems prefer to go to substance abuse counselors. They think that
mental health professionals do not have the expertise to help them.
However, with the changing climate created by the managed care
systems, patients are sent to facilities that take their insurance, regardless of the clinic's therapeutic specialty. Consequently, those with
substance abuse problems are increasingly being sent to mental health
clinics for treatment. If there is a clinician on staff who specializes in

the addictions, he may get the referral. If not, any available therapist may be expected to provide treatment, regardless of his knowledge and training regarding substance abuse.

A fourth situation happens occasionally when the individual does not admit to having either a mental health or substance abuse problem. Most often, the person's drinking or use of drugs has gotten him into trouble with the legal system, his boss, or his spouse. The judge, boss, or spouse informs the person that some behavior, not necessarily recognized as related to drug use, is unacceptable. They may even make an ultimatum that unless the person gets help and changes that behavior he will be incarcerated, fired, or divorced. That threat is sufficient to bring the person to treatment, even though he may not admit any problem or have any intention of changing. He feels coerced into treatment and comes to appease the threatening party. Therapists who perform evaluations for the courts encounter many such people who are eventually recognized as dually diagnosed. They are referred by their lawyers or judges because they have broken the law, driven under the influence, been caught with an illegal substance, or done something disruptive. These patients come to avoid further legal sanctions, not to change their lifestyles.

The chronic mentally ill substance abusers can be included in this category. They may have some awareness of their problems, but have neither the will nor internal resources to address them. Treatment is maintained as long as a family member provides the needed support and encouragement to participate.

Considering the typical situations in which clinicians encounter the dually diagnosed in outpatient settings, these patients can be divided into four groups according to whether or not they are seeking help for their substance abuse and/or mental health problems. There are four possible combinations of patient characteristics, that can be portrayed by a two-by-two matrix with four cells: 1) those seeking help for both their mental health and substance abuse problems; 2) those seeking help for their mental health problem, but not their substance use disorder; 3) those seeking help for their substance abuse problems, but not their mental health problems; and 4) those not seeking help for either their substance abuse or mental health problems. Each of these groups presents particular clinical challenges.

TABLE 2–1   Help Seeking Behavior in an Outpatient Mental Health Setting

		For a Substance Abuse Problem	
		Yes	No
For a Mental Health Problem	Yes	1	2
	No	3	4

Different Therapeutic Strategies

The first group, comprised of those dually diagnosed patients who are seeking help for both their substance use and psychiatric disorders, is seen frequently in the outpatient setting. If the sobriety is well established, little alteration of the therapist's usual treatment approach is required, and the therapist can focus on the psychiatric disorder. However, if the sobriety is recent, the therapist must monitor carefully a return to substance use, particularly if too much anxiety is aroused in the therapy.

The second group, comprised of those who seek help for their mental health problems, but do not acknowledge any substance abuse problem, also appears frequently in outpatient settings. The most common diagnosis for this group of patients is alcohol abuse or dependence with depression and/or anxiety. The clinician faces difficulties in assessing precisely the nature of the psychiatric disorders because the substance abuse tends to mask and mimic psychiatric symptoms; conversely, the psychiatric symptoms may also disguise the substance abuse. The therapist must devise strategies to address the patient's denial regarding his substance abuse before that problem can be treated. In doing so, the therapist must significantly modify his usual treatment approach, particularly if the substance abuse problem is severe.

The third group, comprised of those who seek help for their substance abuse, but not for any mental health problem, although rare, is increasingly encountered in present day outpatient practices. If they do present themselves, the therapist may refer these patients, who are often primary substance abusers, to substance abuse specialists and invite them to return later if they want to address any mental health problem. Preferably, to maintain the continuity of treatment, the clinician should learn how to treat substance abuse issues and work with these patients himself; he can also address any mental health problems that may arise.

The final group of patients, comprised of those who seek help neither for their substance abuse problems nor mental health problems, are seen less frequently by outpatient mental health clinicians. These coerced clients come because of pressure from the courts, their spouses, their friends, or their work. Their substance abuse problem is often primary, and they are frequently character disordered or chronically mentally ill individuals. The challenge to the clinician with this group is to engage these individuals in treatment, confront their resistance, and address their denial regarding both their substance abuse and mental health problems. Most treatment failures occur with this group of resistant patients.

Recognizing the heterogeneity of the dual diagnosis population and the diversity of their treatment needs is the first prerequisite for developing effective treatment strategies with these patients. The following chapters will elaborate some principles,strategies, and practical techniques for treating them.

3 | THE CHICKEN OR THE EGG? THE RELATIONSHIP OF THE DISORDERS

Clinicians working with the dually diagnosed have found it necessary to develop a conceptualization of the interaction of the psychiatric and substance use disorders to guide their treatment approach and clinical decision making. However, because of the complexity of the interactions of the disorders and because research on this question is in its infancy, there are few firm conclusions. Yet practitioners develop their own positions on this controversial issue because of the necessity of operating from a theoretical base to make sound and consistent clinical judgments. How therapists view the interaction of the disorders will inevitably have implications in how they treat their patients.

VIEWS OF THE RELATIONSHIP

Correlational Studies

The largest and most comprehensive study to date on the comorbidity of mental disorders with substance abuse is the Epidemiologic Catchment Area (ECA) Study referred to previously (Regier et al. 1990). The researchers gathered data on over 20,000 persons from five metropolitan areas. Although causality cannot be inferred from correlation because of possible intervening variables, these authors propose hypotheses regarding the interaction of the disorders. They state: "The finding of a statistically significant association between two disorders in epidemiologic studies suggests that one disorder may cause the other or that an underlying biologic vulnerability to these disorders exists in affected individuals" (p. 2511).

Looking at specific psychiatric disorders, the study found a life-time prevalence of those diagnosed with schizophrenia and some form of substance use disorder to be 47%. The researchers distinguished between abuse and dependence, alcohol and other drugs, and specific types of drugs abused. Within the schizophrenic group, 33.7% met criteria for an alcohol disorder and 27.5% for another drug abuse disorder. Some form of substance abuse was identified in 83.6% of individuals with antisocial personality disorder. Substance misuse tended to be more severe in this group; a higher percentage of persons were diagnosed with dependence. More than half exhibited signs of alcohol dependence (51.3%), while nearly a third were drug dependent (30.8%). For those with any anxiety disorder, the lifetime comorbidity rate was 23.7%; for those with panic disorders, 35.8%; for those with obsessive-compulsive disorders, 32.8%; and for those with phobias, 22.9%. In all of the anxiety disorders, the odds ratio of having a substance abuse problem were notably higher for any other drug diagnosis than for any alcohol diagnosis. Some form of substance abuse or dependence was found in 32.0% of individuals with at least one affective disorder diagnosed. The rates of alcohol diagnoses and other drug diagnoses were nearly equal. Those with any bipolar disorder had a 56.1% lifetime prevalence of comorbidity; those with major depression had a rate of 27.2%; and those diagnosed with dysthymia, a rate of 31.4%.

The most abused drugs were alcohol, with a lifetime prevalence rate of abuse or dependence of 13.5%, marijuana (4.3%), amphetamines (1.7%), and barbiturates (1.2%). Looking at specific substance use disorders, the study found that among those with an alcohol disorder, 36.6% had a comorbid mental disorder. The most common lifetime prevalence rates of mental disorders associated with alcohol problems were anxiety disorders (19.4%), antisocial personality disorder (14.3%), affective disorders (13.4%), and schizophrenia (3.8%). Among those with drug abuse (other than alcohol) disorders, more than half (53.1%) were also diagnosed with a comorbid psychiatric condition. Anxiety disorders (28.3%), affective disorders (26.4%), antisocial personality disorder (17.8%), and schizophrenia (6.8%) were the most common comorbid conditions. Individual drugs of abuse were associated with rates of psychiatric disorders ranging from 50.1% for marijuana to 76.1% for cocaine abusers.

Many authors have investigated the relationships between substance abuse and different psychiatric disorders. For example, in his review of the literature, Bolo (1991) notes the growing interest in the coexistence of substance abuse and various anxiety disorders, especially panic disorder, agoraphobia, and post traumatic stress disorder. Alcohol is often used to self-medicate anticipatory anxiety, and withdrawal symptoms may mimic or cause panic symptoms. Cocaine abuse is highly associated with panic attacks and may cause a panic disorder that persists many years beyond abstinence. The frequency of the co-occurence of thought disorders and substance abuse has been observed by many researchers (Giannini and Collins 1991). Drugs may induce psychotic-like states and be used to cope with the dysphoria of psychotic episodes. Researchers also note the association of substance abuse with a variety of neurological disorders, such as seizures, neurovascular problems, dementia, headaches, attention deficit disorder, and epilepsy. Drugs may both cause organic brain syndromes and complicate these disorders (Kushner 1991). There has been extensive research on the interrelationships between substance abuse and mood disorders, about which is primary, which is secondary, and how the disorders interact. In particular a common genetic predisposition toward both alcoholism and affective disorders is being investigated (Schuckit 1986). The association between drug abuse and anorexia nervosa and bulimia nervosa has gained attention in the last decade (Newman 1991). Finally, clinicians observe the frequency of personality disorders with alcoholism and drug abuse, particularly antisocial and borderline personality disorders (Daley et al. 1987).

Models of Interaction: Primary/Secondary Dimension

Although there is no consensus about precisely how the use and abuse of substances and these various pathologies are related, three basic models are proposed along a dimension of primary and secondary (First and Gladis 1993). Other authors propose variations and refinements of these basic models (Lehman et al. 1989, Meyer 1986, Nunes and Deliyannides 1993).

1) Primary Psychiatric Disorder

In the first model, the psychiatric disorder is primary, and the substance use disorder is secondary, resulting from the mental health problem. This perspective appeals to those working in the mental health field who tend to view the psychiatric disorder as preceding and causing the abuse of substances. Some researchers propose that individuals may use substances to self-medicate because of the dysphoric affects caused by the mental disorders; they may even choose particular types of drugs to alleviate the symptoms of specific disorders (Khantzian 1985b). For example, persons with mood disorders often use depressants to feel better. In other cases, individuals may use drugs to help them cope with the stresses of life because they have a particular intolerance to pain.

As a refinement of this model, it is proposed that the psychopathology may be a risk factor in the development of the drug problem. The risk factors for addictive behavior may be the low self-esteem, negative affect states, impaired cognition and judgment, poor impulse control, impaired social skills, poor coping skills, and lack of social supports that are often associated with mental illness. These psychological vulnerabilities may also modify the course of the drug problem in terms of the rapidity of its course, symptom picture, and response to treatment. Substances may initially provide relief from these painful symptoms. Over time, however, the substance abuse may develop into a full-blown addiction and take on a life of its own.

For diagnostic purposes, attention to the temporal order of the development of the disorders and to family history can give valuable clues to the applicability of this model. If the psychiatric disorder precedes the development of the substance use disorder and the psychiatric symptoms persist in the absence of drug use, it is a reliable indication that the mental illness is primary. If there is a family history of mental illness in the absence of drug problems, this is also a good sign of the likelihood that the psychiatric problem is primary.

2) Primary Substance Use Disorder

In the second model, the substance use disorder is primary, and the psychiatric symptoms are considered secondary to the substance use. This perspective appeals to those in the addiction field who are accustomed to treating the drug problem and anticipate that the residual psychiatric problems will remit with abstinence. Research on the psychophysiology of substance use suggests that the brain undergoes profound changes under the toxic influence of the substance. Stages of intoxication and withdrawal are distinguished for each substance, and the psychological sequelae are different in each stage. For example, a person intoxicated with cocaine may appear to be manic and may manifest symptoms of paranoia. However, in the state of withdrawal from cocaine, the person may become profoundly depressed, and this depression may last several weeks.

According to this model, the secondary psychiatric symptoms are usually transitory and remit after a period of abstinence. However, there are increasing reports of cases where the symptoms persist for extended periods of time. For example, 3 percent of heavy marijuana users manifest schizophrenic symptoms many years after they have stopped using. Long-term use of some drugs can result in permanent damage to the central nervous system, resulting in a psychiatric syndrome that persists long after the acute effects of the drug have subsided. For example, prolonged and heavy alcohol abuse may lead to a persisting dementia. The persistent psychiatric symptoms suggest that the substance use may be a risk factor in the development of an independent mental disorder. Substance use causes severe physiological stress and social disruption. It may well trigger a mental or emotional disorder in vulnerable individuals.

Attention to the temporal sequence of the development of the disorders can give indications that this model applies. If a period of significant substance abuse precedes the development of the psychiatric symptoms, it is likely that the substance use disorder is primary. A period of abstinence is necessary before making a diagnosis with some certainty so that the clinician can be sure that the symptoms of intoxication and withdrawal have subsided. Furthermore, attention to family history can help in making the diagnosis. A family history of substance abuse without a corresponding history of mental illness is also an indication that the substance abuse is primary.

3) Dual Primary Disorders

In the third model, both the psychiatric and substance use disorders are viewed as primary. The dual primary hypothesis pertains to those cases in which the symptoms of both disorders appear to run independent courses. There are periods in which the psychiatric symptoms occur in the absence of substance use, and vice versa. Family history may be variable, with instances of either mental illness or substance abuse, or the presence of both disorders in family members.

Although according to this model both disorders are initially unrelated and independent, over time they may interact and exacerbate each other. The interaction of these disorders may alter the presentation of either illness, making diagnosis and treatment difficult. Various causal links may develop over time. For example, bouts of depression may trigger drinking episodes as individuals attempt to self-medicate, or drug use may precipitate an episode of a recurrent depression.

A variation of this model is the one that suggests that both disorders, although independent of each other, may result from a third underlying etiological factor. Genetic studies suggest that alcoholism and affective disorders are familially linked (Schuckit 1986). There may also be a common genetic vulnerability to both antisocial personality disorder and substance abuse (Meyer 1986). Common psychosocial factors, such as homelessness, may predispose individuals to mental illness and drug abuse. There are also investigations of common biological factors, such as defects in various neurotransmitter systems, that may make individuals vulnerable to both disorders.

Models of Interaction: Separate-Linked Dimension

In my interviews with therapists who have treated the dually diagnosed for many years, I was not surprised to find that all had conceptualizations of the relationship between the disorders to guide their treatment approaches. However, I did not anticipate finding that, instead of focusing on the primary-secondary dimension regarding their interaction, as is frequently reported in the literature, they underlined how the disorders are either relatively separate or linked together. In fact, these interviewed practitioners appeared to adhere to two contrasting positions regarding the relationship between the disorders. One group tended to conceptualize the disorders as relatively separate. For them, dual diagnosis patients manifest a comorbidity. Substance abuse is viewed as having a "life of its own," and not necessarily related to any preexisting pathology. Their position was more dualistic. The other group of therapists tended to conceive of the disorders as "inextricably linked," and their position was more unitary. Substance abuse is viewed as a "way of self-medicating" some underlying pain or pathology. How the therapist viewed the relative separateness or linkage of the disorders had a significant impact on how they treated their patients.

1) A Dualistic Position

A representative of the first group, which views the disorders as relatively independent, stated:

> I think they're comorbid. I don't think we have psychiatric problems causing substance abuse. We might have some substance abuse causing some character disorder kinds of adjustments. I think that everybody starts using for the same reason. If you have the genes, you got it. You may have a major depression or obsessive compulsiveness that goes with it. You may be psychotic with it. You may be any of these things. But you have to treat them both.

One member of this dualistic group, who began his career working in an inpatient substance abuse unit, observed that the disorders may be linked initially, but over time, substance abuse often takes on a life of its own:

> Again, it's something evolutionary. Gordon Allport talks about functional autonomy of motives. What he would point out is that what may have begun as a symptom then becomes a disease. It comes to take on a life of its own. In the hospital, what was obvious to me was that most of the people had developed a lifestyle that centered around alcohol. Typically, you'll hear from alcoholics that they were shy and introverted and when they drink it brings them out more. They began drinking for that reason. But then they

begin to build a lifestyle focused on the substance abuse. They become habituated to it.

He continued, giving an example in which situational drinking takes on a life of its own:

> For example, in the military almost everybody drinks. It is a drinking culture. When they leave the military, most give up the drinking pattern developed there. They return to a more normal drinking pattern. But some continue to drink heavily, and the drinking begins to take on a life of its own. These become alcoholics. . . . So substance abuse becomes functionally autonomous and takes on a life of its own over time. There may have been a linkage at first between the disorders, but over time, with enough drinking, the substance abuse problem takes on a life of its own.

These therapists tended to embrace the disease concept of alcoholism and substance abuse. They view alcoholism as biologically based and as a progressive, chronic, and fatal disease. For example, one clinician of this group stated: "I'm a believer in the disease model of alcoholism. I believe that alcoholism has a biogenetic basis. I think there are some people who drink heavily who are not alcoholic. I think the pattern is different." She observed that certain individuals are addiction prone, but was careful to distinguish between addictions and compulsions:

> One thing I always look for is addiction substitutions. What happens is that if the addiction has some sort of ameliorating effect on symptoms, when the person stops drinking, he is likely to engage in other addictive or compulsive behaviors to try to cover up the symptoms. So the person will go from alcohol to drugs to food, which are, by the way, the only things I will call addictions. I don't think there are shopping addicts. I don't think gambling is an addiction. I don't think spending money is an addiction. I think those are compulsive behaviors. For me, I am just comfortable distinguishing addictions as something that has a biological, biogenic basis. People who are with me who give up the chemical dependency often switch to something else, to another addiction or compulsion, or sometimes go through a progression. They will go through alcohol to a drug to food to spending money and even to compulsive sexuality.

These therapists were less inclined to accept the self-medication hypothesis regarding substance abuse. For example, one of those interviewed, a recovering alcoholic, related:

> I think everybody starts drinking for the same reason. Self-medication may be true when it gets to the point of combating withdrawal. Then you self-medicate to avoid withdrawal. Self-medication in terms of dual diagnosis—I don't think so. Except it would be the same thing as if you started drinking because of the depression and then got hooked on it. That may be true. But self-medication implies an underlying psychopathology. I'm not willing to buy that totally. That implies, too, that if you analyze the depression away, then you won't have to drink or even have the urge to drink.

As a way of contrasting the dualistic position with the unitary position, one therapist of this group offered the examples of Eugene O'Neill and Ernest Hemingway: "That's [the unitary position] a more neurotically based thinking. That's like the old Eugene O'Neill story. The guy saw Eugene O'Neill and said, "You're an alcoholic because of these conflicts with your father." Eugene O'Neill never took another drink in his life. But how often do you see that happening? A lot of people begin drinking that way, but by the time you're an alcoholic, someone has a separate habit strength that has to be dealt with also." According to him, the more common scenario is represented by the famous Hemingway story, in which drinking results in depression: "We know that it is a very common feature of individuals who drink over long periods of time that they begin to have mood swings. That may be the chemistry of the alcohol, and nothing else. The famous story, of course, is Hemingway, who killed himself when he was 60 years old, after having electric shock treatments. But he drank a fifth of vodka every single day for about forty years. It was probably alcohol that caused his mood swings."

2) A Unitary Position

The second group of therapists held a different position on the relationship of the disorders. They considered them to be linked to one another. One clinician, who follows a cognitive-behavioral orientation, proposed that the substance use is a way of self-medicating:

"What I have found is that the substances they are using, typically alcohol more often than not, are actually a way of self-medicating themselves. They don't necessarily realize this. They just know that when they are high they don't have so many problems. At least, it doesn't seem that way." He commented further that he does not believe that the disorder of alcoholism is an entity distinct from mental health problems:

> But I don't believe that it's a disease and that people can't help themselves. I believe that most alcoholics don't know how to help themselves. It has become such a learned innate behavior that they don't know what other tools to use in terms of maintaining sobriety. So I don't see it as a distinct entity. I see it as a way of coping with their environment, as a way of self-medicating. I don't view the disorder of alcoholism as a distinct entity, distinct from the mental health problems. When you have people who are dually diagnosed, they clearly have disorders of alcoholism and other problems. But it's my feeling that they're not two distinct entitites which have to be treated separately. It's really all part of the same entity.

Another therapist, who is psychodynamic in orientation, reported that he considers the disorders inextricably linked. He described an addiction process that begins with the utilization of the substance to blunt the impact of painful experience and progresses to become a disease:

> If you take substance abuse as an addiction process, then you assume that anyone can become addicted because of the nature of the substances involved, regardless of the reasons they start. . . . Life is a painful process. That's true for all people. It doesn't matter what the structure of the personality is. There are painful events in people's lives, both physically and emotionally. Many of the dually diagnosed lack tolerance for pain. In somebody who becomes a substance abusive or dependent person, whether they are healthy or severely disturbed, they stumble upon the strategy of utilizing substances in one way or another to blunt the impact of painful experience. . . . People will gradually start to have anxiety about that pain such that they fear the pain almost as much as they can't stand the pain. The fear generalizes and spreads. Typically, the substance abuser's dependence spreads as well, such that the

occasions they feel justified in consuming substances will generalize and spread to other things because that's the way pain and
trauma works. It tends to spread, and so will the remedies.

What began as a way of coping with the stress of life can progress to
become a full-blown addiction:

> Certainly, there are predispositions to the development of addic-
> tion in people that are biological. At some point, any person who
> utilizes substances excessively runs the risk of becoming addicted,
> which means the disease assumes a life of its own that no person is
> reasonably expected to be able to manage. It begins gradually to
> organize their personality and life, rather than vice versa. We're
> used to people organizing and managing their lives according to
> their personality structures. People who become addicted become
> more and more alike for a reason, because the addiction has a logic
> and progression of its own.

He further observed that those who are able to participate successfully in outpatient treatment are probably not so far along in the
addiction process, and substance abuse and personality issues are
inseparable: "If somebody is so far into an addiction process that it
has taken on a life of its own, they are unable to stop drinking in the
context of outpatient treatment. Then it is necessary to contain the
disintegrating effects of the addiction before one is going to be able
to do outpatient treatment. If somebody is able to be treated as an
outpatient, then I don't believe it's possible to extricate substance
abuse problems from personality problems."

In general, this group of therapists did not embrace the disease
concept of alcoholism. One therapist, in fact, strongly rejected the
disease concept as a way of minimizing personal responsibility for
drinking:

> I do not think of it as a disease, because I think a disease is a cop-
> out. I tell people it's less important that they worry about whether
> it's genetic and more important that they understand what hap-
> pens when they drink, the circumstances when they drink, and what
> they need to do to avoid drinking. . . . If they see it as a disease,
> they may say, 'I have alcoholism like I have appendicitis or diabe-
> tes,' and tend to see it as something they're not responsible for. I
> think the problem with most alcoholics is that they look for any

excuse to put the blame on others. . . . So I try not to facilitate the concept that it's something they have that they can't do anything about. I'd rather focus on what kinds of things they can do.

IMPLICATIONS FOR TREATMENT

Particular treatment strategies follow from the conceptualizations of the relationship of the disorders. The primary-secondary distinction suggests which disorder needs to be given initial therapeutic attention. On the one hand, if the psychiatric problem is viewed as primary, then it must be treated first. Without the personal stresses generated by the psychiatric problem, it is presumed that the secondary substance abuse behavior will disappear. There will no longer be a need for the person to drink or use drugs to self-medicate or cope with stress. Typically, mental health professionals prefer this approach. On the other hand, if the substance use disorder is seen as primary, then it ought to be treated first. With abstinence, it is presumed that the secondary psychiatric symptoms will remit. Many substance abuse specialists follow this approach. In the third model, where both disorders are thought to be primary, of course, both must be treated concurrently from the beginning.

The therapists interviewed described the treatment implications of their views of the interaction of the disorders. Those who viewed the disorders as relatively separate suggested a sequential approach to treatment, addressing first the substance abuse problem, then the psychiatric problem. For example, one therapist stated: "True alcoholism is biogenetically determined and must be treated first. I cannot think of an instance in which I would say we'll deal with the alcoholism later." Those who thought of the disorders as inseparable, suggested a simultaneous approach, treating both disorders together at the same time. For example, one of this group stated: "I think it's a spurious distinction. They [the disorders] develop together, and they have to be treated together. They're too entwined."

In individual cases, it is often unclear which model applies, particularly in the beginning of treatment.

Rhonda, a 38-year-old married woman, came to see me because she was depressed and having marital problems. She seemed to have lost sexual interest in her husband after their son was born four years previously. They talked rarely and had been living parallel lives for some time. Upon further inquiry, she reported that she had had periods of depression and difficulties sleeping since her early teenage years. These bouts of depression would come and go. She admitted that she began drinking heavily when she was 17. Throughout college, she worked at a bar and partied with friends practically every night. When she graduated from college, she got married to her present husband. She continued to drink with him, but not quite as heavily. Now they were in a pattern of drinking two or three drinks every night before bedtime. She said it helped her to sleep. She reported that her father was an alcoholic who physically abused his wife and children. Her mother suffered bouts of depression throughout her life, although she had never been treated for it.

In this case, as in so many others, it is not clear if Rhonda's substance abuse or depression is primary, or if both are primary. It is also unclear if the disorders are independent or inseparable. Furthermore, diagnosis is difficult because, over time, the relationship between the disorders can change. What initially appeared to be independent disorders can become linked and mutually interactive, altering the course and presentation of both disorders. If initially drug use was a means of self-medicating an underlying primary pathology, over time it may become a full-blown dependence and assume a life of its own.

In the initial phase of treatment, it is not useful to distinguish which disorder is primary or secondary. Often this distinction cannot be made with certainty because of the lack of data and the unreliability of the patient's self-report. If a premature judgment is made, there is also a danger of subordinating the treatment of one of the disorders to the other. This may result in a disjointed treatment in which the patient is referred back and forth between different psychiatric and substance abuse treatment programs. Both disorders should be treated together from the beginning of treatment, although the therapeutic focus may shift to address more intensively the more severe problem. Over time, it may become clear which disorder is driving the other, and the treatment focus can be altered accordingly.

In the lived world of the patient, of course, the disorders are experienced as inseparable and mutually interactive. However, in the thinking world of the patient, it may be beneficial to present the disorders as distinct and in need of specific treatment. Patients may fail to see the need to address both disorders in treatment if they are not clearly seen as two different problems calling for attention. Furthermore, in a mental health facility, the addictive diagnosis may be lost if it is not given sufficient emphasis as a separate and important problem. As treatment progresses, it will be didactically useful to show the patient the relationship of the disorders. For example, patients can be shown how a relapse in one disorder will lead to a relapse in the other and how substance abuse is used to self-medicate underlying pathology.

As will be elaborated in the following chapters, a thorough assessment for both disorders must be made from the beginning of treatment. In that assessment, the clinician will inevitably develop hypotheses regarding the relationship of the disorders. However, it is crucial to remember that an accurate diagnosis takes time, since the presentation of the disorders will vary over time. Evidence must be continually gathered either to confirm or alter the initial hypothesis. Therefore, the assessment needs to be an ongoing process throughout treatment and to be attentive to the development and mutual interaction of the problems.

4

SHIFTING PARADIGMS: MODIFYING THERAPEUTIC TECHNIQUES

One of the principal difficulties in treating the dually diagnosed is the lack of an integrated treatment model for this population. Substance abuse counselors propose one approach for addictions, while mental health practitioners follow another model for addressing psychiatric disorders. The strategies and techniques of these two groups of professionals are irreconcilable at many points. Those treating patients with coexisting disorders must then create their own models through trial and error experimentation.

Ries and associates (1994) compare and contrast the treatment approaches of practitioners in both the mental health and addiction systems. For mental health professionals, the use of medications is central to the management of psychiatric disorders in all its phases, whereas addiction specialists are reluctant to use medications except for acute detoxification. Clinicians in the mental health field are sensitive to the fragility, limitations, and deficits of their patients and tend to assume more responsibility in gradually facilitating the recovery of their patients. They also tend to avoid becoming confrontational and aggressive in their approach because of their recognition of the vulnerability of the patient. In contrast, clinicians in the addiction field emphasize the individual responsibility of their clients, including the responsibility of accepting help. The use of therapeutic confrontation of the client's denial of a drug problem is a central technique. In psychiatric treatment, the focus is often on past developmental issues, and it is assumed that drug problems are a result of underlying unresolved psychological problems. In addiction treatment, the focus is often on the "here and now," and it is presumed that any psychiatric symptoms will disappear once the patient has achieved a stable sobriety. Most substance abuse counselors insist on total abstinence from all mood altering drugs, while mental health clinicians tend to accept controlled drinking as a treatment goal. Both treatment groups recognize the importance of group therapy and supportive self-help groups for patients and their families. Participation in twelve step programs has long been a central feature in substance abuse treatment, while only recently mental health practitioners are recognizing the value of twelve step groups for emotional problems.

The burden of integrating the insights of both these treatment communities falls to the individual therapist in treating the coexisting disorders of the dually diagnosed. While substance abuse specialists must alter their usual approaches in addressing the psychiatric problems of these patients, mental health professionals must adapt their treatment models to address the addiction problem. Clinicians working in mental health settings typically need to learn about the treatment of addictions and incorporate elements from that tradition. At the same time, being sensitive to the psychological fragility of their patients, they need to modify the standard addiction approach to treatment in order to create an integrated and individualized treatment model for their dually diagnosed patients.

Treatment Principle One: The effective treatment of most dual diagnosis patients requires some modification of techniques and an integration of treatment approaches from both the mental health and substance abuse fields.

This chapter will present a brief overview of the necessary modifications of technique to treat the dually diagnosed and a rationale for these changes. The subsequent chapters will explain in more detail the principles, strategies, and techniques for addressing specific clinical issues with this population.

MAKING A PARADIGM SHIFT

Since the recognition of the treatment needs of the dually diagnosed is so recent, the literature does not offer an integrated treatment model for this population, particularly in the outpatient setting.
However, those clinicians who work with this group soon realize the
inadequacy of their usual therapeutic approaches and the need to make
modifications. One necessary change is to address the substance abuse
problem directly. Some therapists refer to this modification as a "paradigm shift."

One therapist, who has been working with the dually diagnosed
for over 20 years, described the case of a woman whom she initially
diagnosed as suffering from post traumatic stress and later came to
discover was addicted to prescription medication. This case illustrates
for her how the paradigm shifts.

> A very neurotic and depressed woman, named Mary, came to see
> this psychologist. She had been depressed for many years and suf-
> fered extremely low self-esteem. She referred to herself as a "shit
> worker." The therapist worked for many months with her on her
> low self-esteem and discovered that she had an abusive childhood.
> Mary kept mentioning that for pain she was taking "222s," which
> are Codeine tablets that can be purchased over the counter in
> Canada. The therapist inquired carefully about Mary's use of this
> medication and did not think that she was abusing it or addicted
> to it, although she remained suspicious. Her initial diagnosis was
> post traumatic stress disorder. Then one day Mary brought in her
> pills and said, "I think I'm hooked."

The therapist described how the therapy shifted from that
moment on:

> It shifted from an attempting to figure out what was going on
> with the post traumatic stress to what to do with the substance
> abuse. I found that the shift became less dynamic and more
> cognitive to the point where I completely shifted roles. I became
> more of a teacher for a while, rather than a passive screen. I
> referred her to a hospital for lectures and group, because I only
> do individual therapy. I also referred her to AA meetings. Then

the role changed, too, because when we do psychodynamic
therapy, we mobilize the anxiety. But now there was an attempt
to put down the anxiety so she would not use.

Those who are psychodynamic in their approach speak of intro-
ducing parameters when the substance abuse is recognized as being
severe and interfering with treatment. One therapist whom I interviewed specified some of the parameters he introduces: "Do you treat
people entirely differently? Not really. It's just that you have different tools in your tool box to deal with them because they are addicted.
You think of medications in different ways. You think of different kinds
of treatment settings. You think of enlisting support groups or networks in different ways."

Those who are cognitive behavioral in orientation envision less
of a paradigm shift. One brief therapist reported that his general
cognitive-behavioral approach to therapy was effective with substance
abusers and required little alteration of techniques, only of focus, when
substance abuse problems arise. He summarized his approach with
this population: "For anybody that has a substance abuse problem,
insight-oriented approaches simply do not work with most of them.
You need to be more directive. You need to be more educationally
focused. It's also helpful to have them get some outside assistance and
attend AA."

In working with the dually diagnosed, three basic technical changes
are called for. First, the therapist must be more active and directive.
Secondly, structure and support need to be provided for the patient.
Finally, there needs to be an educational focus regarding substance
abuse and its interaction with the patient's psychiatric disorder.

Being Directive

Because of the tendency of substance abusers to deny their drug
problems and because of their frequent substance induced cognitive
impairments, therapists need to be clear, straightforward, and direct
with these patients. One therapist interviewed described her approach,
which also reflected her personality: "I have been known to be very
directive. I think that might make a difference in the way you work
with chemically dependent people and the way you work with non-

chemically dependent people. It's how directive you are. . . . I tell them, 'My diagnosis is that you are alcoholic, and this is the treatment of choice. This is what you have to do, if you want to get it together. No *ifs*, *ands*, or *buts*. These are the meetings I require, and this is what you ought to do.'"

Another therapist, who has over twenty years experience working with this population, described how he challenges his substance abusing patients: "If someone came in, and I saw there was a pattern of drinking that constantly got him into trouble, I would say, 'AA is the most effective way because of the group process and because it is a life long commitment.' If the person wasn't doing that, I would say, 'What does that mean? To me, it means that you don't want to change. If you know it's effective and you say you really want to change, but you're not going to meetings and working at it, then what's the point in being here?"

Another therapist, experienced in working with the mentally ill substance abusing patient, related how he communicates with his patients in clear and simple terms. He repeats to his patients time after time: "You suffer from two disorders. You have a diagnosis that fits each disorder. That's why you're here. Not just for one, but for both. If you see yourself as mentally ill and not drug addicted, you won't make it. If you see yourself as alcohol dependent and not mentally ill, you won't make it." He further explained: "I do it rigidly, authoritatively, after I'm convinced it's true, in order to convince them it's true. I make it as clear and simple as possible."

Being Supportive

Because the dually diagnosed patient is more fragile while he is not using his drug of choice to cope, he needs more support and structure in his life. Often the patient uses the substance to cope with the disturbing thoughts and affects of the psychiatric disorder. Because he has used the drug as a primary coping mechanism, he may not have developed the inner resources to cope with the internal or external stresses of his life. He then becomes more vulnerable in the treatment as he makes efforts to abstain from drug use.

The therapist needs to be especially supportive while the person is adjusting to life without substances and to be conscious of not creating too much anxiety for the patient to bear. Therefore, he ought to refrain from exploring issues that are too sensitive or anxiety provoking for the patient. He must be careful not to be too confrontative with the patient's defenses, which, even if they are immature and only moderately effective, still protect the patient from being overwhelmed. If either the psychiatric or substance use disorder is severe, the patient may need more support and be seen more frequently than once a week.

One of the most important supports is offered by AA groups. Participation in a twelve step group can complement the support and structuring provided in therapy. Therapists should also facilitate their patients' participation in the group by answering questions about it, explaining its importance, and exploring resistances to attending. The group is important because it can offer support and understanding by others who have shared the same painful experience of drug dependence. This support can be continuous between sessions and ongoing after the therapy ends. One therapist, a recovering alcoholic, commented on the importance of the ongoing relationship with AA: "If you are talking about the therapy as a journey that the patient and therapist take together, then you have to be able to say good-bye. If you think of drug dependency as a life long illness that needs a lot of support, then you have to have somebody to take my place. I think that's one of the most important things. I don't think an individual can do it himself."

If the problem, either psychiatric or substance abuse, becomes so severe that it causes a significant disruption in the patient's life and interferes with his capacity to participate in treatment, it may be necessary to recommend the support and structure of an inpatient program. Outpatient therapy provides a relatively unrestricted environment for the exploration of issues. Its effectiveness depends on the motivation of the patient and his ability to control his acting out behavior.

Being Educational

Finally, an educational focus regarding the disorders and their interaction must be included in the treatment of the dually diagnosed. First of all, the patient needs to learn about the nature of substance abuse, its progression, signs, and symptoms. This knowledge can be used to help the patient assess himself regarding the problem. The best way of confronting denial is indirectly, by providing the individual with enough information that he can make a judgment for himself concerning whether or not he has a problem. A direct confrontation of the denial will often lead to an increased defensiveness on the part of the patient and/or a withdrawal from treatment. Once the person has achieved sobriety, information about the precipitants of relapse can be helpful to prevent relapse. Relapse prevention education includes an awareness of the persons, thoughts, feelings, and circumstances that frequently lead to the urge to drink or use drugs. After a relapse, the goal is to keep a temporary relapse from becoming a full-blown one. A nonjudgmental and exploratory approach can help the patient learn from the experience and not suffer more sobriety threatening damage to his self-esteem.

It is also beneficial to have patients attend twelve step meetings where they can learn about themselves and their drug problem in ways appropriate to their capacities. One therapist commented on the concreteness of AA advice, which she includes in the therapy sessions:

> You've got to be concrete enough and cognitive enough to give the substance dependent person some tricks to use. That's where AA helps you out a lot, because they have all these little sayings: "first things first," "one step at a time"—those kinds of things. And you can use them in your therapy with substance abusers. . . . Now there's also the sensory motor level of activity that happens at AA: the activity, the emptying of ash trays, the making coffee, the going to meetings. I think all that's important. It's like going to school.

A second important area of education concerns the psychiatric disorder and its relationship with the substance abuse. Patients, especially the more disturbed, may have difficulty accepting that they are mentally ill. The therapist needs to educate them about their symptoms, the progression of the illness, and the medications and their side effects. These patients also should be educated about their need to continue taking their medication and be warned about not drinking or using other drugs. They may be confused when they hear conflicting advice from their fellow recovering addicts at twelve step meetings that they must remain entirely drug free. The therapist needs to distinguish clearly between the medication prescribed for the psychiatric illness and the drugs abused by the patient. It is also helpful to discuss with patients how they used drugs to cope with particular disturbing affects or experiences, and how the use of medication can serve that purpose in a more effective way.

RATIONALE FOR SHIFTING PARADIGMS

Images of the Dually Diagnosed

The dually diagnosed suffer from a double vulnerability. Because of their psychiatric disorders, they are psychologically fragile. Because of their substance abuse, they experience many cognitive and emotional impairments. A recognition of this double vulnerability has lead sensitive clinicians to introduce modifications in their usual therapeutic approaches in treating these patients. The specific needs of this patient, particularly with his substance abuse problem, warrant these shifts in technique. The experienced therapists I interviewed offered several intriguing images of the dually diagnosed that guide their treatment: as learning disabled, trauma victims, developmentally arrested, and habitually addicted. Of course, these images are not aptly descriptive of all the dually diagnosed, but pertain especially to the more severely impaired.

One therapist believes that because the alcoholic bathes his brain in alcohol, his cognitive functioning is compromised: "My sense is that everybody who is chemically dependent acts as if they're learning disabled. So what you have to do is to deal with the learning disabled person. . . . Even with professional people, they are learning disabled, and you can't expect that much. You have to go over, and over, and over things." She suggested that because of these drug-induced cognitive deficits, the therapist must be very concrete, repetitive, and directive.

A second clinician had the image of a dual diagnosis patient as someone who is a trauma victim because the substance abuse problems are so inextricably linked with the personality and psychopathology of the user. He observed: "What substance abuse does is have a net effect of making them like trauma patients. Their affective development gets stunted, almost like a developmental arrest in terms of learning how to manage affects. The presence of the substance abuse is linked with that in short circuiting their cognitive development in the area of their affective internal life." He elaborated the implications of this view of the dual diagnosis patient for the treatment: "It's not so different from treating a trauma patient in many ways. You have the problems verbalizing affects, problems with somatization, same sort of pain anxiety equivalents, intolerance of dysphoric affects, the same propensity to generalize the fear and to underestimate their capacity to cope with situations." The therapist's task is to help the traumatized patient identify triggers to a reflex panic and to verbalize affects. In that way, he helps the person contain his overwhelming feelings and contain behaviors that are maladaptively avoidant of affects.

Another experienced practitioner conceptualized substance abuse as a self-reinforcing symptomatic pattern, sustained by habit strength, that can most effectively be broken by direct behavioral interventions:

> The substance abuse itself is a self-reinforcing symptomatic pattern that has to be broken before you get to deeper issues. So you need a behaviorally oriented approach. I modified my approach because when I first got into practice I tried to do analytic therapy and found that it was largely unsuccessful. I first had to deal with the habit strength of the substance abuse. I also had to deal with some of the characterological patterns that go along with it. Analysis is really a tool for dealing with neurotic patterns, although a lot of people have tried to modify analyses to deal with character pathology. When you deal with substance abusers, you're dealing with the habit strength of drinking and the character pathology which maintains that drinking pattern. In order to deal with that, you have to make direct behavioral interventions.

A final image of the dually diagnosed is to view him as a developmentally arrested person. Treatment typically progresses in stages that correspond to the maturity level of the patient. One therapist, a recovering person, employed an Eriksonian model of development to explain her paradigm shift in treating the dually diagnosed patient. She related this model of development to the twelve steps of AA:

> I like to use a developmental model. In fact, the steps of the AA program can be analyzed with Erikson's model of development, if

you stop to think about it. You start out with the first step, which is developmentally getting back to the helplessness stage. 'I'm powerless over alcohol, and my life has become unmanageable.' If that doesn't put you back into infancy, I don't know what does. Then you begin to believe in the parents; that's the second step. Slowly, you get into your own autonomy and build it up from there. I like to think of that as my real developmental model for therapy.

Because of the interfering effects of a reliance on drugs to cognitive and emotional development, the addict is developmentally disabled and must be guided through different stages of growth in the treatment. Before working on the relatively more advanced issues of autonomy in therapy, the treatment must first focus on breaking the patient's infantile reliance on the substances.

Neuropsychological Evidence

The neuropsychological effects of substance abuse have been extensively studied during the past few decades. Most of the research has focused on the effects of alcohol abuse. There is clear and convincing evidence of neuropsychological impairments that are a direct result of alcohol abuse and some evidence of impairment caused by polysubstance abuse. In their extensive literature review of studies on the neuropsychology of alcohol and drug use, Parsons and Farr (1980) concluded that many alcoholics who present for treatment are mildly to moderately impaired neuropsychologically for their age and educational levels, as measured by the Wechsler Scales and Halstead-Reitan Battery. The few studies that have been done on polysubstance abusers suggest that they also suffer some cognitive impairment. A pattern of impairment emerges for the alcoholic after prolonged drinking. Besides the most severely brain damaged alcoholic who suffers the memory ravaging Korsakoff Syndrome, the typical alcoholic tends to have intact verbal abilities, but impaired nonverbal abstracting and problem solving abilities. These authors observed that the pattern of impairment is characterized by relatively poor performance in visual-spatial (Block Design, Object Assembly, Picture Arrangement) and tactual-spatial (TPT-Time and TPT-Location) constructional tasks. Performance on nonverbal abstracting and set flexibility tasks (Category Test and Trails B) and visuo-motor speed (Digit Symbol) are also affected. However, these cognitive impairments, according to them, tend to be reversible over time with abstinence.

In a more recent review, Lishman (1987) concluded that while there is evidence of a recovery of cognitive functioning in the first few weeks of abstinence, it is likely that some deficits still persist even after a year of total abstinence. Deficits on tests of psychomotor speed, perceptual-motor functioning, visuo-spatial competence, memory, and measures of abstracting ability and complex reasoning can be observed. Lishman noted that the vulnerability observed on tests related to frontal lobe function are particularly noteworthy. He surmised that the prolonged alcohol abuse would likely set the stage as the alcoholic gets older for more serious and irreversible damage as other pathologies, such as those of aging, trauma, vascular changes, and hepatic dysfunction develop.

McCrady (1987) called for a careful assessment of the substance abuser's learning ability and recovery related skills when involved in treatment. This assessment may have a profound effect on the clinician's approach to treating the person. She lists those skills affected by neuropsychological impairment:

1. The ability to remember information presented in treatment;
2. The ability to remember why drinking is a problem and why abstinence is necessary;
3. The ability to find the treatment program, find one's way around the treatment facility, and find AA meetings in the community;
4. The ability to associate names with faces of people met in AA or group therapy;
5. The ability to listen to discussions and sort the relevant from irrelevant information in therapy and group discussions;
6. The ability to identify situations that could provide difficulties in terms of maintaining abstinence;
7. The ability to generate ideas about how to handle life problems that have arisen because of or independent of drinking;
8. The ability to select possible solutions to problems, to try them out, to evaluate their effectiveness as solutions, and to assess other solutions if the first ones prove ineffective;
9. The ability to converse with people; and

10. The ability to recognize consequences of continued drinking and act accordingly. [p. 387]

If these cognitive deficits are combined with the affective limitations described above, it is obvious that the substance abusing patient
presents enormous difficulties in treatment, requiring substantial
modifications in approach.

There have been a few studies recently on the neuropsychological
picture of the dually diagnosed patient. For example, Oepen and
colleagues (1993) investigated whether patients experiencing both a
major psychiatric disorder and a concurrent substance abuse problem manifest greater neuropsychological dysfunctions than patients
with a major psychiatric disorder alone. They compared the psychiatric records of 50 dual diagnosis patients and 36 chronically hospitalized non-dual diagnosis psychiatric patients. They found that the
dually diagnosed patients manifested significantly greater neuropsychological impairments. In this group, there were more cases of
attention deficit hyperactivity disorder (28%), neurodevelopmental
disorders (48%), seizure activity (32%), head injuries (58%), and impulsive eating disorders (28%) than in the singly diagnosed group. Over
half of the dually diagnosed abused a variety of different substances.
The dual diagnosis group also showed a greater range of psychiatric
diagnoses and diagnostic fluidity than the single diagnosis group.

INTEGRATING TREATMENT MODELS

Because of the unique needs of the dual diagnosis patient and the
lack of appropriate treatment models for this population, clinicians
must take what insights they can from existing therapeutic approaches
and integrate them into new creative models. One therapist, experienced in working with the mentally ill substance abuser, related his
treatment philosophy and the components of his treatment model:

> This is my philosophy. I try to take what's most helpful from each
> system and bring it into an integrated system. From the psychiat-
> ric system, we learn the importance of the correct prescription and
> the controlled environment, protecting people from their own

behaviors in a locked ward. From the substance abuse system, we learn the importance of twelve step groups, group therapy, and the involvement of the family. Psychologists in outpatient settings could benefit by using some of the approaches used in the inpatient setting, particularly family contact and sessions involving the family.

The integration of mental health and substance abuse treatment approaches will require a modification of the traditional practices in each. Because of the cognitive and affective limitations associated with the substance abuse of the dually diagnosed, therapists need to modify their usual approaches and incorporate some of the strategies and techniques employed by substance abuse specialists. As elaborated above, therapists need to be more directive, supportive, and educational with their dual diagnosis patients than with clients who have only mental health problems.

Another interviewed therapist articulated his appreciation of the substance abuse professional community's work:

> The substance abuse field has had a fair amount of success with their approach to their clients. If you look at the residential treatment centers that have focused on abstinence as a demand for recovery, you'll notice they do a much more comprehensive and whole environment job than most mental health professionals typically. They find it quite acceptable to do a lot of didactic teaching about how to structure and manage life. They have the historical tie in to self-help groups in which they involve people in a social milieu that is very supportive and educational. People are sometimes going to one or two meetings a day. They're getting input about how to manage, structure, and change their lives behaviorally in concrete ways. In some respects, the ongoing treatment milieu extends way beyond the treatment center into a lifestyle change that plays an ego auxiliary role in the lives of their clients.

Because of the fragility associated with the psychiatric problems of the dually diagnosed patient, it is necessary to modify the incorporated elements from the substance abuse treatment model. First of all, attention must be paid to the uniqueness and personality dynamics of the patient. There is a tendency among substance abuse specialists, who are often recovering persons themselves, to use their own recovery as a model for treatment. However, one recovery model does not fit all. As one therapist stated: "You can't treat everybody the same. The one thing my analytic training really taught me is an individual approach. You have to get a feeling for a person as to how best to approach him. For some, you can be very confrontative and say, 'Stop, or else don't come back.' For others, you have to say, 'Wait a second; this person's more fragile,' and you have to deal with it in a different way."

Secondly, the treatment approach with the dually diagnosed must be more gradual and less confrontative than that with the typical substance abuse client. One interviewed therapist highlighted the difference:

> It's different in that I'm willing more patiently to work through the defensive functions that the problems with drugs and alcohol play in a person's life. I don't expect that a person can just give up drugs without having some reasonably confident sense that there's something to replace them with. The kind of confrontational, immediate abstinence demands that are associated with residential treatment centers are inappropriate and unrealistic for outpatient treatment, particularly in the context of somebody who has more or less severe emotional and psychological problems.

Thirdly, there must be a more flexible attitude towards the use of medications. Traditional substance abuse treatment discourages the use of any mood altering substances. For some, because of the fear of fostering an addictive mentality, this has become a rigid stance. However, many psychiatric disorders are best treated with medications, which should, however, be prescribed with care regarding their addictive potential.

Because the dually diagnosed form a heterogeneous population, there must be an openness to the unique needs of each patient and a flexibility in addressing those needs. Because of the existence of co-existing disorders with traditionally different treatment protocols, the therapist needs to be open to learning from different treatment traditions and creative in integrating the insights, strategies, and techniques of various approaches.

Clinical Issues

5

THE SQUEAKY WHEEL GETS THE GREASE: SHIFTING THE THERAPEUTIC FOCUS: THE ORDER OF TREATMENT

Most mental health and addiction professionals fail to ask the question about which disorder to treat first because their therapeutic approaches are dictated by their specialized training and expertise. They are alert to the problems to which they are personally and professionally attuned and treat what they know how to treat. Consequently, when a clinician encounters a patient with a coexisting substance use and psychiatric disorder, he treats the problem he is trained to recognize, and frequently overlooks the coexisting disorder. For example, on the one hand, addiction counselors typically address the substance abuse problem in their clients and expect that any residual psychiatric symptoms will eventually remit with continuing sobriety. If these symptoms persist, it means that the patient needs to be referred to a mental health professional. On the other hand, mental health personnel treat the psychiatric disorders in their patients and expect that the substance abuse problems will disappear with the resolution of the underlying psychological problems. If the alcohol or drug use continues as a problem, a referral is made to an addiction specialist.

A young student therapist told me about an interesting case. He had interviewed a middle aged man who came to a walk-in crisis clinic because he was depressed and suicidal. This man said that his wife wanted a divorce because of his bizarre behavior. She had caught him taking in wine by enema. He said he never drinks much now, but gets drunk frequently by enema, taking in as much as three gallons of wine each time. He explained that he learned 15 years ago that he could get drunk quicker through his anus. My colleague, who was psycho-dynamic in orientation, was fascinated by his story and speculated on the dynamics of anal intoxication. He thought it would be most helpful for this man to be involved in insight oriented therapy for this bizarre behavior. I viewed the case differently and suggested that this man had a severe substance abuse problem that probably needed to be addressed first before he would be able to explore fruitfully the under-lying dynamics of his behavior.

PERSPECTIVES ON THE ORDER OF TREATMENT

There is a growing consensus among those who treat dual diag-nosis patients that both disorders must be addressed from the begin-ning and throughout treatment. Their experience with this popula-tion indicates that a relapse into drinking or drug use will almost inevitably lead to an exacerbation of psychiatric symptoms, and con-versely, an increase of emotional or mental disturbance will result in a return to substance use. If the substance abuse problem is ignored or overlooked, the effective treatment of the psychiatric disorder will not be possible because of the cognitive, emotional, and functional impairment caused by the continued drug use. If the psychiatric prob-lem is not addressed, there is an increased risk that the patients will continue using drugs or relapse in order to cope with their unresolved problems.

Treatment Principle Two: It is necessary to address both the psychiatric and substance use disorders from the beginning and throughout treatment.

Different Treatment Models

While there is agreement on this basic treatment principle regard-ing the necessity of addressing both disorders, there are differences of opinion on strategies for implementing this approach. In the lit-erature, three basic models for coordinating addiction and psychiat-ric treatment have been distinguished: sequential, parallel, and inte-grated (Ries 1993a).

1) Sequential Model

In the sequential, or serial, model, the treatment for either the psychiatric disorder or addictive disorder begins first, followed by the treatment of the other disorder. Treatment usually occurs in two different settings. For example, a bipolar alcoholic may first be stabilized in a mental health hospital for a manic episode and then referred for substance abuse treatment following discharge.

There are advantages and disadvantages to this approach. The advantage of this model is that it utilizes the present system in which mental health and substance abuse services are separate. No cross-training of treatment personnel or exchange of resources is required. If the more severe disorder is addressed without neglecting the other disorder, this approach can be effective with some of the dually diagnosed. However, it often occurs that the secondary disorder is either ignored by the clinician who does not have expertise outside his field or neglected by the patient who does not follow through with treating the other problem. For example, once stabilized, the bipolar patient refuses to enter a substance abuse treatment program and prefers to drink rather than taking his medication. He feels better on alcohol than Lithium. Even if he does seek help for his alcohol problem, he is confused when he hears from substance abuse specialists and other alcoholics that he should remain completely drug free and discontinues his Lithium. Consequently, many of these patients fall between the cracks, end up half treated, and inevitably relapse.

2) Parallel Model

In the parallel model, the patient is treated concurrently for his psychiatric problem in a mental health clinic and for his addiction problem in a substance abuse program. For example, someone being treated in a psychiatric ward attends Alcoholics Anonymous meetings outside the unit. This model is used frequently in outpatient settings where the therapist recognizes the substance abuse problem, feels unqualified to treat it, and requires his patient to attend AA meetings or see a substance abuse counselor while he addresses the psychiatric problem in therapy.

Like the sequential model, this approach utilizes the existing separate systems. However, some knowledge of the philosphy and approach of the other treatment field is required of the therapist because the patient invariably receives conflicting information from the clinicians from the two treatment systems and may bring his concerns to the sessions. Thus, an advantage of this model is that it begins a cross-fertilization of ideas between the two often competing treatment systems and opens the doors to communication between personnel. A serious disadvantage of this approach is that the treatment is fragmented and often confusing for the patient who bears the burden of integrating the different treatment approaches to his problems. The patient may also feel overburdened by the requirement to participate in two separate treatments at the same time and give up altogether.

3) Integrated Model

The preferred approach of those experienced in treating the dually diagnosed is the integrated model. In this model, the same clinician provides both mental health and substance abuse treatment in the same setting, and both disorders are treated concurrently. This approach offsets the disadvantages of the other models. The therapist rather than the patient bears the burden of integrating the opposing treatment philosophies and makes sure that both disorders are addressed in treatment according to the needs of the patient. A single treatment is also more economical in terms of resources, time, and money. The patient does not have to utilize two separate treatment systems and risk having one disorder or the other go untreated. The disadvantage of this model is that the existing systems do not accommodate it. Staff must be trained in two different disciplines and integrate traditionally competing treatment philosophies, conceptual views of the nature of the disorders, and therapeutic techniques. Programs need to be altered to include the treatments that have for years been separate domains, sometimes jealously guarded by their practitioners. The bureaucratic changes required to implement this integration of programs can be daunting, given the long history of antagonism and lack of communication between the mental health and substance abuse treatment communities.

What little outcome research there is supports the greater effectiveness of the integrated model over the others. For example, Kofoed and collegues (1986) conducted a treatment outcome study with thirty-two dually diagnosed patients who participated in a unique outpatient pilot program that used techniques drawn from both psychiatric and substance abuse treatment approaches. The patients participated in weekly support groups in which education was provided regarding the dual disorders. They also attended AA meetings, individual therapy, day treatment, and skill training groups as needed. The thirty-two patients represented a severely dysfunctional population with diagnoses of major mental illness and substance abuse. Although twenty-one of the patients dropped out of treatment within two months, those who remained had a reduced rate of hospitalization. In another study, Nigam and colleagues (1992) described the successful use of weekly group therapy with eight dually diagnosed patients. The group was conducted in a mental health setting and utilized a psychoeducational approach aimed at substance abuse recovery. Six of the eight patients achieved periods of stable abstinence, continued group attendance, and improved social functioning.

THE VIEWS OF SOME OUTPATIENT THERAPISTS

The above models for treating both disorders have been developed through working with the mentally ill substance abuser, most frequently in inpatient or intensive outpatient settings. Practically nothing has been written about the efforts of outpatient therapists to treat the dually diagnosed in an integrated fashion, addressing both disorders. In my discussions with fellow therapists experienced in the outpatient treatment of the dually diagnosed, I learned there was a consensus that both the psychiatric and substance use disorders must be treated for a successful therapy. All agreed that the substance abuse problem must be addressed from the beginning of treatment and made part of the treatment plan. Furthermore, because of the disruptive potential of the substance abuse problem, these therapists concurred that their dually diagnosed patients needed to be monitored for relapse thoughout the therapy.

While these practitioners unanimously agreed on the basic principle that both disorders must be treated from the beginning and throughout therapy, they disagreed on the timing of the therapeutic focus in addressing these issues. Some of the therapists were insistent that the disorders ought to be treated sequentially, first the substance abuse, then the psychiatric disorder. Others proposed that the disorders needed to be addressed simultaneously.

It should be noted that all these therapists follow the integrated model above described. They treat both disorders of their patients in the same setting, although they may employ adjunctive services, such as AA. They attempt to integrate the treatment models derived from both the mental health and substance abuse treatment communities. Even those who follow the sequential approach are mindful of both disorders throughout the therapy with their patients.

A Sequential Approach

Those who espoused the sequential approach follow a two-part strategy. They address first the substance abuse problem, then the psychiatric problem. As one therapist with over 18 years of experience treating dual diagnosis patients stated:

> My approach has always been that you must treat the alcoholism first. You cannot overlook the drug abuse, whatever it happens to be. You cannot deal with other issues until the person is abstinent, particularly with something as traumatic as a history of any kind of abuse, whether physical, emotional, or sexual abuse. You need a basis of sobriety. Once I suspect that there's ongoing substance abuse, then that becomes the primary focus. Until they acknowledge their chemical dependency, get help, and stop abusing the substance, I think working on the other issues is secondary.

This therapist related an intriguing case in which she demonstrated her sequential strategy. It is the case of a woman, named Mary, whom she had been treating for several years.

> Mary came to her because of marital problems. After a couple of months, it became clear to the therapist that Mary was an alcoholic. So the therapist told her directly that they could not work on any other issues until she dealt with her alcoholism. Mary was very resistant to going to AA and kept saying that she could not accept the first step in admitting her powerlessness. In exploring her resistance to participating in AA, the therapist discovered that Mary had a long history of sexual abuse and was frightened of

being powerless. Being powerless meant for her the possibility of being victimized. Eventually, she went to AA meetings and became almost completely abstinent, slipping only occasionally. After several months of therapy, she resolved some issues in her marriage, felt better about herself, and achieved a measure of sobriety. They mutually decided to terminate treatment.

A year later, Mary called her therapist for an appointment and complained that she was struggling again not to drink. She was having bad dreams that dealt with sexual assault. Over time, the therapist began to realize that Mary seemed very different from other times. She had asked her to write about her experiences and noticed how the writing appeared to be by different people. The therapist consulted with some advisors and began to suspect that Mary may have been suffering from a multiple personality disorder. Over the next three years, several other personalities emerged in the therapy.

The therapist remarked how fascinating it was that some of the personalities drank socially and were not alcoholic. Some personalities did not drink at all, and others were alcoholic. She related: "So I had to start over with each personality that was alcoholic and deal with the alcoholism before I could deal with the trauma of memories."

There are several good reasons to justify this sequential approach. The first is based on a recognition of the debilitating effects of drug use on the person's capacity to participate in therapy. All the therapists interviewed admitted the futility of seeing patients who are intoxicated and refuse to treat them. However, these clinicians who espouse the sequential approach are particularly sensitive to the long-term effects of substance use that may interfere with the therapeutic process. If therapy is viewed as a process of increasing self-understanding or of solving personal problems, it is clear that drug use interferes with the client's capacity to participate fully and effectively in this work. Alcohol and drugs are often used to medicate the feelings that need to be explored in therapy. If a patient covers up his anxiety and depression, he will not be sufficiently aware of the issues that need to be addressed in therapy. Furthermore, drugs and alcohol have a deleterious effect on cognitive functioning, interfering with a person's capacity to remember clearly, to manage painful affects, and to resolve problems. Depending on one's conceptualization of the therapeutic process, effective participation in therapy requires that the person be able to articulate his experience, understand his feelings, reframe his thinking, and/or work towards resolving his problems. This cannot be done unless the patient's head is clear.

One of the interviewed therapists, a recovering alcoholic with over 20 years of experience working with the dually diagnosed, related some of her own personal experiences of being cognitively impaired because of her years of drinking:

> When people tell me that they have difficulty with memory when they're first coming off alcohol, I immediately think about when it took me five months to memorize the Serenity Prayer. I was at dissertation level, and it absolutely shouldn't have taken that long. . . . When I first came into AA, there was a test in one of the beginner's packets, called, "Who, Me?" If you answered three questions positively, you were alcoholic. I answered four. I took it a year later when my head was clear, and I answered twenty-two.

A second reason for the necessity of treating the substance abuse first is that the abuse makes an accurate diagnosis of the psychiatric disorder difficult or impossible. The problem is that the symptoms of chemical dependency can mimic or mask the symptoms of many psychiatric disorders, particularly depression, anxiety disorders, many personality disorders, and even schizophrenia. These experienced clinicians recommended a period of sobriety, from six months to a year, before an accurate diagnosis could be made.

A third reason is suggested for addressing the substance abuse first. Initially focusing on the psychiatric disorder may support the patient's alcoholic process and denial. It communicates to the patient that his substance abuse problem is not that important and that it is all right to continue drinking or using drugs. Some patients are even relieved if they are told they are dually diagnosed, because then they can entertain the illusion that they might be able to continue drinking once the psychiatric problem is resolved. They might think that they drink so much only to cope with the mental health problem, and once that is resolved, their drinking behavior can continue without difficulty.

The fourth reason for addressing the substance abuse problem first is that it is important to recognize that the exploration of sensitive personal issues in therapy usually raises anxiety, which may cause the individual to relapse, especially if his sobriety is not well established. Often these patients use drugs or alcohol to cope with uncomfortable affects and have not developed more effective means of coping. Their tolerance for anxiety is not very high. Psychotherapy can pose a danger for these patients, unless they are strong enough internally to address painful issues. Therefore, the first goal of treatment is to help the person become sober and begin to develop ego strengths and a supportive network that will enable him to confront his other problems. The initial strategy is then to diminish anxiety and offer support until the person is able to engage in the difficult and anxiety-provoking work of personal exploration.

Addressing the substance abuse issue is only the first stage of treatment, however. After sobriety is achieved, the underlying problems need to be addressed in a cautious fashion. Shifting too quickly to address the mental health problem might raise more anxiety than the person is able to handle comfortably and lead to a relapse. It is helpful to explain to the patient that the therapeutic focus is shifting to the psychiatric issue and caution him about the danger of relapse. Relapse is a particular danger if the underlying issue is one of traumatic abuse, which can stir up overwhelmingly painful memories and affects. Furthermore, the newly sober person might get so caught up in these other issues that he neglects working his recovery program and becomes more vulnerable to relapse. Consequently, while addressing the psychiatric problems, there is always the need to monitor closely the substance use and shift back to that problem if a relapse occurs.

Realistically, it must be admitted that there are occasions when it is necessary to address the psychiatric disorder before the recovery program is firmly established. There are times when a particular problem, such as physical abuse or traumatic memories, are foremost in the patient's mind and cannot be ignored. A current situation, such as an abusive relationship, may demand an immediate response because of the physical or emotional danger. If the person has become psychotic or suicidal, these problems demand an immediate response. As a criterion to determine the need to shift focus, attention should be paid to the level of urgency of the psychiatric problem.

Even after the focus has shifted to the mental health problem, however, the therapist must keep an eye on the substance abuse problem and always be conscious of the possibility of a relapse. In particular, the level of anxiety has to be closely watched, because it often leads to a return to drinking or drug use if it is too high. One therapist described walking a tightrope regarding anxiety in addressing both issues: "You have to keep one eye over here on the substance abuse and the other over there on the mental health problem when you do this work. But the most important thing is the anxiety. How do you walk that tightrope of anxiety? When we're dealing with a mental health problem, we want to mobilize that anxiety. When dealing with substance abuse, we don't want to mobilize it, because that will lead to drinking. Therefore, you have to walk a tightrope."

A Simultaneous Approach

Another group of therapists followed a simultaneous approach, insisting that the disorders are inseparable and must be treated together. One of those interviewed, a psychodynamic therapist, provided the rationale for treating both disorders together:

> The disorders develop together, and they have to be treated together. They're too entwined. Basically, when you are talking about the utilization of a substance to maladaptively tolerate an intolerable affect, idea, or circumstance, then there's no way in which you can take away that defense without providing some treatment for the intolerable affect, idea, or circumstance. They are inextricably linked. It's true that until a person stops utilizing the substance to avoid something that you cannot deal with what is being avoided. But it is just the flip side of the coin. Inevitably, you find yourself bouncing back and forth between dealing with the symptoms of the withdrawal from the substance and the symptoms of the psychological or emotional disturbance that are more raw and exposed at the point at which the substance is not functioning defensively anymore.

While these practitioners prefer addressing the disorders simultaneously, they recognize occasions when their attention must be focused on the substance abuse problem. Like their sequentially minded colleagues, they believe it becomes necessary to shift the therapeutic focus when the drug use is so severe that it interferes with the patient's ability to participate in therapy. According to them, such interference occurs when their drug use causes significant disruptions in their lives so that they are unable to contain their acting out behavior.

What all these experienced outpatient therapists have in common is their recognition that both the substance abuse and psychiatric disorders must be addressed for the treatment to be successful. Contrary to the practice of many psychologists, those interviewed insist that the substance abuse problem be treated from the beginning and throughout the therapy. They are aware of the disruptive potential of substance abuse, its debilitating effect on the individual, and the ever present danger of relapse. Therefore, they monitor the drug use of their patients closely throughout the treatment. When the consequences of drug use are severe enough to interfere with the person's life and capacity to participate actively in treatment, the substance abuse problem becomes the primary focus of treatment.

SHIFTING THE THERAPEUTIC FOCUS

All of these experienced outpatient therapists attempt to integrate the treatment of both the substance use and psychiatric disorders in their approaches. However, each group of clinicians highlight a different aspect of the integrated approach. Those who espouse a simultaneous strategy emphasize the first treatment principle, that both disorders must be addressed from the beginning and throughout treatment. Those who follow a sequential strategy suggest that the therapist needs to shift his therapeutic focus according to the severity and urgency of the problem, whether it is the substance use or psychiatric disorder. They are careful to emphasize that, while they are focusing on one disorder, the other cannot be neglected. One disorder may be in the foreground of treatment, while the other remains in the background. Their approach suggests a third treatment principle.

Treatment Principle Three: While maintaining attention on both the substance use and psychiatric disorders, the therapeutic focus ought to shift to address the more severe or threatening disorder.

Bill, a 35-year-old man, came to see me because he was having severe marital problems. He had been separated from his wife for a year and had just learned that she was filing for divorce. He was feeling overwhelmed and depressed and was having sleep problems and suicidal thoughts. In the initial interview, I learned that he had been drinking since his teenage years and had been drinking six to eight beers about three times a week on average. He admitted that his drinking was a problem for his wife and one of the reasons she wanted a divorce. I suggested that he might have a substance abuse problem and recommended that he abstain from drinking and attend AA. Bill admitted that he was concerned about his own drinking and had thought several times about quitting. So he readily agreed to abstain and attend AA. We began addressing his depression and suicidal thoughts at that point. It turned out that he had been depressed for many years and felt demeaned by his stern and critical father. Our initial focus was on addressing the relatively more severe symptoms of depression.

Bill was progressing well in treatment and feeling less overwhelmed. He was attending AA meetings regularly and maintaining his sobriety. About a month into treatment he had a face to face confrontation with his wife, became upset, and went on a drinking binge. When he came into the session following the relapse, we shifted focus to his substance abuse problem. We talked about what led to the relapse, what he thought, what he felt, and what circumstances surrounded his return to drinking. I also tried to relate his increased feelings of anxiety and depression to the underlying psychiatric issues we had been discussing for the past month. Bill gained some valuable insights into himself following the relapse and has maintained his sobriety since.

An ongoing and accurate assessment of both disorders is crucial in implementing this treatment principle regarding the shifting of therapeutic focus. The severity of either disorder may fluctuate over time, and the therapist must be aware of these changes in symptomotology. Furthermore, it is not always clear what is causing the observed symptoms, whether it is the substance abuse, the psychiatric problem, or an interaction of the two. Consequently, it may be difficult to determine which disorder demands a focus of treatment. There is also a continuum of severity for both disorders which may defy precise determination.

Four Diagnostic Situations: The Severity Factor

Along the continuum of severity, both disorders may be classified as either high or low (Ries 1993b). There are four possible combinations of diagnoses, which can be represented by a two by two matrix with four cells: 1) those with both substance use and psychiatric disorders of high severity, 2) those with severe psychiatric disturbances and substance abuse problems of low severity, 3) those with severe substance abuse problems and psychiatric disorders of low severity, and 4) those with both substance abuse and psychiatric disorders of low severity. Each of these groups requires a different therapeutic focus in addressing the problems.

In the first situation, in which both disorders are severe, the patient may need to be hospitalized, preferably in a dual diagnosis unit where both disorders can be treated aggressively in an integrated manner. If the person is acutely unstable and unable to control his drinking, he may well be a danger to himself and/or others and need to be placed in a protected environment. He may need to be referred to a place where he can be detoxed and closely monitored for his medical condition. An individual must be stabilized before he can be helped in the less structured outpatient setting.

TABLE 5–1   Order of Treatment According to the Severity of the Disorders

		Severity of the Disorders Substance Use Disorder	
		High	Low
	High	1	2
Psychiatric Disorder			
	Low	3	4

In the second situation, in which the psychiatric symptoms are severe while the substance abuse is less severe, the focus must be on the psychiatric problem. Any severe mental or emotional disturbance will interfere with the patient's ability to control his drug use if he is disposed to abuse, since the urge to self-medicate his feelings may be powerful. If the patient has acute psychotic symptoms or becomes suicidal, he may have to be referred to a psychiatrist for medication or inpatient admission. If the patient is feeling overwhelmed because he is being flooded with memories of abuse, for example, that issue must be addressed at the moment until the patient is relatively stabilized.

In the third situation, in which the substance abuse is severe and the psychiatric problem of a lesser severity, the therapeutic focus is directed to the substance abuse problem. Regarding the drug use, it is important to determine if the diagnosis is one of abuse or dependence. If it is a severe dependence, the cessation of substances may cause a medical emergency that needs to be addressed immediately through detox. If the drinking is uncontrolled, as the sequentially minded therapists explain clearly, it will interfere with the person's ability to participate in the treatment and must be addressed before exploring other issues. If relapses occur during the treatment, they too will need to be addressed. A decision must be made whether or not the severity of the drug problem requires a referral to a medical doctor or an inpatient substance abuse program.

In the fourth situation, in which both disorders are relatively mild, the therapeutic focus can shift readily between the disorders as the occasion arises in sessions. For example, if the person is mildly depressed and anxious and drinks occasionally to self-medicate, both disorders can more easily be treated together. The therapist may request that the patient remain abstinent, address the psychiatric issue, and respond to any returns to drinking.

Since there is a shift of therapeutic focus throughout the treatment according to the assessed severity of the disorders, it is clear that there is no rigid order of treatment of the disorders. However, even in the process of shifting attention to one disorder or the other, it is of paramount importance that the less severe problem not be ignored, because an exacerbation of symptoms can easily lead to a relapse of the problem being addressed. It might be more accurate to say that the more severe disorder is in the foreground of therapeutic attention, while the other disorder recedes into the background. In each session, there might be a sort of budgeting of attention to the problems according to the need of the patient at that moment.

For the purposes of analysis, these disorders are presented here as if they were clearly separate. However, in the real life of the patient, these disorders are not separate. They are inextricably intertwined and mutually interacting. Furthermore, the severity of these disorders cannot be so precisely measured and categorized within four discrete categories; rather, there is a continuum of severity for both disorders. The disorders interact in too complicated a fashion for such a clear and simple categorization. In the real clinical situation, there is no simple and precise correlation between symptom severity and therapeutic focus as is presented here. The clinical judgment of the therapist regarding the needs of the patient in all his multifaceted presentations becomes the final touchstone for determining the appropriate time for shifting therapeutic focus.

6

IF YOU DON'T ASK THE QUESTION, YOU WON'T GET THE ANSWER: ASSESSING THE DISORDERS

The accurate diagnosis of both the substance use and psychiatric disorders is essential for effective treatment. If the substance abuse problem is overlooked or ignored, the treatment will eventually reach a standstill. If the psychiatric pathology is not addressed, there is an increased risk that the patient will continue or return to drug use to cope with his problems. Furthermore, the diagnosis of both problems is complicated by the interaction of the disorders and may require an extended period of time before a final diagnosis can be made. In this chapter, strategies and techniques will be presented for assessing for a dual diagnosis. Since mental health professionals are more thoroughly trained for the assessment of psychiatric rather than substance use disorders, more attention will be given to how to recognize a substance abuse problem in those who present themselves in outpatient mental health settings.

Treatment Principle Four: It is necessary to assess fully for both substance use and psychiatric disorders with every patient from the beginning and throughout treatment.

Because of the prevalence of coexisting disorders in the psychiatric population, the therapist needs to maintain a high index of suspicion that those who present themselves for treatment of their mental health problems may also have a covert and unadmitted drug problem, particularly with alcohol. Every patient needs to be assessed carefully for the possibility of coexisting disorders. This assessment will rarely be simple and straightforward because of the interactions of the disorders. Patients tend to minimize their drug use and deny its negative consequences. They usually need to establish a trusting relationship with a therapist before revealing the full extent of their substance use, particularly of an illicit drug. Furthermore, substance use tends to mask and mimic many psychiatric disorders, particularly in the intoxicated state and early stages of withdrawal. These complications suggest another treatment principle regarding diagnosis.

Treatment Principle Five: The assessment process must be ongoing because an accurate diagnosis for both disorders may take time.

ASSESSING FOR SUBSTANCE ABUSE

Complications

In the mental health setting, it is not always easy to make a dual diagnosis. The substance abuse problem often goes undiagnosed. There are few studies and some estimates of how often mental health professionals fail to detect a substance abuse problem in their clients. In talking with my colleagues, I estimate that about 25 percent of those who come for help in outpatient clinics have problems significantly affected by drug use, particularly alcohol. I further estimate that less than a fifth of these patients are diagnosed and treated for their substance abuse, resulting in at least partial treatment failures.

In one study of the effect of unrecognized drug abuse on diagnosis and therapeutic outcome among psychiatric outpatients, Hall and colleagues (1977) discovered that drug abuse was often undiagosed and was a major factor in distorting the accuracy of diagnosis. Furthermore, they found that therapists behaved very differently with those patients who were covert drug abusers. In their study, these researchers collected urine samples from 195 consecutive community mental health center outpatients and tested for the presence of drugs other than alcohol. Thirty-one patients refused to participate in the study, leading to the suspicion that they may have been covert drug users. Of the population screened and not diagnosed with a substance use disorder, 13.3 percent were found urine positive for drugs of abuse. Patients with positive urines were significantly more likely to be misdiagnosed than those with negative urines. Therapists perceived them as being "brittle," helpless, dependent, and sicker than their level of social functioning would seem to indicate. Marked differences in the behavior of the clinicians towards these covert drug users were noted. Therapists were seven times more likely to cancel appointments with this group, thirteen times more likely to transfer them to other therapists, and six times more likely to terminate treatment prematurely. Obviously, countertransference issues arose with these patients. Not surprisingly, those patients who remained in treatment were significantly less likely to benefit from therapy than were nonabusers matched for initial diagnosis.

This study suggests some of the difficulties in diagnosing the substance abuse of outpatients. First of all, people come to therapists in mental health settings primarily for help regarding mental health problems. Rarely do they seek help for their drinking or drug use in these settings. Their attention is focused on getting relief from the distress that they identify. In discussing the patient's presenting problem, however, the clinician may become aware of problematic drug use which the individual may or may not be ready to address.

Secondly, patients may be resistant to recognizing and admitting that they have a substance abuse problem. Many will frankly deny that their drinking or drug use is causing them any difficulties. They may admit that they drink on occasion and even get drunk, but they may see this as a long standing pattern that does not interfere with the quality of their lives.

Even therapists experienced in working with the dually diagnosed lament that they are fooled because they must rely on the self-reports of their patients who may minimize or hide their drug problems. One clinician confessed: "I remember treating someone when I first started whom I treated for years. She finally admitted to me that she would sober up the day before she came to see me. I never knew she had a substance abuse problem. That is the case at times. She came with chronic marriage problems and depression. She never really admitted to me she was drinking until later." Another therapist concurred:

If the addiction isn't severe yet, it's much easier to hide from you. I don't have a crystal ball. I don't always see it. I remember Fr. Quinn (a recovering alcoholic and national speaker) saying, "Watch out for the person who says 'I only have one drink a day.' I used to have only one drink a day. So I learned to pour it into a great big glass. I had only one drink, but it was most of a fifth." So people say they only have one drink a day, but it may be a water glass, and that's three fingers high. They are not in their own minds lying to me.

A third complication concerns the attitude of the therapist. Hall and his colleagues noted how therapists responded differently to their substance abusing clients. Furthermore, these clinicians related that they were not consciously aware that these patients had a drug problem or that they themselves were acting differently towards them. Clinicians may engage in patterns of denial similar to those of their patients. This denial keeps them from recognizing and inquiring about substance abuse. One therapist, who confronted his own denial, confessed: "I started to feel more comfortable with substance abusing patients. I also started to see that unconsciously I was ignoring all the substance abuse issues in patients who were coming in without a substance abuse complaint. Somehow, without knowing it, I was sometimes colluding with them to avoid talking about something very obvious, I later found out. . . . I realized I had a whole population in my own practice that potentially had substance abuse problems I hadn't detected yet." Furthermore, many mental health professionals have not been specifically trained in the treatment of substance abuse and feel incompetent to diagnose and treat it. They may even be reluctant to recognize it because they would not know what to do if they did.

A final difficulty is that psychiatric symptoms may mask and mimic some substance abuse problems. Many psychiatric symptoms such as depression, anxiety, mood swings, irritability, and paranoia can be caused by substance abuse. The toxic effects of drugs on the brain cause neurochemical and neurophysiological changes that manifest themselves in commonly seen psychiatric symptoms. Both patients and therapists can easily attribute these symptoms to psychiatric illnesses and fail to recognize their true etiolology as substance induced.

In summary, the complications in assessing the substance use disorders are the following:

1. Patients generally come to mental health settings for the treatment of their psychiatric problems.
2. Patients tend to minimize and deny their drug problems.
3. Therapists may share the denial of their patients and lack training in the assessment and treatment of substance abuse.
4. Psychiatric symptoms may mask and mimic a substance abuse problem.

Therapeutic Tasks

1) Is the Drug Use Problematic?

There are several tasks in the substance abuse assessment process with the potential dual diagnosed patient. First of all, it is important to determine if the patient's use of substances is problematic and in need of therapeutic attention. In our culture, almost everyone will use mind altering drugs at some point in their lives for some period of time. Most will use them with social support, and their use will be controlled. This judgment about whether or not their drug use is problematic is made by noting the consequences of use in the total context of the person's life. Even if the consequences appear minimal at first glance, the substance use needs to be carefully monitored because of the user's tendency to minimize. There are both external and internal consequences that can be observed. The external consequences are more evident, such as marital conflicts, failed relationships, getting fired from a job, or legal problems. The internal consequences concern the individual's feelings about his drug use, whether he has ever felt concerned, guilty, or ashamed about it. A clinician needs to ask himself: Does this person's use of drugs cause him problems in his life? Does his drug use enhance or interfere with his well-being?

2) What Is the Severity of Drug Use?

If a drug problem is discerned, the next step is to evaluate its severity. Research suggests that the distinction between abuse and dependence has important treatment and prognostic consequences. For example, Bartels and colleagues (1995) studied the long-term course of substance use disorders among patients with severe mental illness. A baseline study group of mentally ill patients was followed up seven years later to determine if there were significant changes in their drug use over that period of time. Of the original group, 148 (87%) were fully assessed seven years later. These researchers discovered that almost all patients without a substance use disorder at baseline had no signs of abuse at follow-up. Among those with alcohol or drug dependence at baseline, two-thirds had substance use disorders seven years later. The greatest change was noted in the substance abusing group. About two-thirds (67%) of the alcohol abusers were abstinent or nonproblematic users at follow-up, and over half (54%) of the drug abusers were in remission. The researchers concluded that the difference in outcome between patients who were abusers and those who were dependent suggests the need for different intensities of treatment for the two types of patients. Those who are dependent may require inpatient or intensive outpatient treatment, while substance abusers may be successfully treated on an outpatient basis.

There are many models for making the diagnostic distinction between abuse and dependence. Some clinicians focus on the pattern of use: the amount, frequency, and type of drug used. *DSM-IV* presents diagnostic criteria based on physiological signs and the degree of social, occupational, and personal disruption caused by the use. One of the therapists interviewed offered an alternative model based on the person's relationship with the drug and the experience of a loss of freedom:

> The distinction between dependency and abuse is very important. Philosophically, the distinction is between loss of freedom or not over the use of substances. When that occurs, I consider the person addicted. It can be a subtle transition. Initially, the person may have been using the substance to medicate a mental or emotional disorder. Depending on the addictive potential of the substance, increasing numbers are going to pass over that invisible line of loss of freedom, or loss of control. It's tougher assessing that. I don't think it's fair to just go by the amount or frequency of drug use. I think a clearer indication is use in spite of adverse consequences. It appears to the objective observer that this person had very good reason to stop—been arrested, lost jobs and families—yet returns to using. They will admit their troubles from using, but will con-

tinue to use. That's a clear indication of loss of freedom. Every time a person gets into trouble for using and continues using, it's that much more evidence for addiction as opposed to simple abuse.

He continued by describing the kind of psychological attachment that indicates an addiction: "Physical dependence alone doesn't make an addiction. You also have to have the psychological. That means you have to explore a person's attachments. Do they feel like they need it in order to function? Are they panicked at facing certain situations without it? Do they only feel good under the influence of substances? This is all evidence of a full-blown addiction. When people have your confidence, they will talk about their relationship with the substance."

3) What Is the Interaction of Disorders?

A third assessment task is to determine which model of interaction between the disorders applies. Is the substance abuse primary or secondary to the psychiatric disorder, or are both disorders primary? The distinction may be made by considering the temporal relationship of the disorders and the family history of the patient. One of the experienced therapists I interviewed offered this view on making the diagnostic distinction:

If the substance abuse is secondary, you can usually trace it to some situational behaviors. For example, someone has lost his job and is under a great deal of stress. So he starts drinking. There is a clear cause and effect relationship to some stressors in a person's life. Now the drinking may begin as something reactive and develop into something with a life of its own. If the substance abuse is primary, you can see the effects across the board in a person's life. It has become a habituated behavior that is not related to any particular event in the person's life. So you have to look at the pattern of the drinking. If the substance abuse is secondary, the drinking will be more episodic.

This distinction is important, if it can be made with assurance, to guide the focus of treatment. However, as observed previously, most cases are not so clear, and it normally takes some time for the true nature of the disorders to reveal themselves.

4) What Is the Meaning of Use?

A final assessment task is to understand the meaning of the client's substance use in the context of his personality dynamics, life, and other symptoms. The therapist needs to learn how the patient uses substances, under what circumstances, and to cope with what kinds of feelings or stresses. One of the clinicians interviewed offered an example of how he explains to his patients the relationship of the disorders:

> Let's just say it's depression, and they're alcoholic. What I will do is help them see the relationship between the mental health problem and the substance abuse problem. Even though people often are reluctant to define themselves as having a substance abuse problem, they are more likely to focus on the depression because of some family or personal crisis. I will try to help them understand how they use the alcohol to substitute for some type of antidepressant medication. Even though alcohol is a depressant, it also helps them to forget their problems. So they think it's helping them, because they don't feel so overwhelmed anymore.

In summary, the therapist faces many assessment tasks in diagnosing the substance abuse problem. A careful assessment requires that the therapist

1. Determine if the use of alcohol or drugs is problematic,
2. Assess the severity of the substance use disorder,
3. Distinguish if the substance abuse problem is primary or secondary to the mental health problem, and
4. Understand the meaning of the substance use in the context of the person's life and symptom picture.

Some Assessment Strategies

1) Ask Questions

In assessing for the possibility of a substance abuse problem, the first requirement is to ask the patient about his use of drugs and alcohol. All patients should be questioned in the first session. This recommendation might seem too obvious to mention. However, many mental health professionals fail to inquire about the substance use of their patients, perhaps because of their own denial or lack of training in substance abuse. Or their questioning may be done in a cursory manner, just to fill out a form, without any exploration of the person's responses. One therapist, experienced in the treatment of the dually diagnosed and of the sexually abused, commented on the importance of asking the questions:

> I have had people referred to me by other psychologists and social workers where they'll say, "Therapy isn't working, and I'm sure it's because this person has been sexually abused." They'll come in and I'll start asking them about their use of substances and find out there's a good likelihood that this person is addicted. The previous therapist will never have asked these questions. It's not often that a person comes staggering into your office. Most people are smart enough not to do that. So if you don't ask the questions, you probably won't get the answers.

In assuming an inquisitive posture, the therapist needs to develop a high index of suspicion regarding substance abuse, particularly if the patient has a history of abuse. The research on the prevalence of the dually diagnosed in all treatment settings also warrants a suspicious attitude. A psychiatrist related to me a story that illustrates the importance of being suspicious and assuming nothing. He was interviewing a woman who had brought in a covered 32-ounce cup from a fast food restaurant. Throughout the interview, she sipped periodically from the cup through a straw. The doctor noticed that the woman's face was flushed and asked her what she was drinking. She said it was liquor.

There are, of course, many ways of asking about a patient's drinking and drug use. Because of temperment or therapeutic orientation, therapists may vary in their manner of questioning. Some are more direct than others. One therapist, who is straightforward in personality and therapeutic approach, described what she does:

> If you ask the questions, you're going to get the answers. This is the directness. You do not go into the symbolism. You go into what is in front of you and ask questions. Of course, you're not going to ask the question if you're afraid of what the answer is going to be. I think that psychologists don't know what to do with it, so therefore they don't ask the question. They're afraid of what the

answer is going to be. The other thing that psychologists are known for is obsessive-compulsiveness. We analyze everything. We analyze and analyze and we're afraid to come to any conclusions. It's almost as if we want to have all the knowledge, but we're afraid of knowing. So we get caught up in analysis. I think that's one reason why psychology has not been successful with chemical dependency. It's that we analyze too much and don't listen for answers.

Other therapists prefer a more indirect approach to learning about the substance use of their clients. For example, one psychodynamic practitioner commented:

I have never met anybody who had a substance abuse problem who didn't tell me about it in the first session in one way or another. I certainly may have missed it, thinking back in my memories of people I've known over the years. I realized it's there. It's always there, even if they don't talk about it directly. It's there in the disguise of marital tension, or work problems, or fatigue and malaise. In the course of talking with people, they will mention alcohol or drug abuse in the conversation. It may not be about themselves. They may talk about being at a party and their brother did this, their father did that, and their mother or spouse did this. But somewhere, a substance abuse problem is mentioned. I just take the lead and ask them more about it right then. Ten years ago I might not have asked about it. Now I ask. "You said your dad's got a drinking problem. How about you? You said you guys have been fighting. Does alcohol play a part in this?" It's amazing, when I think back on it, if they've got a problem, everybody brings it up somehow. Just listen for it. . . . I just find that I don't have to bring it up. It's there. If somebody really didn't know it or I missed it, now I would ask about it. I'd get it indirectly. "What do you do for fun?" They tell me about their hobbies or interests, "I like to go out to dinner." I ask them to tell me more about it. They say, "I like a great restaurant, a great wine. I really like wine." You find out a lot of different ways people use drugs and alcohol.

The types of questions asked of the potential dual diagnosis patient are similar to those used in the routine assessment for substance abuse. The first area of concern is the individual's personal pattern and history of drinking or drug use. When did they have their first drink, and what was their experience? When was the first time they got high? What is the most they have ever put away in an evening? What drugs have they experimented with? What has been the progression of their drinking or drug use? Did they have any periods of abstinence or treatment for substance abuse? It is also important to establish the current pattern of drug use. How much do they drink? How often? Do they usually drink alone or with others? When was the last time they drank or used drugs? What happens when they drink? Does their personality or behavior change? Do they evidence signs of addiction: blackouts, tremors, loss of control? Have they ever been concerned about their own drinking or drug use? Have people close to them been concerned? Of course, these questions are asked regarding the various types of drugs of abuse, particularly if the person indicates even a minimal use of the drug. In the case of the dually diagnosed, it is important to determine the temporal sequence of the psychiatric symptoms and substance abuse behavior to determine which is primary.

It is helpful to assess the personal meaning that the drinking or drug use has for the patient. Individuals perceive positive benefits from their substance use that motivate the continuation of their using. Therapists can ask directly what their drug does for them. What was life like for them before using drugs? What do they imagine life will be like without it? The circumstances surrounding their substance use—where, when, and with whom—can give clues as to its meaning. The clinician can also form hypotheses about what disturbing thoughts and feelings the patient has difficulty coping with and tries to avoid with drug use.

2) Be Alert to the Consequences of Use

Another important area of exploration is the negative consequences of drug use. Often the patient does not associate these problems with his drug use, but there is a typical pattern of disruption that can alert the therapist to the possibility of a drug problem. Is there a history of acting out or assaultative behavior? Are there significant marital problems? Have they had work related problems, an inconsistent work history or many job changes? Have they ever been arrested for drunk driving or drunken behavior? Have they ever neglected family or work responsibilities because of their drinking or drug use?

3) Review the History

Knowing the patient's psychiatric history can give valuable information about the possibility of a drug problem. Studies of the comorbidity of disorders, as indicated previously, suggest that particular psychiatric diagnoses are associated with substance abuse problems to a degree far greater than chance. For example, if the patient's childhood history revealed disruptive behavior, poor school performance, and hyperactivity, the therapist might suspect that the patient suffered attention deficit disorder and that there was a good chance that he now abuses substances. Research indicates a strong association of attention deficit and conduct disorder with substance abuse in later life.

A review of the family history of substance abuse can yield information regarding the likelihood of the patient's having a drug problem. Research has firmly established a genetic contribution to chemical dependency. Coming from a substance abusing family poses a significant risk for a person to develop an addiction problem. For example, the son of an alcoholic father has a four-times greater chance of being alcoholic than the son of nonalcoholic parents.

A careful review of the person's medical history can give important clues regarding a possible drug problem. Some pathologies, for example, are frequently associated with the chronic abuse of depressants such as alcohol: gastric ulcers, hepatitis and cirrhosis of the liver, neuropathy, hypertension, memory problems, sexual performance problems, and general dementia. Seizure disorders, strokes, hypertension, and restlessness are associated with the abuse of stimulants, such as cocaine. Infections and AIDS are frequently found among intravenous drug users. The therapist might also note if patients have frequent headaches in the morning, a history of head injuries, make frequent visits to the doctor for vague complaints, or call in sick a lot from work. If the patient presents these types of physical complaints and symptoms, the therapist can explore them further and possibly relate them to a covert drug problem.

4) Use Questionnaires

How questions are asked can contribute to the building of a trusting relationship and enhance the reliability of the patient's responses.

By no means can these questions be asked in a judgmental way, which will only make the patient more defensive. The questions should be posed in as matter of fact, disarming, and nonthreatening a manner as possible. Using the questions of standardized questionnaires with proven validity, such as the Michigan Alcoholism Screening Test (MAST), can be helpful. It is not necessary to read the questions to the patient in a formal way. However, the content and style of the questions can be useful guides for the therapist's own interviewing. The CAGE questions have shown themselves to be a nonthreatening and brief diagnostic tool. The patient's responses to the four CAGE questions can be explored further with other questions:

Question 1: Have you ever felt the need to cut down on your drinking or drug use? The therapist can explore the person's response by asking: What was it like? Were you successful? Why did you decide to cut down?

Question 2: Have you ever been annoyed at criticism of your drinking or drug use? Further questions might be: What caused the worry or concern? Do you ever get irritated by their worry? Have you ever limited what you drink in order to please someone?

Question 3: Have you ever felt guilty about something you've done when you were drinking or high from drugs? Further explorations might be: Have you ever been bothered by anything you have done or said while you've been drinking? Have you ever regretted anything that has happened to you while drinking?

Question 4: Have you ever had a morning eye-opener to control the shakes? Some follow-up questions: Have you ever felt shaky after a night of heavy drinking? What did you do to relieve the shakiness? Have you ever had trouble getting back to sleep early in the morning after a night of drinking?

5) Seek Collateral Information

Most of this information depends on the self-report of the patient. However, substance abusers are notoriously unreliable in accurately describing their frequency, amount, and pattern of drug use. Besides the tendency to deny and minimize their drug use, these patients, if they are chronic abusers, also suffer significant cognitive impairments.

They often cannot remember what they have done. They also lack the insight to connect their life problems with their drinking or drug use. In my own mind, I usually double the amount and frequency of alcohol use reported by the patient to obtain a more accurate picture of the pattern of use. I recognize also that the abuse of illicit drugs is seldom reported or drastically minimized because of the feared legal repercussions for the patient. A trusting relationship must first be established before most people will reveal the true nature of their illicit drug use.

The cognitive and emotional impairments that lead to a distorted reporting of drug use are compounded with the dually diagnosed. Mentally ill individuals may have a distorted perception of the world around them and be unable to report accurately their personal histories of drug use. Their memories may also be profoundly affected by their psychiatric disorders. Therefore, it is unrealistic to expect many of these patients to answer the therapist's questions accurately. The therapist can facilitate the patient's recall of his drug history by helping him relate incidents of use to significant life events, such as high school or college graduation, the wedding day, the birth of children, and so on.

Because of the patient's reluctance and inability to give an accurate history, collateral sources of information are often sought in some treatment settings. In inpatient and substance abuse treatment settings, the family is typically involved to offer support to the patient, help monitor his progress, and learn about the disease. Furthermore, substance abuse is viewed as a family illness that affects all the members who may in some way be enabling the abusive behavior of the addicted member. Consequently, the whole family is often brought into treatment with the substance abuser.

In the outpatient mental health setting, however, it is not so usual to enlist the help of family members for the patient's recovery. Because of confidentiality and the individualized treatment model of most therapists, the family remains uninvolved. Since the outpatient setting works most effectively with those who are motivated and functional in the world, the family's support is not seen to be as essential as it is for the more disturbed hospitalized patient. Nevertheless, family members, if the patient gives permission, can be helpful in the diagnosis and treatment of the dually diagnosed. For example, if the patient complains of marital problems, the therapist can suggest that the spouse come in for a collateral session. At that time, the therapist can get an idea if a drug problem is contributing to the marital conflict. The spouse is usually quite aware of, and verbal about, the substance abuse that the patient is reluctant to admit.

6) Drug Screens

Drug screens are also more appropriate for substance abuse and inpatient treatment settings than for the outpatient mental health clinic. Normally, the necessary facilities are not available in the clinic to perform, monitor, and analyze the results of the drug screen. The patient, who generally comes for a mental health problem, may resent the intrusion of a drug screen and terminate a therapy for which he has come voluntarily. It would interfere with the therapeutic alliance that the therapist is trying to establish with his patient. Furthermore, since most patients are voluntary, the therapist has no leverage to require them to get drug screens. Even if the therapy is court ordered, the therapist may be reluctant to require a drug screen because that would ally him on the side of the court rather than with the patient in the patient's eyes and, again, interfere with the establishment of a therapeutic alliance.

7) Be Intuitive

Those who have worked with substance abusers develop an intuitive sense about the presence of the problem. There are seemingly insignificant signs that when put together with other such signs, can suggest a problem. For example, the lack of eye contact, the frequent wiping of the nose, and the vague self-report of the patient alert me to the possibility of drug abuse. One experienced therapist, who is a recovering person, admitted that she relies on intuition in making a diagnosis: "That's the way I diagnose alcoholism or chemical dependency. It's something you pull out of the sky." She related that she is attentive to details that might suggest a drinking problem:

> If it's a non sequitur, it doesn't fit. A patient may come in, and
> things just don't fit. Let me give you an example. I had a patient

who came in to talk about her 3-year-old. I had never seen her before, and she arrived in a jogging suit and tennis shoes with a coke. That's one way you can tell, whether they bring in a coffee or coke to a session. If they bring in a coffee or coke, you wonder why they have to drink so much. Of course, you get near them and smell. Anyhow, I thought something was wrong. There is alcoholism in this family, and this lady is an alcoholic. Now her husband, an attorney, comes in, very meticulously and appropriately dressed. I didn't think it was appropriate to come into a psychologist's office for the first time dressed like that. So after we finished the whole interview, I said, "By any chance, is there any alcoholism in the family?" They looked at each other, and it was the man. I'm not quite sure why the woman dressed like that unless she was trying to send me a message of some sort. But they didn't do anything about it. That's not why they came for therapy. I thought it was interesting that I was able to pick that up. That was just one of those threads you like to follow.

This therapist reflected further:

You just notice little things, like the person bringing in a coke or coffee. That's the data that you get to give you a hypothesis. Then you have to test the hypothesis, because I don't want to go ahead and say, "This guy wipes his nose; therefore, he is a cocaine addict." I tuck things in the back of my head, which is really that I compartmentalize it. I wait until I get another hunk of data. Then I put them together. Then I keep adding to it. Then pretty soon I can question more. Or I question and get more data. Then you analyze it and question and get more data.

Eventually, she reaches a conclusion and makes a diagnosis, which she presents to the patient.

Anyone attentive to the possibility of their patient's having a substance abuse problem has similar experiences that resemble informed clinical guesses. A mother and her 15-year-old son came to see me because of family problems. The mother was at wit's end because her two boys were fighting constantly, and she did not know how to stop it. The older son, who was 17, refused to come to the session with his mother and brother. I asked the boy what he was fighting with his brother about. He said that his older brother suddenly began picking on him two months previously. I asked him what he thought the reason was, and he replied that he had no idea. I asked him if he thought his brother might be drinkng or using drugs. At that point, the mother spoke up and objected vehemently that I asked her son that question. She said, "Why ask him? I'm his mother, and I know better!" I became suspicious that there indeed was a drug problem in the family and that it belonged to the mother. In later sessions, I learned that the mother herself did not abuse drugs, but that she was caring for a severely alcoholic brother and experienced much personal turmoil because of him.

For the accurate assessment of a substance abuse problem, the following suggestions can be helpful:

1. Maintain a high index of suspicion regarding substance abuse with every patient who comes for treatment.
2. Be aware of the person's tendency to deny and minimize a drug problem.
3. Ask nonjudgmental and probing questions about the patient's substance use.
4. Be alert to the negative consequences commonly associated with substance abuse in the areas of marital, family, interpersonal, employment, legal, and medical problems.
5. Look for substance abuse in the family history.
6. Consult with collateral sources if the patient gives permission.
7. Develop an intuitive sense of things not fitting together that might suggest a drug problem.

An Ongoing Process

The assessment for substance abuse is an ongoing process that requires time. Sometimes, the problem can be diagnosed to the satisfaction of the therapist within the first two to three sessions. Oftentimes, the therapist becomes suspicious of a problem and continues to probe and be alert for confirming evidence. One clinician related that the patient's denial often delays her picking up the problem immediately: "Usually, I would say within the first half-dozen sessions something feels like—I hate to say it's intuitive—but I feel suspicious that something's not right, the pieces aren't fitting together right. As people get more comfortable with me, they'll talk about their drinking and drugging more openly. When people come to see me, by and large, they don't come to see me because they believe they have an addiction problem."

Because of the patient's denial, it may take several months before the therapist's suspicion regarding substance abuse can become a certainty. As an example, one therapist related an experience with a long-term patient she was seeing:

> I had been concerned about her drinking from the beginning. By the time I was seeing her, I did an assessment of everyone I saw in terms of chemical dependency. I had been concerned about her answers at that point. I just didn't think they were honest. So I kept monitoring her drinking. By four or five months, I was convinced she was an alcoholic. She denied it and minimized her drinking. Then she came to me one day and told me that she had a horrible experience, and maybe I was right. This was an extremely successful professional lady who made $300,000 a year. She had gone to some woman's professional meeting, came home, and drove her car onto the lawn, narrowly missing her house. She was frightened by that. She had been drinking.

An accurate assessment for substance abuse may also take time because the patient must first learn to trust the therapist before he will reveal the true nature of his use of substances. People are particularly reluctant to talk with a relative stranger about their use of illegal substances because of the possible legal ramifications. Furthermore, many patients have been so mistreated by the significant people in their lives that they have trouble trusting anyone. They may have felt criticized and judged by so many people for their behaviors that they expect the therapist to react in the same way. They keep what is shameful or embarrassing in their eyes to themselves. Those who suffer paranoia are even more resistant to revealing any possibly incriminating facts about their lives. Consequently, the therapist must work at establishing a trusting relationship with patients before he will be able to learn more about their pattern of drug use and make an informed and accurate diagnosis.

ASSESSING THE PSYCHIATRIC DISORDERS

Complications

The presence of a substance abuse problem greatly complicates the assessment and diagnosis of psychiatric disorders. Corty and colleagues (1993) examined the interrater reliability of diagnoses made on the basis of a structured interview for psychiatric patients with and without substance use disorders. Forty-seven patients were evaluated by pairs of interviewers. There was a notable difference in diagnostic reliability when substance abuse was present. Interrater reliability in diagnosing the patient was high when there was no substance abuse problem, with the percentage of agreement around 90%. However, reliability decreased substantially when there was a dual diagnosis, and the percentage of agreement was in the 70% to 80% range. Furthermore, the interviewers did not seem aware that the coexistence of a substance use disorder might affect the accuracy of their diagnoses and were just as certain of their assessments, whether or not a substance abuse problem was present.

Several factors contribute to the difficulty of assessing for the mental health problem. First of all, the substance use and psychiatric disorders interact in ways that are little understood and may influence the course and presentation of both illnesses. As elaborated in the chapter on the interaction of the disorders, the disorders may have begun separately, but over time become intertwined and mutually interactive. One therapist interviewed employed the image of a lens: "Now, they may start by using these substances for different reasons, and it may have different effects on them, which affects the nature of their psychopathology. Substance abuse is going to become a lens that in some ways exaggerates, intensifies or distorts people differently depending on how they start."

Secondly, substance abuse masks and mimics psychiatric disorders, making an accurate diagnosis difficult. Because the drugs of abuse are psychoactive, they influence the mood, thinking, and behavior of the user. Many have observed that the symptoms of chemical dependency are similar to the symptoms of a great variety of disorders in the *DSM-IV*, including anxiety, depression, mania, and schizophrenia.

Thirdly, because of the changing course of substance abuse states and the diverse symptomotology of the various classes of drugs, the symptom picture can change over time. Each type of drug, whether stimulant, depressant, opioid, or hallucinogen, has unique physiological effects on the brain that result in different behavioral manifestations. There is an immediate effect that is influenced by the route of administration and dosage and a later rebound effect that is the opposite of the initial reaction. Thus, it is important to distinguish what drug is being abused, what state the patient is in, and how long he has been abstinent to make an accurate diagnosis.

An Example: Cocaine

Cocaine, whose use has increased in the past decade, is a good example. Two distinct phases with vastly different symptom pictures can be discerned in the aftermath of cocaine use. The first phase is that of intoxication, the "high." The euphoric effects occur almost immediately and last about 30 minutes. With low doses, the effects are euphoria and sometimes improved performance on cognitive tasks. With high doses, the symptoms resemble a manic episode: hyperactivity, grandiosity, hypersexuality, impulsivity, impaired judgment, extreme psychomotor activation, irritability, and distractibilty (Baxter et al. 1988). As the binge lengthens, anxiety, hyperactivity, and irritability may increase.

Mood disturbances, delirium, and psychotic states can also result from cocaine use. During intoxication, states of severe transient panic accompanied by a terror of impending death can occur. Individuals intoxicated on cocaine report a mixture of elation and dysphoria similar to a cycling affective illness. They may become delerious and out of touch with their surroundings. Finally, while intoxicated, persons might develop paranoia and suspiciousness. When the paranoia is severe, reality testing becomes markedly impaired, delusions develop, and aggressive, even homicidal, behavior can result. These cocaine-induced paranoid psychotic disturbances may resemble any of the psychotic disorders of the *DSM-IV*, from delusional disorder to schizophrenia.

Following the period of intoxication is a phase marked by abstinent symptoms of withdrawal. Based on their study of the abstinent symptoms and psychiatric diagnoses of thirty chronic cocaine users, Gawin and Kleber (1986) have divided this phase into three periods. Immediately following the intoxication from the binge, the user experiences a "crash," which may last from hours to days. Initially, the user experiences agitation, depression, anorexia, and high cocaine craving to relieve dysphoria. These symptoms soon give way to fatigue, exhaustion, hypersomnolence, hyperphagia, and a lack of cocaine craving. A final period of euthymic mood and episodic cravings follows. During this withdrawal phase, individuals manifest symptoms of depression that are the inverse of the acute effects of stimulants: decreased energy, limited interest in the environment, limited ability to experience pleasure, psychomotor retardation, and suicidal thoughts (Baxter et al. 1988). In the early phases of withdrawal, it is difficult to determine whether the observed symptoms of depression represent a primary affective disorder or a drug-induced mood disorder.

Those who work with the dually diagnosed in outpatient settings are well aware that specific symptoms can be related to either the substance abuse or the psychiatric disorder. One experienced clinician noted that symptoms of anxiety and depression are found commonly among alcoholics and others suffering post traumatic stress and depression:

> But even something like post traumatic stress has so many anxiety symptoms that could be related to the alcoholism that I can't say that the post traumatic stress is there. I think probably the most common dual diagnosis is chemical dependency and dysthymia or major depressive disorder. Again, alcohol is a depressant drug. So, if I see someone who is actively using, I don't know how much of that is going to go away after they stop drinking. So I may have a suspicion that they're depressed and perhaps self-medicating with alcohol, but I really don't make a full psychiatric diagnosis until the person stops the chemical abuse.

She further remarked that restlessness, the inability to concentrate or remember, and agitation may be caused by withdrawal, by post traumatic stress, or a bipolar disorder: "As I said, it's very hard to make an accurate multi-axial diagnosis when the person is still actively chemically dependent. It disguises the symptoms. If somebody comes in here who can't sit still and can't concentrate and doesn't remember a lot, is it because of the withdrawal or because of the post traumatic stress?

If they are real agitated, is that because they are bipolar or are these withdrawal symptoms? So I am very careful in diagnosis."

In summary, the assessment of the psychiatric disorder is complicated by the presence of a coexisting substance use disorder for the following reasons:

1. The substance abuse disorder interacts with the psychiatric problem and changes its usual course and symptom presentation.
2. Substance abuse masks and mimics psychiatric disorders.
3. The symptom picture can change drastically over time because of the changing states of the substance use disorder and the type of drug abused.
4. Mental health professionals generally lack knowledge about the manifestations of substance abuse and how the disorders interact.

A Diagnosis Over Time

The usual methods for assessing the psychiatric disorder can be used with the dually diagnosed. The therapist can make his own version of a mental status examination. A history of the presenting problem, a thorough psychiatric and social history, and an assessment of the patient's psychosocial supports and stressors are taken. A generational family history including occurences of mental illness and treatment yields valuable information. Because of the cognitive deficits associated with many mental illnesses, the therapist may have to aid the recall of the patient and consult with collateral sources. After a careful gathering of information, though, only a provisional working diagnosis can be made if the patient is still abusing substances. Because of the ways that substance abuse masks, mimics, and distorts psychiatric disorders, it is wise to be cautious in making this initial diagnosis.

One of the therapists interviewed, a recovering alcoholic, employed the image of a cookie to describe how she sees the interaction of the disorders: "Chemical dependency is like an Oreo cookie. The bottom layer of chocolate has your genes, your life experiences, your learned behavior, your IQ. Then you put the vanilla in, the alcohol or chemical. Then you have the resultant behaviors." She stressed the importance of waiting to make a dual diagnosis, waiting to get the drugs out of the patient's system:

> I am well aware of how addiction masks and mimics other diagnoses in the DSM-III-R. So I think waiting is very important, but being cognizant of all the possibilities. . . . The image I like is that of the oreo cookie. The vanilla is the alcohol or drugs. We have to wait to get that out to see how the cookie crumbles. It's essentially the same thing when you are trying to make a dual diagnosis. It's my sense that we all have a dual diagnosis when we're using. But part of it can be, particularly when you get into the personality disorders, from learning what to do to get our drugs. So we have to wait till that passes.

It is necessary to wait before making a dual diagnosis because people may look very different after a period of sobriety. One therapist observed that people can look either healthier or crazier once they stop using substances:

> What you don't know, of course, is what they're going to look like after they withdraw from their substance of choice. There's a pressure towards need satisfying object relationships in all addicts. That's part of the addiction process. They all begin to look that way because their substance is a need satisfying object. It short-circuits object relationships. . . . People look much healthier when they stop using drugs. In this group [of my patients], they stopped having temper tantrums, looking not quite so narcissistic and brittle. They stopped using and exploiting other people and expecting other people to cater to them. They seemed more like well rounded people. It can work both ways, though. Sometimes people will look much crazier when they stop using because they are forced to use other kinds of defenses, and they may not have the ego to use more mature defenses.

There is a controversy about how long to wait in order to make an accurate dual diagnosis. Evans and Sullivan (1990) recommend waiting a month after the patient is sober before making a dual diagnosis because most psychiatric symptoms induced by the substance abuse will remit in that period of time. They also noted that several lab tests have indicated that the drugs are no longer detectable in the system after a month of abstinence. Anthenelli (1994) advises a two to four week period of observation before considering the use of psychotropic medication, and in the meantime, uses supportive and cognitive-behavioral therapy. He makes this recommendation because research shows the resolution of most major psychiatric symptoms with abstinence over this period of time. Furthermore, he is reluctant to commit patients to a regime of psychoactive medication unless it is absolutely necessary. One of the therapists interviewed, who had worked on an inpatient substance abuse unit, recommended six months to a year of abstinence before making a final diagnosis:

> So you need a period of time. I generally recommend six months to a year before you really know what's going on with that individual. In some of the work I did at X Hospital, we found that after you detoxified alcoholics most cognitive functions came back after a couple of weeks. We also found that there were sequelae that might last for months and months. We basically had a rule, that I always stuck with, that you don't make a final diagnosis for about six months until after the person is sober. It's only at that point that you can really know what's going on underneath without being complicated. It really has to be a two-part strategy. First, you have to get the person off the substances. Then, secondly, you have to make the diagnosis.

If a clear dual diagnosis cannot be made in the initial sessions after considering the patient's psychiatric and substance abuse history and the temporal relationship of the disorders, I recommend waiting two to four weeks before making the diagnosis. As research indicates, the major symptoms of substance abuse are generally resolved within a month, or sometimes sooner with some drugs, such as cocaine. If depression, anxiety, or psychotic symptoms remain after two to four weeks of abstinence, there is probably an independent psychiatric disorder that also needs to be addressed. I prefer not waiting too long to address the psychiatric disorder because the distress it creates for the patient may make him vulnerable for a relapse into drug use. Of course, as mentioned previously, acute and severe psychiatric or substance abuse symptoms must be treated immediately, even if a dual diagnosis is not made. If the patient is extremely depressed and actively suicidal, the depression must be addressed aggressively with medication and hospitalization, even if these symptoms may be substance-induced. If the person is acutely psychotic, he must be stabilized on medication first, no matter that these symptoms are not clearly related to an independent mental disorder.

Assessment is a dynamic and ongoing process. Even after a month of sobriety, when the clinician is relatively certain of a dual diagnosis, he must continue to observe the patient carefully. The symptom pictures of each disorder may vary in severity over time, and the therapist may have to shift his therapeutic focus according to the discerned needs of the patient. Furthermore, the clinician must determine the relationship of the disorders—whether one or both are primary—and learn how the disorders interact. Nevertheless, making a diagnosis is only the first step in the treatment process. The next step is to convince the patient of the diagnosis and engage him in the treatment process.

7

DO YOU SEE
WHAT I SEE?
ADDRESSING DENIAL

Once therapists arrive at a diagnosis through the assessment process, it becomes their task to convince their patients of the validity of their diagnosis and to elicit an agreement to a treatment plan. Ideally, the patient recognizes himself in the therapist's description of his problem and agrees to work with the therapist to resolve it. However, the clinician's proposal of a diagnosis and treatment plan often meets with resistance on the part of the patient because of his tendency to deny or minimize his substance abuse problem. Furthermore, particularly with the more severe psychiatric disorders, there is a similar tendency on the part of some patients to deny their mental illness and the necessary treatment.

Denial is a primitive defense mechanism. It is used adaptively by infants and by some adults in situations of overwhelming stress. Denial is an avoidance of something painful, usually a painful affect state. As a defense, it shares common characteristics with dissociative defenses and is equivalent to saying, "I choose not to think about that because I can't handle it now." While everyone uses denial on occasion to protect themselves, it is a prominent defense used by substance abusers who cannot imagine coping with life without their drug of choice. Substance abusers typically establish a whole range of tactics to justify, hide, or protect their drug use, to block treatment, and to deny responsibility for the consequences of their behavior. Because of their experience of loss of control, their despair about being able to stop using, and the terror of the consequences of abstaining, the addict sets up an elaborate psychological protective structure to preserve his access to his drug of choice. He may minimize the obvious negative consequences of his use and employ bizarre rationalizations to justify his continued use. To the outside observer, this system of denial may appear to be ridiculously maladaptive, but to the addict, these evasive tactics are perceived as necessary for survival.

Treatment Principle Six: Once a substance abuse problem is diagnosed, the therapist must begin to address the patient's denial for treatment to progress.

The process of breaking down denial begins with informing the patient clearly of the substance abuse diagnosis and attempting to include the cessation or curtailing of drug use in the treatment plan. The process of addressing denial may take time and should be done in a manner that does not arouse too much anxiety. An overly confrontative approach may cause the patient to flee treatment or to withdraw defensively. Many of the dually diagnosed are quite fragile psychologically, and their defensive structure should not be exposed, uncovered, or modified too rapidly before the patient is helped to develop other more adaptive defensive mechanisms. Therefore, the therapist must gently educate the patient about the effects of drug use, help him become aware of the negative consequences of his use, and offer support and alternative means of coping with the stress of life. Yet the therapist must be persistent in addressing this denial. If the clinician does not help the patient see the negative consequences of his drug use, it is not likely that the patient will admit the problem and begin the recovery process. If the substance abuse problem is not addressed, the treatment of the psychiatric disorder will probably not progress to a successful conclusion.

THE THERAPIST'S DENIAL

For the therapist to be able to address the denial of his patient, his first and crucial task is to confront his own prejudices regarding substance abusers and his own denial regarding drug use. One of the therapists interviewed candidly related his personal journey in treating dual diagnosis patients. He admitted: "The basic attitude I had toward someone whose primary problem appears to be substance abuse related is that they are simply not insight-oriented, not only not capable, but highly resistant to it. They really don't want to know anything about themselves. They externalize the responsibility for what's going on in their lives to an outside agency, in this case, alcohol. I didn't like those people." He further admitted that he had to address his own denial: "I started to feel more comfortable with substance abusing patients. I also started to see that unconsciously I was ignoring all the substance abuse issues in patients who were coming in without a substance abuse complaint. Somehow, without knowing it, I was sometimes colluding with them to avoid talking about something very obvious, I later found out."

There may be several reasons why a therapist might overlook the substance abuse of his clients. First of all, he may be abusing drugs himself and be as blind to the negative consequences in his patient's lives as in his own. Research indicates that over a fourth of the American adult population (26.6%) have a lifetime prevalence of some substance use disorder, either abuse or dependence. Since mental health professionals are not immune from drug problems simply because of their training, it is not unlikely that nearly a quarter of these practitioners have experienced a problem at one time or another in their lives. Secondly, I suspect that a large number of therapists may exhibit codependent behavior because they grew up in alcoholic homes where the drug problems were denied. From my discussions with people in human service professions, I have learned that many are adult children of alcoholics. They assumed caretaking roles in their families and chose professions that allowed them to continue this role in the service of others. Their self-esteem became associated with their ability to help others in need. Thirdly, because of their lack of training in the assessment and treatment of addictions, therapists may easily overlook signs of a drug problem. Since they are trained in the treatment of psychiatric disorders, those become the focus of their attention. Finally, the therapist may have many countertransferential reactions to substance abusers, who tend to be dependent, grandiose, hostile, manipulative, and provocative.

Imhoff and colleagues (1984) describe several common countertransferential reactions induced by addicts that affect their evaluation and treatment. In a common scenario, the therapist may assume the role of a "good parent rescuing the bad impulsive child." Such a thera-pist may become overinvolved, protective, and permissive toward his patient. The therapist takes pride in the recovery of his patient, but reacts with a sense of anger, hurt, and betrayal when the patient sud-denly relapses or acts out. Another common scenario takes place at the beginning of treatment when the patient exhibits almost imme-diate and remarkable improvement. The therapist may attribute this success to his therapeutic skills. However, when the patient unexpect-edly relapses and becomes resistant to treatment, the clinician may feel like a failure and harshly judge himself "a bad therapist." Another type of countertransferential attitude occurs when the therapist over-identifies with the "underdog" status of his patient. He may identify with the anti-authoritarian and victim role of the addict, expressing his own unconscious feelings of inferiority and hostility. Finally, many mental health professionals experience "burnout" in attempting to respond to the intense and demanding dependency needs of these patients. The result is that the therapist withdraws from the thera-peutic relationship and becomes tired, bored, and indifferent.

ADDRESSING THE PATIENT'S DENIAL

Dually diagnosed patients employ defensive strategies, similar to those of any substance abusers, to protect their access to drugs. How-ever, a particular strategy of denial that these individuals use is to fo-cus on their mental health problem in a way that deflects attention from their substance abuse problem. As mentioned previously, persons typi-cally come to mental health professionals for help regarding their psy-chiatric difficulties and not for substance abuse complaints. In the ses-sions with the therapist, they will often discuss at length their emotional problems and refer to their drinking or drug use as a way of coping with these problems. For example, Steve, a 22-year-old man, came to therapy at the advice of his lawyer, having been arrested for drunk driving. In our sessions, Steve admitted that drinking was a problem and that he intended to cut back, but not abstain. He thought his main problem was his depression and his inability to relate well with women. He felt lonely and depressed because many of his relationships ended in failure. In fact, four years previously Steve had attempted suicide after his girlfriend left him for another guy. I told him that his depression may well be related to his alcohol use and that we had to address that first before we could work on his difficulties in relating with women. Interestingly, I noted that the more I focused attention on his drinking, the more he wanted to talk about his problem with women. Of course, I brought this diversionary tactic to his attention. We were able to maintain a focus on the impact of drinking on his life, and Steve eventually admitted his need to quit altogether.

Addressing denial is a process that may take time because it depends on the establishment of a strong therapeutic relationship and the development of alternative coping mechanisms. It begins with informing the patient of his diagnosis and what he needs to do to treat his substance abuse problem. If the patient is resistant to accepting the diagnosis, which is typical, the therapist must undertake various strategies to convince the patient of the validity of his diagnosis. Mental health practitioners often feel untrained to undertake this task, which requires a modification of their usual therapeutic techniques. As described previously, the technical modifications require that they become more directive, educative, and supportive. Therapists need to become directive in alerting their patients to the consequences of their drug use, in inviting them to question their perceptions and judgments, and in undertaking an experiment to limit their drinking. Furthermore, they need to educate their patients regarding the nature and effects of substance abuse and its interaction with their psychiatric disorder, and to provide a supportive context in which they can safely address their problems.

Informing the Patient

The first step in addressing the patient's denial is to present clearly the diagnosis of a substance use disorder. The therapist cannot wait for a chemically dependent person to make his own diagnosis, because that generally will not happen. For example, the therapist needs to say quite clearly: "From what you have said (list reported signs and behavioral consequences of drinking), I think you have a problem with alcohol. You may be depressed or anxious and have these other problems, but they may be related to your drinking. I think we have to work first on the drinking before we can address these other problems." Then see how the patient responds. It never works to argue with the patient about the diagnosis because the disagreement will become the focus of attention and distract from the real problem. If the person objects strenuously, the therapist might propose that they keep an open mind and view his drinking as a potential problem. The therapist can then proceed to help him understand his behavior and its possible connection with drug use.

The ideal situation is one in which the patient comes to the realization himself of a problem through the questioning of the therapist. One of the therapists interviewed, who is psychodynamic in orientation, said:

> In general, if it's an active substance abuse practice, I would comment directly on the difficulty in just working together without addressing that. Usually, I'll be able to get them into that position without my having to say, "I think you've got a drug problem that you're not talking about." Usually, it pops up in the metaphors enough. There are enough people who think they have a problem. I can just say to them, "You talk about these things, but you also mention a lot of people who think you have alcohol problems. There's got to be something there. What do you think about that?"

On rare occasions, the individual may readily admit he has a drug problem and be eager to find out what he has to do about it. One therapist told me about an anthropologist who came to her for treatment: "I took her history and had a feeling that she was probably alcoholic. So I said to her, 'What would you say if I told you I thought you were alcoholic?' She said, 'I know I am.' I thought, 'What am I doing here?' I didn't have to break through any denial or anything. Then I said, 'What would you say if I said the treatment of choice is to see me and to go to AA?' And she said, 'Where do I go?' That is unusual, really unusual."

It is important that the therapist elicit an explicit agreement from his patient to include the substance abuse issue in his treatment plan. Patients may say the words in admitting a drug problem, but they do not fully accept the diagnosis until they are willing to work at changing their behavior. If the therapist and patient do not explicitly agree on how they are going to address the substance abuse problem, an effective treatment never really begins. If the problem is not discussed explicitly, the patient's avoidant defenses will sabotage the treatment because in most cases people will not spontaneously talk about their drug problems.

Discussing the Consequences of Use

If the patient does not accept the substance abuse diagnosis and is not willing to work on that issue, the clinician must begin a process of attempting to convince the patient of the validity of his diagnosis. This involves a persuasion process that may take time. The first strategy is to alert the patient to the consequences of his drug use. One of the therapists interviewed described how he helps his patients see what happens when they drink:

> If they don't see it as a specific problem, I try to get them to understand what happens to them when they drink. There may be times when somebody gets pulled over for a traffic violation, for driving while intoxicated. There will be a requirement that they go for counseling for a certain amount of time. They will often say, "I really don't have a problem with it; it just happened this one particular time." Rather than attempt to argue with them about whether it's a problem or not, I will try to help them understand that these are the things that happen when you do this. . . . One of the things I've found to be effective is to help people understand that oftentimes something that they do not perceive as a problem really is a problem. It's a problem because of what it does to them economically, physiologically, with regard to the impact it has on one's family and those closest to them. Since the tendency is to deny, I try to get them to look at the impact of their behavior on their own body systems, on the economics of the family, and on their family and loved ones. Rather than calling it denial, I'm getting them to recognize, "I guess I do have a problem." I've found it more effective to help them understand the consequences of their behavior. . . . I try to get them to understand that what they do has an impact on, not only themselves, but on others.

During the assessment process, which is ongoing, the therapist becomes aware of how the patient's drug use has a significant impact on his life and functioning. In addressing the patient's denial, he tries to help the person realize the impact of his behavior on himself and others and how it undermines what he values most. Another therapist interviewed offered an example of how she brings the consequences of the drinker's behavior to his awareness:

> I use whatever works. With one man, who ultimately stomped out of my office, I tried to use the one tool that I thought would work. He had a 10-year-old daughter whom he adored. I had been talking to him about the daughter hearing the abusive things he said to his wife, and I tried to make him understand that this would affect the daughter's perception of herself, because as a girl, she identified with the mother. All the things he said about the mother and women in general would affect his daughter's self-esteem. "What's the message you're giving your daughter when you come home drunk, when you sleep on the couch, when you can't get up the steps, when you are drunk and abusive of your wife?" That same approach worked with other people. Nothing worked with that man.

There are opportune moments when the patient is more inclined to admit the consequences of his drinking or drug use, and the therapist can use these times to press the patient. The best time for the therapist to focus attention on the drug use is when the patient is wondering aloud himself about it or when he is in a lot of pain because of the collision he has had with the outside world because of it. For example, individuals respond more readily after they have suffered the indignity of spending a night in jail because of drinking and received a large fine, or after a spouse has threatened to leave because she cannot tolerate his drunken behavior. These are opportune moments to point out the negative consequences of the drinking. If this interpretation is made with an acknowledgement of the pain the patient is experiencing, it can be effective.

The therapist needs to be very direct with the patient about the consequences of drug use if he is drinking and driving. The situation is potentially lethal, and the responsible clinician cannot be silent. One of those interviewed commented:

> If someone is drinking to the point that they are driving drunk, I won't lead around to it indirectly. I'll go right at that and say, "You say that you don't have a problem, but if you are drinking and driving, that's a problem. At least start there and don't drink and drive. Can you do that?" That's the most remarkable breakthrough

I've ever had, when I first realized I could say to a spouse, "Don't let him drive home. If he's going to drive home, don't get in the car." I've been able to influence the partner to the extent that they won't get into the car. Despite all the threats and swearing and out-and-out bad behavior, usually the person stops trying to drive the car.

Inviting the Patient to Look Inward

A second strategy in addressing denial is to lead the patient to question his perceptions and judgment. The dually diagnosed tend to deny their substance abuse problems by projecting blame onto others. In response to this defense, it can be beneficial to invite patients to look inward and accept responsibility for their own behavior. One of those interviewed related how he shapes the interviews to get the patient to look inward, rather than blame:

> I ask people each week to come in and be spontaneous and talk about things. I listen to them and begin shaping the interview along certain lines by pointing out aspects of their functioning, their character structure, by trying to get this person to look inward, rather than blame. That's always an essential element of therapy. People come in blaming circumstances and other people for their problems. I begin to get people to look at it. That's part of the intermediate step that may help get people to look at their substance abuse problem. The real primary step is whether you can orient them to look at themselves as the cause of their difficulties, rather than external things. . . . So you get some person to reflect internally that his own behavior is the cause of his problems. If you can get that, that's an important step in breaking down denial. When someone takes responsibility for himself, he also may begin to see that he drinks and maybe that's one of the causes of his problems.

It may also be helpful to point out the inevitable consequence of not taking responsibility for themselves and blaming others for their behavior. Not taking responsibility is an admission that they have no control over their destiny. They view their lives in a passive way, as though their destiny is completely in the hands of others. Consequently, espousing such a view results in the relinquishing of power and control over one's own life, a sort of voluntary enslavement.

Inevitably, if a person has a substance abuse problem, it has caused conflicts in at least some of his significant relationships. Part of the conflict is rooted in the differing perceptions the patient and the significant people in his life have of his drinking or drug use. One of the interviewed therapists related how he invites his patients to question their own perceptions and judgment by noting the discrepancy between what they and others say about them:

> Typically, there are places in the substance abuser's life where they are encountering difficulties, either at home in their relationship with their spouse, with their children, at work with their employers or coworkers, where others have a perception of them that is highly discrepant from their perception of themselves. So there will inevitably be some work around the issue of reconciling the discrepancies between what they say of themselves and what others say of them. . . . But for those patients who have retained the integrity of their egos, you can generally work through their empathy with other people in their lives, to the extent they are capable of it, in order to point out areas to question their own perception and judgment. People in their lives will typically have a clearer perception of the substance abuse part of the problem than the patients themselves.

If spouses are brought together for conjoint sessions, there is a good opportunity to confront the disparity of the couple's perception of the drinking problem. The therapist can talk with the couple both together and separately for an assessment and to get a history of the problem. He may discover that alcohol is perceived as a problem by one partner, but not the other. A useful technique is to point out the disparity of their perspectives, "You say that he has a drinking problem, while he says he does not. What should we do?" The partner may get defensive and keep denying the problem. In such a case, the therapist should just continue talking with the couple about the issues that come up and point out how the conflicts may be related to his drinking behavior.

Experimenting with Abstinence

A third strategy in addressing the denial is to request that the patient cut back or refrain from drinking for a certain time and to discuss the experience in the sessions. If an individual comes to see me and drinks to any significant degree, I usually ask that the patient abstain from drinking while in therapy. If they complain that they are feeling depressed or anxious or are having mood swings, I explain how alcohol use will exacerbate these symptoms. I further explain how drinking will interfere with the therapeutic process. Often alcohol is used to cover up or cope with uncomfortable feelings. For therapy to be effective, those feelings need to be felt and explored during sessions. Drinking also clouds the mind and makes people less able to understand and resolve their problems. Finally, drinking may interact adversely with any medications they may be taking.

If I suspect that the individual has a drinking problem and he denies it, I challenge him to prove to me that he does not have a problem. I invite him to undertake an experiment with abstinence. I tell the patient, "OK, you don't have to change a thing about your life. Continue to go to the bar with your friends. Continue to do everything you do normally, but, since the alcohol is not that important to you and you can quit at any time, drink Coke or club soda or anything other than alcohol and come back and tell me what it feels like when you do." I invite patients to experience life sober and to come back to therapy to talk about the experience. I want them to talk about their thoughts, feelings, fantasies, and struggle to abstain from drinking. If they can do that, they often convince themselves that they have a problem, because they see all the reasons they have been using the substance. In my experience, patients are relatively honest about their success or failure at maintaining abstinence and gain a new understanding about their drinking and the purpose it serves in their lives.

One of the therapists interviewed related that she uses a slightly different sort of experiment: "People sometimes tell me that my diagnosis is not correct. Then I ask them to drink two drinks a day for two weeks, no more and no less. If they can do that for two weeks, then I am willing to rethink my diagnosis. I've never done that when it is not successful." Her reason for employing this strategy is her belief that if a true alcoholic begins drinking, at some point he will lose control and be unable to limit himself to two drinks. She believes it is easier for an alcoholic to maintain abstinence for brief periods of time than to maintain strict control when exposed to alcohol.

Keeping a Journal

One experienced therapist proposed another useful technique for helping patients be more aware of their drinking behavior:

> If people say, "I can control this," I tell them: "I don't think you can. But if that's something you want to try, I'm willing to work with you, provided you're willing to chart your drinking behavior, keep a journal. If this doesn't work, and you are not able to control your drinking as you say you can, then you are willing to follow my recommendations." The reason for the charting and journal is so they become observers of their behavior. I'm also getting information about what their life is like. Usually, they can visually see the decline. Sometimes the family members, especially the wives who are in Al Anon, get upset with me when I consent to controlled drinking. They don't understand that I am doing this to keep their spouse in treatment and help them see their problem.

Substance abusers have often been scolded for their behavior, rather than helped to observe it. They also seek the immediate gratification offered by the mood-altering drugs, and have not learned to wait and observe themselves. Therefore, they tend to be experiencers, rather than observers, of themselves. If the therapist can help them to observe themselves, it will aid in reducing the defensiveness and enable them to see themselves more objectively and accurately.

Educating the Patient

A fifth strategy is to educate the patient regarding the nature, signs, effects, and psychological functions of substance abuse. The therapist needs to do some basic didactic work on the progression of the disease of alcoholism so that the patient can identify in himself the signs and symptoms of a drug problem. By presenting the facts about substance abuse in a nonthreatening manner, the patient is invited to assess himself for a problem. Some useful resources regarding the signs and symptoms of substance abuse and dependence are the Jellinek chart, the *DSM* criteria, and the questions of the *MAST*.

Practitioners who are recovering persons have an advantage in addressing the patient's denial because they are more sensitive to the avoidance tactics, which they themselves have relied upon in their drinking or drugging days. "You can't con a con," as they say at AA meetings. Another advantage for recovering persons is their experience with other addicted persons at meetings. One therapist interviewed related how she shares with her patients stories she hears around the AA tables or from friends and colleagues: "I use tales I have heard at meetings or from friends or from other people who treat alcoholics. For instance, this one woman drank one time a year and got so drunk that she messed her bed, urinated in her bed. And she was clearly alcoholic because that was the consequence. Here was a very well-dressed, well-to-do lady who did this. So you use these kinds of analogies, metaphors, and stories."

It is helpful to instruct the patient on the precise way in which he uses alcohol or drugs to cope with disturbing affects and thoughts. Many people utilize drugs as a medication to treat underlying pain that does not seem to them resolvable. Drugs are also used as mood elevators or stabilizers. However, addiction is paradoxical in that substance abusers, in an attempt to survive and cope with life, kill themselves. Often they have not learned any other way to face the stresses of their lives. The therapist can help them find an alternative way of dealing with the pain of life and their psychiatric disorders. The first step, by alerting them to the negative consequences of their use, is to demonstrate to them that their using substances is not adaptive. Then they can draw the linkages more clearly between their behavior and use. Once they see their use as a medicine and understand that there are more effective medicines, then the denial can be broken through.

Offering Support

A final strategy in addressing denial is to provide a supportive context in which patients can feel secure enough to give up their denial. The primary support comes through the relationship with the therapist, which needs to be fostered by an attitude of warm acceptance and empathy. The relationship is built up through expressions of empathic understanding, particularly of their struggle to give up their substance of choice and face the pain of life without it. In discussing how he confronts denial, one clinician commented:

> That can be very tricky for a couple of reasons. One is that you
> often have to build up a therapeutic alliance first before you can

confront the denial. Remember, when you confront, then people run often if they're not prepared to deal with something. If you try to break through a defense before they're ready to deal with it, then what you have is someone who runs from you. I've had cases where I had to say, "OK, that's something we'll have to watch." You deal with the person, then he gets a drunk driving ticket. And you say, "What about that; what do you think?" You have to build up enough evidence sometimes to show the person that you have a valid issue here. You have to work with them.

The strength of the relationship enables the therapist to interpret more directly the substance abuse problem. As one clinician remarked: "I don't care if I'm making the same interpretation more directly, if you have enough of a relationship with the person, he tends to survive psychologically what you are saying to him. You work through that, and he begins to think about some help. If you've got a strong enough relationship with them, most people stick in through that period of time and then get some treatment for it." The relationship provides some leverage by which the therapist can confront, challenge, and ask the patient to prove that his substance use is not a problem.

The psychological fragility of the dual diagnosis patient makes a supportive relationship essential in order to address his defensive use of denial. One therapist elaborated the reason for the importance of such support:

> You don't ask somebody to tolerate pain without being able to provide them with some kind of assistance that's adequate to the task, even if the pain does not look like it ostensibly should be that great from the outside. Who's anybody to tell anybody else how bad their pain is? Typically, in these cases, there's practically a phobia about pain of any kind, whether it's physical or emotional. The anxiety is so pervasive about experiencing that pain, that they're afraid of the anxiety. They have to feel like there's some kind of context to support them in going through that and reassure them that it's time limited and going to change before they're going to be willing to give up their substance use.

In short, the dually diagnosed are unwilling to give up their primary coping mechanism, alcohol or drugs, unless they have the assurance that they will have the necessary support to survive without their accustomed crutch.

Attending AA Meetings

Attending AA meetings can also provide the needed support and facilitate the process of breaking down denial. Sometimes I recommend that patients, who in my estimation are substance abusers, attend meetings. I propose to them, "Would you be willing to attend an AA meeting to see if you fit, just to see if you fit?" I refrain from calling them alcoholics because patients in denial cannot identify with that label, consider it a stigma, and become increasingly defensive. If they come back and say that they didn't feel like they fit in, depending on how certain I am about my diagnosis, I will ask them, "Would you be willing to try another meeting?"

Attending AA meetings can offer support in several ways. First of all, the group itself offers support. The members are all individuals at different stages of recovery who know personally the ravages of addiction. They are invariably empathic, warm, and welcoming of new members. The substance abuser often feels alienated from others and filled with guilt and shame. It is a relief for him to feel such acceptance from a group of strangers who offer friendship. Secondly, participating in the meetings can give the individual an opportunity to talk with others who have similar problems. Many members have years of experience with struggling to overcome their addictions and can offer helpful advice to the novice. Thirdly, a person's stereotype of an alcoholic or drug addicted person can be challenged by meeting them personally. Commonly, people think of alcoholics as "skid row bums" and the drug addicted as part of the criminal element of society. Embracing such a stereotype makes people very resistant to identifying themselves as alcoholics or drug addicts. At meetings, there is an opportunity to meet ordinary people who have drug problems, people with whom the new members can easily identify. Finally, at meetings people learn basic facts about the disease of chemical dependency and the process of addiction. Such knowledge can free them from ignorance and an overriding sense of guilt.

How Confrontative to Be

An important clinical issue is deciding how confrontative to be in addressing the denial of patients. John Wallace (1985) points out that denial serves a valuable purpose in sustaining the fragile self-esteem of alcoholics. He cautions against confronting the denial too aggressively and forcing a premature self-disclosure. A premature self-awareness can heighten the alcoholic's anxiety and lead to a return to drinking in order to cope. Because of their reliance on substances, these persons have not typically developed other, more effective, coping mechanisms. Therefore, the therapist must be content with a gradual deepening of self-awareness in his patients and be careful not to arouse too much anxiety in the process. A further consequence of being too confrontative too soon in the outpatient setting is that the patient will feel overwhelmed and decide either not to return to treatment or to become more defensive and withdraw emotionally.

While substance abuse specialists tend to be more aggressive in confronting denial, mental health professionals tend more to move with the patient, be reluctant to confront substance abuse problems, and wait for the person to raise the issue. Such a passive, nonconfrontative approach, however, may collude with the patient's defenses that help to maintain the drinking or drug use. One of the therapists interviewed acknowledged that he had to learn to be more confrontative in his work with the dually diagnosed: "My worst experiences have been from not confronting and letting things go too long. I think the biggest growth I've had in being a therapist is being more comfortable confronting things, not in a hostile way, but pointing out this person's behavior and demanding in vivo changes when they're with me."

The therapist must maintain a balance in how he approaches the denial of the patient. On the one hand, he must be confrontative enough to keep the drug problem and its consequences in view of the patient. Otherwise, the problem will go unaddressed. On the other hand, he must be gentle enough to avoid arousing too much anxiety in the patient, which may lead to a relapse, a withdrawal from treatment, or increased defensiveness. Several factors influence the decision about how confrontative to be in a particular case, such as the personality and pathology of the patient and the severity of the drug problem.

One outspoken therapist with over twenty years experience in working with substance abusers and the dually diagnosed related how he varies his approach according to the individual needs of the patient, particularly in terms of how neurotic the person is:

How confrontative I am depends on the person. You can't treat everybody the same way. The one thing my analytic training really taught me is an individual approach. You have to get a feeling for a person as to the best approach. For some, you can be very confrontative and say, "Stop, or else don't come back." For others, you have to say, "Wait a second, this person's more fragile," and you have to deal with it in a different way. . . . It's just clinical feel in terms of how much neurosis the person has. If I think the person is a character disorder, then I can be very blunt and tell him, "You're lying to yourself." There are other people who are much more anxious, much more neurotically based, that you have to treat in a different way. That's the main thing, how much it's driven by anxiety.

Because of the emotional fragility of many of the dually diagnosed, a more gradual, "soft," approach in addressing denial is called for. The confrontational, immediate-abstinence demands that are associated with traditional residential substance abuse treatment centers are inappropriate and unrealistic for the outpatient treatment of individuals with psychological problems. The therapist might begin by labeling the drug use as a hypothetical problem and help the patient change his definition of himself and his behavior. Work over a period of time by alerting the patient to the adverse consequences of his drug use and by leading him to question his own perception and judgments can help him change the way he views his drinking or drugging behavior.

One therapist, who is psychodynamic in orientation, stated that he prefers an interpretative to a confrontational approach: "If you feel that there's denial taking place, you point out the possibility of it. I don't see it as my role to try to ram it down their throats. I might have ignored it myself ten years ago. I won't ignore it anymore. I also won't get on the bandwagon. I appreciate what my supervisor used to say: 'People do whatever they're going to do. It's not your job to make them do anything else. Just interpret what they say about it.'" However, he acknowledges that he does become more confrontational, depending on the severity of the drug problem: "I already mentioned the criteria for pushing real hard. If the disruptions are severe and frequent. If anger and hostility are coming out and interfering with their life. Third, if somebody's endangering their job because of alcohol or substance abuse, I tend to push a lot harder right then. I know how devastating it can be to lose a job. The fourth thing would be driving and drinking. I see that as a major problem in their judgment, a potentially fatal problem."

In summary, the following are some strategies for addressing the patient's denial regarding a substance abuse problem:

1. Inform patients of the substance abuse problem and ask them at least to consider it as a hypothetical problem.
2. Alert patients to the adverse consequences of their drug use; help them to see the connection between their drinking and drugging behavior and these consequences.
3. Invite them to question their perceptions and judgments by noting discrepancies between what they and others say.
4. Request that patients undertake an experiment in abstinence.
5. Recommend that patients keep a journal of their drinking and drug use.
6. Educate them about the nature of substance abuse and how it interacts with their psychiatric symptoms.
7. Provide a supportive context in which they can give up their denial.
8. Invite them to attend AA meetings.
9. Take a gradual, but persistent, approach in addressing the denial.

WORKING WITH THE RESISTANT PATIENT

The most difficult cases in the outpatient setting are those in which the patient is coerced into treatment and refuses to acknowledge either the substance abuse or psychiatric problem. In fact, many people who come for treatment with a primary substance abuse problem do not come voluntarily. They come because they have had a drunk-driving ticket, and their lawyer or the judge mandates treatment. Their wives threaten divorce unless they stop drinking. Their bosses threaten to fire them if they do not change the behavior that is directly related to their drinking or drug use. Their doctors warn them that they will die if they continue drinking. External pressures bring the individual to treatment.

Rollnick and Morgan (1995) describe an approach to addressing resistance that they call "motivational interviewing." They note that traditionally resistance has been conceived of as a motivational deficit within the client, but suggest that the therapist also has a role and responsibility regarding resistance. The interviewing style of the clinician can either increase or decrease the client's resistance to change. They further observe that ambivalence about change is at the heart of any addictive problem. All clients experience ambivalence about the prospect of change in their lives; they simultaneously desire and avoid it. At some level, they recognize that their drug use is destructive, but they cannot imagine living without their substance of choice. All persons seeking treatment can be viewed as manifesting different degrees of readiness to change. It is the task of the therapist to recognize where the patient stands along this continuum of willingness to change. The authors suggest the following working definition of motivational interviewing: "a directive, client-centered counseling style for helping clients explore and resolve ambivalence about behavioral change" (p. 182). They recommend that therapists express empathy, avoid arguing, and roll with the client's resistance. Therapists should also highlight the ambivalence their clients feel and explore the gap that exists between the clients' future goals and current behavior. A final strategy is to support the clients' self-efficacy, their personal beliefs about their ability to change their lives.

Understand the Resistance

Those with experience treating the dually diagnosed have had to develop strategies to engage the patients and work with their resistance. The first step toward engaging resistant patients is to understand why they are resistant. Is it because of their personality, their pathology, or ignorance about substance abuse? The nature of their resistance to treatment will determine what approach will be most effective in engaging them. For example, if the individual is personality disordered and demonstrates ingrained self-centered, manipulative, and oppositional tendencies in relating to others, the therapist may need to be more direct in addressing the resistance. If the person is neurotic and so anxious that he cannot imagine life without his drug of choice, the approach must be more gentle. If the patient is mentally ill and paranoid, the therapist needs to be particularly sensitive to the person's fragility and refrain from confrontation.

An Experience of Sobriety

One experienced clinician described an approach he uses with patients whose resistance is more characterological. He recommended accepting the fact that treatment has been imposed upon the patients and attempting to transform the motivation by giving them an experience of sobriety:

> You may have to impose treatment on them in some way with the hope that after they have been sober for a long enough time, the fear motivation will switch to positive motivation. They all stop drinking because they're afraid of something. They don't want to lose their license, go to jail, lose their job, lose their marriage. If they have enough sobriety under their belt, oftentimes they begin to become more positive and say, "I haven't had a drink for a year. I feel so much better about myself. I don't want to go back to drinking because I feel better."

He further elaborated how he helps patients transform their motivation and make it more internalized:

> First of all, I have them stop drinking. After they have the experience of being sober, they begin to like it. They feel better, and they like it. You have to set up a pattern of reinforcement. After all, they have developed a habit strength for drinking that must be broken. It can only be broken by an experience of abstinence for a length of time. . . . Insight is also helpful in getting them to recognize the benefits of sobriety. It helps to maintain the habit strength. They say they never realized before until they were sober for a while the effects of drinking. They come to realize the impact it had on their jobs, their marriage, their relationships, their health. The more they appreciate how it feels, the more reinforcing is the experience. So I try to get them to experience abstinence for a period of time until they become motivated to accept it for themselves.

Make Demands

This experienced therapist does not hesitate to make demands upon these patients so that they will work at maintaining sobriety:

I confront them right away and say, "Look, if you just want someone to meet your probationary requirements, this is the wrong place
for you. I insist that you deal with problems. I insist that my bill
be paid. There are lots of people you can see once a month and
report in like a probation office, but if you want to see me, that
means you want to change." That's my contract at the beginning.
If I see instances that they're resistant to change, I confront that
right away. I tell them that they really don't seem motivated to do
this kind of work, and maybe they should think about whether they
really want to be here or not. I'm very nonjudgmental. If a guy
wants to drink himself to death, he's going to drink himself to
death. If he comes into treatment, he's going to get better.

Such a direct and demanding posture is frequently associated with
traditional substance abuse treatment. It has some advantages, particularly with patients who are personality disordered. It confronts
directly their externalizing tendencies and conveys clearly the message that the responsibility for change rests with the patient. It can
also impress upon the patient the seriousness of the therapist's commitment to the patient's well-being. Gradually, the patient may begin
to experience the therapist as an ally in his recovery as he begins to
feel better about himself. However, a potential drawback of this approach is that the patient may experience the therapist as another
persecutor in his life and become even more defensive.

Use Empathy

A second therapist advocated a less confrontative, more patient,
approach and emphasized the importance of establishing trust with
the resistant patient:

For some, there is an explicit distrust when they come through
the door. They are here because some event has catalyzed them
coming through the door. What they want to be rid of is the event,
not the addiction. The wife says she will divorce him; the boss says
he will fire him; the police say they will put him in jail; a doctor
says his liver is failing. For them, the idea is that if they come here,
it takes the pressure off. It's a sanctuary of sorts. Recognizing that,
what I have to do with them initially is roll with that and develop
trust. I'm not going to tell them what, how, and when to do it.
Eventually, that's what we do as clinicians, but we get them to say

it. In a word, with the resistant patient, I use empathy. I tell them, "I can understand that if my wife were going to divorce me I'd probably land here as well and not want to be here. Perhaps we can find some other reasons why you might want to be here. I will attempt to help you preserve your marriage." They have to see you as an advocate. If you get into a style of confrontation so you become just like their wife, employer, or judge, you won't be able to create the needed treatment relationship.

Focus on the Trouble

Another therapist emphasized the importance of focusing on the behavior that got them into trouble and of assuming a nonjudgmental stance:

> If someone is continuing to deny problems, it's virtually impossible to be able to help them. What I'll generally try to do is to motivate them to treatment, rather than to go along with the denial. Rather than confronting the denial, if I think it will cause them to withdraw even more, I'll try to get them to focus on the behavior that's gotten them into trouble. We'll talk about that. . . . What makes it difficult is when the person comes in and is oppositional to start with. In other words, they're forced into coming, and they don't perceive it as a problem. So they come in with an attitude as if you're their probation officer, saying, "I have to come here or else I can't get my driver's license back or get off probation." They come in with an attitudinal set against the process of therapy. You really have to get beyond that before you are able to make any headway with them. You have to get them to understand that you're not there to pass judgments on them, but really to help them modify the things that have gotten them into trouble in the first place. If they are willing to start taking a look at some of those things, then you can help them. If they're not willing to take a look at those things and just consider the whole thing a bum rap, there may not be anything you can do with them.

Acknowledge the Ambivalence

It is also important to show patients sympathy for their coerced situation and to address continually their feelings of ambivalence. As one therapist expressed it:

I've begun to approach them the same way I do teenagers who really don't want to come. They are being forced by somebody. I acknowledge they are being forced. After they say, "My wife said this," I ask them what they think about it. Then if they say they really don't want to come, I acknowledge that it makes it difficult for them and we'll just try to work through that. In the past, I would have been more likely to say, "So, don't come." They would have gone away partially satisfied because they didn't want to come anyway. If somebody says that even though they are forced to come they have some interest, I'll tend to feel more positively about the prognosis for working well with me. I will work with the resistant group now. I'll just talk to them, and if it continues to be an issue that they're so ambivalent about it, I keep making the same interpretation over and over. It's up to them. They don't have to come. . . . I show them a little bit of sympathy about the fact that nobody likes to be pushed into doing something against their will, especially when they don't perceive the problem the same way as somebody else. Sympathy seems to be helpful. If you can get beyond that first period of anger at being forced into the situation, they finally like talking.

Some strategies for working with the resistance of the coerced patient are:

1. Try to figure out why patients are resistant.
2. Give them a positive experience of sobriety so that they can transform their motivation.
3. Don't be afraid to make some demands on patients to impress upon them the seriousness of your commitment to treatment and their well-being.
4. Attempt to develop a trusting relationship by assuming an empathic and nonjudgmental attitude.
5. Don't argue with patients. Focus on the behavior that has caused problems.
6. Be sympathic with their feelings of being pressured into treatment.
7. Keep addressing their ambivalent feelings about treatment.

In summary, it is essential to address the patient's denial of substance abuse in a gradual, yet persistent, manner. If the patient is resistant to accepting the therapist's diagnosis of a problem, the clinician must engage in various strategies to help the patient come to a personal awareness of the true source of his difficulties. The effective employment of these strategies, which have been developed by trial and error over many years of experience with the dually diagnosed, depends on the therapist's sensitivity to the personality dynamics and pathologies of the individual patient he is treating.

8 | MATCHMAKER, MATCHMAKER, MAKE ME A MATCH: MAKING REFERRALS

As part of the ongoing assessment process, therapists make clinical decisions about the most appropriate treatment setting for each patient. This decision is based on the clinician's appreciation of the therapeutic potential and limits of the outpatient setting, evaluation of the needs of the patient, and awareness of existing treatment resources. As mentioned previously, the outpatient setting is effective with patients who are motivated, are able to control their acting out behaviors, and have adequate support systems. Depending upon the severity or acuteness of either the psychiatric or substance use disorder, a more structured and protective environment than the outpatient setting may be needed for effective treatment. Typically, referrals may be made to substance abuse facilities, physicians, psychiatrists, and inpatient psychiatric hospitals.

Treatment Principle Seven: Therapists must assess the suitability of treating the dual diagnosis patient in the outpatient setting, and if necessary, make an appropriate referral.

REFERRALS TO SUBSTANCE ABUSE FACILITIES

For dual diagnosis patients, a common referral is to a specialized substance abuse facility. In the past, individuals with severe substance use disorders were regularly sent to inpatient programs for detoxification and stabilization. These programs lasted an average of 28 days. However, today, with the pressures toward cost containment in the health care field, inpatient programs are gradually being replaced by intensive outpatient and day treatment programs. The inpatient programs that continue to exist are reducing their length of stay in order to be more economical. All of these programs provide a protective environment and highly structured programs. Patients receive medical attention, are involved in group and individual therapy, are introduced to twelve step programs, and learn about the nature and impact of substance abuse. Additionally, training in stress management, social skills, proper nutrition, and coping strategies is often offered.

The severity of the substance abuse problem is the principal criterion for making a referral to a specialized facility or program. There are several indications that a severe problem exists and requires more intensive treatment than that offered in an office setting. One indication is the degree of disruption that the drinking or drug use causes. One therapist elaborated on how he decides that more intensive treatment is needed:

> I make a referral if they come to sessions frequently drunk, if they haven't been to work all week because they have been on a binge. I guess the criterion would be that it becomes a major disruption on a frequent basis in their family life, their marital life, their working life. A third one is a history of tickets for driving under the influence. Fourthly, if someone's drinking behavior results in their being physically or verbally abusive to somebody on a consistent basis, I would more likely refer him, than somebody who had the same drinking behaviors, but who was silly, affectionate, giggly, and fell asleep.

In short, if their behavior is destructive to themselves or others and cannot be contained, the therapist must step in and offer the support of a protective environment.

Before making a referral to a specific program, it is helpful to ask patients what has worked for them in the past to control their drinking or maintain abstinence. If people have a long drinking history with serious problems, they have frequently been involved in treatment programs. Such an invitation can encourage the personal involvement of the patient in his own treatment plan and increase compliance. The therapist can facilitate the patient's reentry to a program that has worked for him before and continue to see him until he begins the program and after he is discharged from it.

A second consideration, which will be explained more fully below, is if the person's addiction is so advanced that abrupt abstinence would create a medical emergency. In that case, the person needs to be detoxed and stabilized under the care of a physician. Often this is accomplished in an inpatient setting where the patient is also offered social supports for maintaining sobriety.

A third indication for referral to a more intensive treatment is that the patient has repeatedly failed to control his drinking or drug use through outpatient services. The addiction may be so far advanced that the patient has lost the ability to control his use of substances and requires the added support and structure of an inpatient or intensive outpatient program. The repeated failures may occur because the person is in all-out denial about his drug problem or lacks the motivation to give up using. In this case, the helpfulness of outpatient treatment is limited, because it has shown itself to be effective only with those who are motivated and able to control their acting out behaviors. A more intensive program may address the denial more effectively and help motivate the patient for a life of sobriety. A further possible explanation for repeated relapses may be that an underlying psychiatric problem is not being addressed, and the patient continues to self-medicate with his drug of choice. In that case, the therapist may have to refer the patient for medication. Yet if the drug use continues even after these efforts, inpatient treatment may be called for.

The level of denial is a fourth consideration. One therapist said she evaluates the level of denial and motivation when making a decision about referral to a more intensive setting:

> Basically, I look at the level of denial and motivation. If they're really in denial, if they have been arrested for the third time for DUI and just insist that they don't drink that much and have bad luck that the police just pick them up, if they insist they don't need treatment and don't need AA and don't need to stop drinking, I don't think an individual outpatient therapist is equipped to deal with it. They need more structure and monitoring. When there's dual diagnosis, I'll often want to deal with the substance abuse very

quickly. An Intensive Outpatient Program (IOP) or inpatient program will deal with it much faster. That's the value of that kind of treatment. It's so intensive that it does break down the denial.

A fifth indication of the need for more intensive treatment is the lack of social support for a life of sobriety. Sometimes family members are enablers or are users themselves who actively sabotage the patient's recovery. Another factor is involvement in a drug culture. Individuals may need inpatient treatment in order to get away from the influence of that culture. It is almost impossble to change behavior if individuals are involved in selling drugs and are always around drugs, because the reinforcement is so strong. A period of time away from that culture in a safer environment may be necessary. Involvement in a work culture contributes to maintaining a person's sobriety. If the person is unemployed, he lacks an important support for a life of sobriety. On the other hand, if the patient is employed, referral to inpatient services may be disruptive to his life and be contraindicated.

Realistically, there may be institutional pressures to make an inpatient referrral even if the therapist judges that it is not clinically necessary. One therapist noted the frequency of pressures from the legal system to make this referral: "Inpatient is also used for external problems. Many of the individuals I see have been sent by the legal system. They have been pressured into treatment. You have to do a sort of juggling of the treatment with the demands of the institution. If some judge says that this guy has to go for inpatient treatment, you can't very well say no, that inpatient treatment isn't really all that successful." Pressures may also come from employers who threaten dismissal unless the person gets intensive treatment. I began treating a young man who was suspended from his job for using cocaine. His employer stipulated that he had to participate in an intensive outpatient substance abuse program before he would be reinstated in his job. The employer was not satisfied when the man was involved only in therapy and Narcotics Anonymous.

A sixth consideration in making a referral is whether or not the substance abuse problem is primary, although it is not always easy to determine this immediately. One therapist said:

> Many of the referrals I make now are to people who are purely substance abuse specialists. I still work in a modified analytic frame-

work. The patients I still work with are people who can benefit from that process. If I feel this is a primary alcoholism problem, that basically if this person quits, he will be normal, then usually I don't treat him. I usually refer to someone who works with me and is a recovering alcoholic who basically confronts the substance use, is supportive, and monitors AA programs and Antabuse.

The therapist employs a graduated approach in making referrals for primary substance abusers. If the patient is not able to achieve sobriety working with the substance abuse specialist in the outpatient setting, the therapist refers him for inpatient treatment.

This therapist offered a case example:

Someone came to see me, and he had gotten about six drunk driving tickets and told me that a year before his wife had divorced him. This was a man 57 years old. He was so upset by it that he didn't go to work for 6 months. He looked very depressed to me. Obviously, this man was facing the loss of his license and, concomitantly, the loss of his job and his marriage. But the guy had been drinking so heavily that I had no idea how these thing were impacting him. So what I did was get him into substance abuse treatment, using AA, individual therapy, and Antabuse. Now I have him in treatment with someone else. I'll see him in about 6 months to determine whether in fact there is an underlying depression.

Type of Drug Abused

An important consideration regarding the necessity of making a referral to a specialized substance abuse facility is the type of drug abused. There is considerable literature on the effectiveness of treating alcoholics with psychotherapy in an outpatient setting. While the debate continues, a consensus is emerging that, regardless of therapeutic orientation, psychotherapy can be effective with alcoholics if some modifications of technique are introduced. As has been discussed above, there must be an explicit focus on alcohol use, and the therapist must be active, directive, educational, and supportive.

There is, however, remarkably little research on the utility of psychotherapy with other drugs of abuse. Recently, Richard Rawson

(1995) reviewed the literature on the effectiveness of psychotherapy for substance abusers. The few studies he found on the treatment of acutely addicted or recently detoxified heroin addicts showed little evidence that psychotherapy alone is effective with this population. However, therapy can be helpful as an adjunct to a more comprehensive treatment that includes the use of methadone or naltrexone. Even less is written about the outpatient treatment for cocaine abuse. One conclusion seems clear, however, from the few available studies. The high attrition rates of cocaine abusers indicate that weekly therapy sessions are inadequate as a primary treatment modality. There is a suggestion that psychotherapy can be useful if it is conducted within a more intensive treatment framework that focuses on the achievement of abstinence.

1) Cocaine

The clinicians I interviewed, who had many years of treating the dually diagnosed, reflected on how the type of drug abused influences their decisions about the appropriate treatment setting. Most of this group believe that cocaine addiction can best be treated in an inpatient or intensive outpatient setting, although some treat recreational users in their outpatient practice. For example, one therapist stated:

> I think if the drug is crack or cocaine, it makes an enormous difference. We who work with substance abuse at any level have not had great success in dealing with crack. It is so addictive and so frightening a drug that we really are just finding out how to deal with it. The relapse rate for crack users is enormously high. I don't think in an outpatient setting, meeting once or twice a week, that we can provide the kind of structure and monitoring and intensive treatment that these people need. I have not had much success in dealing with dual diagnosis when crack or cocaine is involved. I have to send them to a specialized program dealing with chemical dependency.

Another therapist believes some recreational users of cocaine can be treated effectively in an outpatient setting. But if the cocaine problem is primary or severe, he makes a referral to an inpatient setting:

> In my mind, and a lot of people will disagree with me, there are a number of recreational cocaine users. There are people who once

in a while use it, and that's it, just like there are recreational drinkers. I've seen lots of people who've used cocaine for ten or twelve
years and never had any problems with it. Once a month they get
together with their friends and toot up. I don't approve of it, but
there are those people who can do that. The people I see generally
are the people who are chronic users, and it's interfering with their
lives. . . . I saw someone a couple of years ago. He was an attorney, and he had a real nice house and didn't have a stick of furni-
ture in it. He was making $180,000 a year, and it was all going up
his nose. He came in for a primary cocaine problem, and I referred
him to a treatment program. He came back later after he was more
free of the addiction, and we started working therapeutically.

Another therapist has attempted to work with some cocaine addicts in his practice but had no success:

In terms of true addiction, where I saw someone long enough to
know it's there, there have only been three cocaine addicts. All
three of them lied to me about their use. That had not happened
before. I'm not used to people lying to me about it. I keep confidentiality, and I'm not judgmental. All three of them told me stories that didn't hold together consistently. In two cases, it actually
turned out that they just flat out lied about their cocaine use. Their
spouses pressed them to have a drug screen, and sure enough, there
was cocaine in their blood. My treatment experience is very limited with anybody truly addicted to cocaine. I've seen a lot of recreational use of cocaine where it's a problem, and they're dealing
with it. There were a couple of cases where they were lying to me
too. The problem was that they were just spending all their money,
and the spouse dragged them in. That's where I really felt helpless, with these cocaine addicts. I felt very helpless. They were all
friendly and agreeable with me. Basically, I got nowhere with them,
and they all quit.

A third practitioner elaborated his understanding of why those
who abuse stimulants are so difficult to treat in an outpatient setting:

The drug that has the most immediate effect is the most difficult to
treat, the stimulant class of drugs. Those are the most difficult patients to intervene with. The immediacy of the effect is so great and
so rewarding that it is very difficult to interrupt. The less socialized
the drug use, the more difficult it is to impact. An example is the
cocaine user who indulges alone versus the alcoholic who drinks in

a bar. It's also my experience with cocaine users that the incidence of mood disorder is much more dramatic. Since they are accustomed to getting relief within seconds with drug use, it is difficult to get them to use an alternative medicine that may take weeks to achieve its full effect. It's tough to gain their confidence so that we will be able to help them with that. I've not been able to work successfully with them in an outpatient setting. Day-treatment or residential programs are alternatives.

2) Heroin

This group of therapists interviewed reported that they had little exposure to heroin users in their practices. They recognized that they worked with a select population because most of their clients worked and had medical insurance. In the experience of two of these clinicians, however, those addicted to heroin need inpatient or intensive outpatient treatment. One therapist stated: "First of all, I don't see many heroin addicts. Most heroin addicts are drawn from lower classes. You do not see and never have seen many middle class people who are shooting smack. For people like that, the physical addiction problem is so great that they almost always need an institutional program, generally because they don't have other things in their lives going for them. They don't have jobs, other families, other ways of dealing with things." Another therapist commented: "I have done some work with dual diagnosis where heroin was the drug of choice. With these people you have to deal with lifestyle issues and self-esteem issues which are so enormous. They have been so degraded by their addiction and other people. You have to send them to an inpatient setting or a methadone setting where the addiction is controlled."

3) Psychedelic Drugs

These therapists reported that they rarely encountered psychedelic drug users. If they did, they attempted to treat it on an outpatient basis. One clinician emphasized the importance of abstinence from drug use to make an accurate diagnosis:

> I hear there's a return of psychedelics, but I haven't seen anybody lately. Back in the seventies I worked with people using psyche-

delics. Again, it was before we talked about dual diagnosis. I was never sure what I was looking at, whether things were drug-induced. I'm sure that some of the people who were tripping on psychedelics had nondrug-induced delusions, hallucinations, and distortions. All I can say is that I certainly wouldn't work with people on issues if they continued to use psychedelics because those are not addictive drugs and used only recreationally. I think if people are serious about wanting to work on their issues, whatever they be, then they have to be willing to give up their recreational drug use. But that's another group of people that I would certainly think about and get a consult on in terms of medication. I would look at the function their psychedelic drug use serves.

A second therapist related that she sees psychedelic drug use as more of a teenager's problem that requires family treatment:

Psychedelics are a whole different story. Very rarely is someone addicted to psychedelics. They don't have that property, although cocaine properly doesn't have it either. Most people who take psychedelics don't take it on a daily basis. You do see problems with young people because they take it and get into trouble. Then you have to try to keep that away from them. But it isn't like alcohol where people drink on a daily basis. People don't drop LSD every single day. That has more to do with the lifestyle they're involved in. It has to do more with family treatment and keeping them away from certain peers and dealing with family issues. Most psychedelic abuse is a teenager's illness, and the treatment of it is quite different. You don't see it much anymore. If some kid is using it frequently, you're dealing with a whole socialization problem.

4) Marijuana

These clinicians frequently see patients who use marijuana, and attempt to treat it on an outpatient basis. One therapist reported that he frequently encounters people who use marijuana recreationally, and his approach is to explore with them if it interferes with their lives:

I have people now who tell me they're smoking pot once in a while. I begin to try to explore with them whether in fact it impedes their day-to-day functioning. I have found that for most people that's not the case. For most, it's a recreational kind of thing, no different than recreational drinking. Let me give you a marijuana example.

Someone was using marijuana a lot. Marijuana has the effect of lowering testosterone. So the sexual life of this couple was suffering because this guy was smoking all the time and then couldn't perform sexually. There was a decision to be made for this individual about what was important to him. Did he want a successful sex life for his own pleasure and that of his wife, or did he want to smoke pot? The therapeutic issue was how much do you value your marriage and your love relationship with your wife? Or would you rather smoke pot? You have to choose.

5) Prescription Drugs

These clinicians also work frequently with patients who abuse prescription drugs, and attempt to treat them in an outpatient setting. They report that most of these patients tend to be polydrug abusers and to overdrink. One therapist noted: "I find that prescription drugs are usually part of an overall pattern of substance abuse. That is rarely primary. People who use prescription drugs are people that are polydrug abusers generally. They use whatever is available. They'll use pot. They'll use cocaine. If they can't float a script, they'll do this or that. But I have had very rare occasion to see someone who is just addicted to one drug. When I first started, there was more of that."

Another therapist commented that prescription drug use may cause little disruption of a person's life and be syntonic with their lifestyle, making the confrontation with denial difficult:

I've seen a number of people who abused Tylenol and Codeine. Usually, not just that. It goes along with alcohol abuse, general substance abuse, but specifically, alcohol and Codeine. Probably the other prescription issues would be the benzodiazepines, Valium and Xanax. I've been working with a number of people who had been taking it for years. By anyone's definition, they were addicted to it. The level of disruption can be quite minor, though, and consequently, taking it is syntonic with them and their lifestyle, syntonic with their spouses, and their employers don't know about it. With geriatric patients, I don't think it's an issue at all. In a situation like that where it's not a disruption of their daily life, I might make comments about it, but it doesn't come up a lot. It's become so syntonic with their routine that they don't see it as any different than taking their morning vitamins.

6) Food

There is another situation of substance abuse frequently encountered by practitioners, addiction to food. One of the therapists interviewed described how she treats those addicted to food:

> I'm convinced that food addicts metabolize sugar differently from other people. In fact, sugar affects the serotonin levels in the brain very much the way alcohol is metabolized differently by alcoholics. I think that is true of sugar and food addicts. So I do see it as an addiction, and not a compulsive behavior. I'm not as stringent with the food addict because food doesn't have the same impact on one's ability to think or reason or look at issues. But it's very much part of my treatment. I talk to people I see who are food addicts with treatment terminology. I talk about "getting high" on sugar. I ask them to work on that. I don't necessarily have the same sense of having to wait a long period of time. I think, by the way, a food addiction is much more difficult for the food addict than alcohol is for the alcoholic because you can't abstain from food. However, you can abstain from certain foods. I use a model, one used by the Willows Treatment Program, with a food plan which eliminates sugar and refined flour from the diet. I have found that that has been very successful for people. I also believe in twelve step programs with food addicts. Again, I would try to focus on the food addiction first, but food is so many things to so many people. For many of the people you see, it is their primary or only source of nurturing. Again, I don't draw quite the rigid boundary that I do with alcohol and other drugs.

In summary, therapists make referrals to specialized substance abuse programs when the drug problem is too severe to be managed in an outpatient mental health setting. Some indications of severity are:

1. The patient's drug use causes a major disruption on a frequent basis in his life.
2. The addiction is so severe that an abrupt abstinence would cause a medical emergency.
3. The patient has repeatedly failed to control his drug use despite outpatient treatment.
4. The individual is in all-out denial of his drug problem.

5. The patient lacks social supports for a life of sobriety.
6. The drug problem is primary.
7. The person is addicted to cocaine or heroin.

The Limits of Inpatient Treatment

The benefits of inpatient treatment for those with severe addictive disorders are evident. The secure and protective environment of the inpatient setting serves several useful purposes. Immediate attention can be given to the medical emergencies caused by detoxification, and the individual's physical condition can be closely monitored. If the patient acts in ways that are a danger to himself or others, the hospital offers a safe and controlled environment. Often it is not clear whether the erratic behavior and acute psychiatric symptoms are a result of the drug use or some underlying psychiatric condition. The inpatient setting allows a period of time for stabilization and observation until an accurate diagnosis can be made. The effects of medications can also be closely observed, and adjustments can be made. If the patient lacks social supports or is involved in the drug culture, he is given the opportunity to begin developing a support network for a life of sobriety. The inpatient programs can be useful for addressing patient resistances in an intensive manner. These programs can also help break the person's well-established, destructive behavior patterns and provide intensive training of alternative, more appropriate behaviors.

Despite these advantages, there are some well-known limitations. First of all, inpatient treatment is by far the most expensive form of treatment available. Increasingly, managed care companies are restricting authorization for referrals to these settings, except in the most severe cases. So far, there is little research on matching patients to treatment settings and determining the most cost-effective approaches with particular types of patients (Kadden and Penta 1995). Secondly, entering an inpatient program is disruptive to the life of the patient. In making a referral, the therapist must balance the cost and benefits of such a referral for the patient. For example, one therapist remarked that she tries to keep women out of the hospital: "I frequently try to keep women out of the hospital, particularly those women wtih families, because that becomes so disruptive, particularly with children.

Not many places provide care for children or youngsters. That's real important. I'm not so sure long, long-term treatment is necessary for professional people either."

Thirdly, inpatient treatment is a temporary and artificial environment. It is just a moment in the continuum of care that must last a lifetime for those who have substance abuse problems. Some people delude themselves into thinking that they are cured if they undergo treatment in a hospital, even though programs try to impress upon their patients the importance of continuing with follow-up treatment. One psychologist, who had worked in a substance abuse unit in a hospital, admitted that he was skeptical about its effectiveness:

> I did the follow-up studies for the hospital. What I found was the key thing was whether people kept up with any outpatient treatment. Individuals who did not, fell off the wagon. Individuals who did, stayed sober. So the key variable was not whether they had been in the hospital or not, but whether they maintained on the program. Some people will tell you that the hospital provides a motivator. But let me tell you, it's a short-term motivator. It's just like sales pitches. Substance abuse, like any other life problem, is a lot of work. You can't go through a program and be cured. You have to work at it. You have to make it part of your day-to-day work.

Finally, successful treatment requires that the substance abusers be socialized into a drug-free culture. One therapist noted that patients enter residential programs seeking to escape the world of drugs. However, ironically, in the hospital they encounter another drug culture:

> It is extremely important to keep any addicted person in the mainstream of life in contact with nonaddicted people. Inpatient units are a lot like prisons. There they are not really in recovery. Recovery begins when they get out. Drug users, as opposed to alcoholics, on the unit often get together and talk about using, not recovery. They may appear compliant and talk the recovery lingo. The residential setting only serves the purpose of getting them off the drug. The sooner you can stabilize them and get them to another level of care, the better off you are. You have to keep the addict mainstreamed and socialized outside the drug culture as much as possible.

REFFERAL TO PHYSICIANS

Occasions arise when it is necessary to refer patients to physicians in order to address the medical problems associated with substance abuse. The first medical problem that requires the attention of a physician is the dangerous effects of withdrawal from some drugs. If a therapist has a concern about the need for detox for a patient, he should consult with a qualified physician. It is a good idea to have a relationship with some doctors who are knowledgeable about addiction medicine. They can be a valuable resource for consultations and referrals.

What guidelines can a therapist use in his office? First of all, if the patient has been abstinent for the past 2 weeks from drugs and alcohol, the time of medical emergency has passed, and there is no need for concern. During the assessment, the clinician should inquire about physical symptoms the person experienced during periods of abstinence. After two days of abstinence, did the patient experience physical symptoms such as vomiting, sweating, nausea, rapid heart beat, hand tremors, or insomnia? Patients with a history of severe withdrawal reactions are at increased risk. One therapist listed his criteria for making a detox referral: "I make a referral for detox when there's obvious signs of addiction and I feel this person stopping on his own could cause problems. For example, if they're getting morning tremors—shakes in the morning—which is typical, excessive blackouts, drinking on a daily basis, if they're having soft neuropathic signs, numbness in their fingers or toes, obvious thinking problems, I would want medical detox because the possibility of someone seizing if they stop on their own is very high." Another therapist uses as a rule of thumb the amount the person consumes daily: "I spent some years doing Employee Assistance Program (EAP) work and learned as a rule of thumb that if the person is drinking a fifth a day, he needs to be detoxed and under the care of a physician to manage the withdrawal symptoms." Another experienced practitioner claimed that he uses a blood alcohol level as a criterion for referral: "If I establish an average blood alcohol concentration of greater than .15, I want a physician to clear them for outpatient treatment. At that level, they are at risk of some level of abstinence syndrome."

Next, the therapist should take note of the drugs the patient has been abusing. Some drugs produce a physical dependence that requires medical detoxification, while others do not. However, overdoses with most drugs can cause a medical emergency and should be attended to immediately. Cases of overdose are seen mostly in emergency room settings and rarely in the outpatient. Cocaine, marijuana, and psychedelics do not produce a withdrawal syndrome that requires medical management or detoxification, although pronounced mood disturbances can be observed. Heroin withdrawal can cause flu-like symptoms that can be extremely uncomfortable, but are not life threatening. Some common symptoms of opioid withdrawal are stomach cramps, achiness, diarrhea, runny nose, chills, restlessness, tearing eyes, and insomnia. The substances of greatest concern are alcohol and other central nervous system depressants, such as barbituates and the benzodiazepines. If a severe physical dependence has developed with these drugs, abrupt cessation of use can be fatal. Therefore, it is essential to evaluate the severity of the patient's dependence on these depressants. When in doubt, it is always advisable to consult with a qualified physician before recommending abstinence and to send the person for a medical evaluation.

A second reason for making a referral to a physician is to help clarify an unclear diagnosis. One therapist noted that some medical conditions can mask and mimic a dual diagnosis: "My rule of thumb is that if they have not had a complete medical workup in the last year that they get one. If they have a family history of an endocrine disorder, such as thyroid, diabetes, or hypoglycemia, those need to be addressed because they can mimic dual diagnosis and aggravate the addiction."

A third reason that substance abusing patients may need to be referred to a physician for a medical evaluation is the physical problems that often develop with the long-term use of drugs. Those who drink excessively often develop liver problems, gastritis, and/or high blood pressure. Alcohol can also exacerbate existing medical conditions. The use of cocaine can cause high blood pressure, strokes, seizures, and heart attacks. If the person has not had a complete physical in a year, it is a good policy to refer the individual to a doctor for an evaluation, particularly if he has a long history of substance abuse. One therapist reported that he regularly sends his patients to a physician if he detects physical problems that he suspects might be alcohol related. He noted that the physician can then effectively confront the patient's denial by pointing out the physical consequences of drinking:

> Certain physical problems can be indications of the abuse of alcohol. When I hear about those problems, I generally don't say, "I think you have alcoholic problems." I suggest that they see the doctor again because there are medical things he can talk to them about. Often that does it. They go back and have a physical. Their liver enzymes are screwed up, and they know something is going on. I know a number of physicians to refer to if they don't have their own private doctor. All the ones I refer to know how to pick those kinds of things up.

REFFERAL TO PSYCHIATRISTS

A common referral made by therapists who work with the dually diagnosed is to a psychiatrist for a medication evaluation. It is necessary to choose psychiatrists who are familiar with dual diagnosis because some psychiatrists tend to focus their attention on the mental health disorder and underestimate the impact of the substance abuse problem on the patient and the effectiveness of treatment. Their limited sensitivity to substance abuse issues may also interfere with their making an accurate diagnosis of the patient. One experienced therapist stated that she will only refer to psychiatrists whom she knows are knowledgeable about chemical dependency: "What I usually do when I'm dealing with chemical dependency is make sure the physician knows about chemical dependency. There are a few of them. I don't care what they tell you, you have to know that they know. This is where I use psychiatrists who are certified by ASAM. ASAM is the American Society of Addiction Medicine. They have a certification program for physicians. They have lists, and you look for the psychiatrists who are certified by ASAM. Then you get to know them." Once the therapist has identified a psychiatrist knowledgeable about substance abuse, it is useful to meet with that person and ask questions about how he treats particular dual diagnosis cases. It is important to develop a comfortable and cooperative relationship with the physicians to whom the therapist makes routine referrals.

Once the therapist has established a working relationship with a particular psychiatrist, he needs to communicate with the physician the reasons for the referral and his concerns regarding the addiction problem. Some clinicians prefer to write the physicians notes, while others prefer to discuss the cases personally. It is important that the psychiatrist understand why the person is being referred for medication and that the person has a substance abuse disorder. Such clarifications will help the psychiatrist make an accurate diagnosis because the substance use disorder can mask and mimic several psychiatric disorders. Furthermore, it helps ensure that the psychiatrist will be suitably cautious in prescribing medications with an addictive potential.

There are several conditions that warrant a referral to a psychiatrist for a medication evaluation. First of all, if the patient has a thought disorder, it is appropriate that the patient be prescribed an antipsychotic medication. Although the substance abuse treatment community is hesitant to endorse the use of any mood-altering drug, there is no reason not to prescribe non-addictive neuroleptic medications to psychotic patients. These medications can allow patients who suffer schizophrenic and severely borderline disorders to tolerate and verbalize affects and to contain their acting out and impulsivity. Secondly, medication can help patients suffering from severe mood disorders, such as major depression and bipolar disorder, to feel less overwhelmed and more able to participate in outpatient treatment. These patients often have suicidal thoughts and need to be stabilized before they can be successfully treated in the outpatient setting. Thirdly, patients who have severe anxiety disorders or are unable to sleep may benefit from medication. However, care must be exercised that these patients not be prescribed medications that have addictive potential. Finally, patients can be referred to psychiatrists for Antabuse, which can be an effective deterent for some alcoholics. If taken regularly and closely monitored, Antabuse can eliminate the impulsive drinking.

Therapists may also refer their patients to a psychiatrist if they are uncertain of the diagnosis or are not making progress in treatment. At times, the drug use of the patient persists despite the interventions of the therapist. The drug use is not severe enough to warrant a referral to a specialized substance abuse treatment facility, and the patient appears motivated to work on his problems. The clinician may then suspect a dual diagnosis. There may be an underlying pathology that is disguised by the substance abuse and that the patient is self-medicating. A referral for a second opinion and an experiment with medication may be helpful. One experienced therapist admitted: "There are times when I'm not sure what's going on, if the substance abuse is contributing or there are other problems. I'm just diagnostically lost and see if an experimental trial on medication would be helpful. That's rare, but I have come into contact with cases that are just not diagnosable by any normal means. I've had to use an experiment to see if this medication helps this person."

REFERRAL TO PSYCHIATRIC HOSPITALS

On rare occasions, an outpatient therapist may have to admit a patient to a hospital. All states have mental health codes that specify the criteria for inpatient admission. In general, those who are a danger to themselves or others or exhibit such severe signs of mental illness that they cannot care for themselves are in need of the protected environment of the psychiatric hospital. In the hospital, the patient is given 24-hour care, and there is a more intensive approach to treatment than can be offered in the outpatient setting.

Clinicians in the outpatient setting may encounter patients who have gotten off their medications and become acutely psychotic. Some mentally ill substance abusers prefer to drink or use drugs at times instead of taking their prescribed medications. When they relapse into substance use, they also relapse in their mental illness. In such cases, if these patients are unable to return to sobriety and resume with their medication, a referral to a psychiatric unit, preferably a dual diagnosis unit, may be necessary for stabilization.

The more frequent experience in the outpatient setting is with individuals who are severely depressed and suicidal. Research shows that people with substance abuse problems are more likely to be depressed and to succeed with suicide. In the literature, the one factor that predicts successful suicide is the individual's using alcohol or drugs when depressed and suicidal. Therefore, the clinician must exercise extreme caution when his dually diagnosed patients threaten suicide, particularly when they are drinking and using drugs.

A thorough assessment for suicidal risk must, of course, be undertaken with every patient. In this regard, questions regarding suicidal thoughts, intent, and plans must be asked. The past history of attempts and the family history of suicidality need to be explored. The degree of depression, impulsiveness, and impaired judgment should also be assessed. Feelings of helplessness, hopelessness, and low self-esteem suggest depression, and the intensity of these feelings indicates the degree of depression. If the person is psychotic and has suicidal thoughts, he is an extremely high-risk patient. Consideration of the patient's history of acting out behavior may help identify the degree of impulsiveness and impaired judgment. Finally, an evaluation of the person's support systems and reasons for not committing suicide must be made.

If the clinician determines that there is a significant risk of suicide, he should make arrangements for the patient to be hospitalized. If the person comes to the office intoxicated and makes a significant suicidal threat, the therapist should call a family member or the police to take the patient to an emergency room for proper care and psychiatric admission. Of course, an intoxicated person should never be allowed to drive, and a suicidal person should never be without a supportive person accompanying him to the hospital. One therapist commented: "Of course, we know that there's a higher probability of suicide when somebody's using. At least, our research has shown that. The question is, I guess, when is this manipulative? That's something you can really never second guess. I don't care whether the patient is borderline, alcoholic, or whatever. I haven't had too much difficulty with that because the patients are not drinking when I work with them. If they are, I send them to the hospital and tell them to go to the emergency if it is that bad." When people threaten suicide, they are calling out for help. The role of the therapist is to help them get the help they need.

In summary, for clinicians to work effectively with the dually diagnosed in an outpatient setting, they must be aware of the potential and limits of that setting for treating their patients. They also need to be sensitive to the severity and acuteness of the substance abuse problems and psychiatric disturbances of their patients. This dual awareness will require that they regularly make appropriate referrals:

1. To inpatient substance abuse programs and to substance abuse counselors, depending on the severity of their patient's drug problem and the type of drug abused;
2. To physicians to address the medical complications from drug use;
3. To psychiatrists for medication evaluation, if the psychiatric disorder is severe; and
4. For hospitalization, if the patient is so disturbed that he is a danger to himself or others or is acutely psychotic and unable to care for himself.

9

A SPECTRUM OF CAUTION: PRESCRIBING MEDICATIONS

There are times when it is necessary to prescribe medications to dual diagnosis patients, particularly when their psychiatric symptoms are severe or when they are in need of detoxification. However, care must be exercised in prescribing medications for this population. First of all, because of the interaction of the disorders, it is often difficult to make an accurate diagnosis. Symptoms of substance abuse can mask and mimic psychiatric symptoms, making the selection of an appropriate medication difficult. Secondly, substance-abusing patients are vulnerable to becoming addicted to other medications and tend to seek drugs to resolve their problems. The problem is complicated by the fact that many commonly prescribed medications have an addictive potential. Therefore, carelessly prescribing medications can lead to other addictions, trigger a relapse to substance abuse, and cause adverse reactions with the drugs these patients are already using to self-medicate. Finally, this population has developed a complex relationship with drugs and may transfer their reactions to medications prescribed by physicians. Patients may either refuse to take the meds or try to titrate the dosages on their own in order to control their moods. Furthermore, because of the adverse effects of some meds, they may prefer to take their drug of choice in order to self-medicate.

There are also dangers in not prescribing medications when they are appropriate. Psychiatric symptoms that could be relieved with medications can persist and worsen, contributing unnecessarily to the suffering of the patient. Furthermore, some individuals have learned the strategy of self-medicating distressing feelings and thoughts with their drug of choice. Patients who are attempting to maintain a life of sobriety may relapse when their psychiatric symptoms worsen. In these cases, appropriate medications may relieve the distress caused by the underlying psychiatric condition and help the patient maintain his abstinence. Therefore, the clinician must carefully weigh the benefits and risks in prescribing medications for any given condition of the dually diagnosed.

Treatment Principle Eight: Care must be exercised in prescribing medication for the dually diagnosed; the benefits and risks need to be evaluated.

A SPECTRUM OF CAUTION

There is a notable lack of research on the effectiveness of using psychotropic medications in the treatment of the dually diagnosed. However, clinicians have accumulated many years of experience in treating this population with medications and developed their own practical guidelines. I interviewed a group of nine psychologists who had a minimum of ten years of experience treating the dually diagnosed and asked them about their attitudes and practices regarding medications. Although none of this group had a medical degree, they were knowledgeable about psychotropic medications. There was a discernable spectrum of attitudes toward medications among these practitioners. All exercised some degree of caution, as manifested in their careful selection of physicians and psychiatrists for referral. Yet some therapists were more cautious than others about the utility of prescribing medication for their dual diagnosis patients.

A few quotes from this group may portray their attitudes. One therapist, a recovering alcoholic, was the most cautious: "I don't like to use medication unless it's absolutely necessary. I think you have a reinforcement that a pill or something will make it better. I think it plays into the whole dynamic of substance abusers. Now that doesn't mean it's not necessary at times. This is where you have to figure out the pros and cons." A second therapist stated: "I'm very cautious in the use of meds. I refer only to psychiatrists who I feel are equally cautious." Another said: "Generally, I am very wary to give out medication until I know what's going to be effective or not. I'm not a real big fan of medication." He offered this case example:

> Years ago, I saw a guy who was a young, talented financial stock-broker who had a repetitive drinking problem. We never got any-place because he just wouldn't stop. He looked depressed to me all the time. But I wouldn't supply him antidepressants or suggest medication for someone like that. He was getting drunk all the time. Who knows whether his depression stemmed from that or not? We certainly know that everybody who drinks goes through mood changes and gets depressed. To say someone is legitimately depressed as an independent entity from the mood changes is very difficult, very hard to know.

Some of this group, while maintaining a cautious attitude, high-lighted the benefits of medication for the dually diagnosed. For example, one clinician asserted that for the neurotic patients he treats he believes medication can be helpful for temporary relief and as an adjunct to, not a replacement for, therapy: "I try to get people to understand that the medication they have is not intended to be medication they take for the rest of their life, but that it's designed to help them get over the rough spots and that it's designed to be an adjunct to psychotherapy." Another therapist affirmed the value of medication for his dual diagnosis patients, if carefully monitored:

> I think medications can be extremely valuable. Some try to self-medicate themselves. They try to control sleeping disorders from developing, to control anxiety disorders by prescription medications. If you can offer somebody something that may not be as gratifying as what they first asked for, but does have some gratification and ultimately has a healthier prognosis, then it makes sense to do that. I'd rather see somebody taking Restoril to sleep at night instead of drinking five shots of whiskey and get up at four o'clock in the morning with a stomach problem. I'd rather treat somebody who's taking Elavil three times a day, than treat somebody who's getting drunk and threatening suicide when he goes home to see his spouse.

Some therapists are worried that you are trading one addiction for
another addiction. I think a careful monitoring of the amount of
medications, a careful selection of appropriate medication, a care in
getting away from the more addicting medications, and identifying
the most addictive prone patients are important.

Finally, one clinician, who has worked for many years with the dually
diagnosed in both inpatient and outpatient settings, admitted to a
change in attitude over the years regarding medication:

I am much more inclined to refer for medication now than ever
before. In the old days, I subscribed to the notion that medication for addicted people was bad news, unless they were psychotic.
To place them on antianxiety meds, meds with sedative or mood
altering effects, was not permitted because you would likely trigger a relapse or transfer the addiction from one chemical base to
another. I don't believe that anymore. Now I believe that anything
we can do to help normalize people's neurochemistry we should
do. The medications used today are different than twenty years ago.
The technology is much more specific in their effects. I'm thinking of the serotonin reuptake blockers for mood disorders.

Adelman and colleagues (1993) conducted an intriguing study
to elicit from a group of 112 psychiatrists their pharmacotherapeutic
strategies with the dually diagnosed. The surveyed psychiatrists were
given ten vignettes, based on clinical experience, which depicted
dilemmas regarding the use of medication in treating the dually diagnosed. Five multiple-choice treatment interventions were offered.
The results showed that there was no unanimity regarding treatment
strategies for any of the vignettes. However, some common features
in their approaches were identified, which reflected cautious clinical efforts to address both diagnoses concurrently. The group tended
to avoid coercive strategies that might result in patients discontinu-
ing treatment. They also shunned treatment choices that involved
prescribing medications to patients who continued to abuse alcohol or drugs. The use of neuroleptics was generally favored for
patients with active psychotic symptoms. The prescription of antidepressants was viewed favorably for patients who were abstinent.
There was no consensus among this group of psychiatrists regard-

ing the use of benzodiazepines for symptoms of anxiety, although those who did allow their use preferred the longer acting ones, like clonazepam (Klonapin).

In a clinician's guidebook for the treatment of the mentally ill substance abuser, Ries (1994) summarized the consensus position of a group of experienced practitioners regarding the pharmacologic management of this population. This group proposed a conservative stepwise approach for mild and moderate mental disorders. They noted that for severe conditions, such as psychotic depression, mania, and schizophrenia, the rapid and aggressive use of medications is needed to prevent the patient's becoming a danger to self or others and further psychiatric deterioration. The first step is to employ non-pharmacologic approaches, such as therapy, support groups, and education. If this approach is unsuccessful, nonaddictive medications, such as antidepressants, antipsychotics, and lithium, may be added. If the first two steps are unsuccessful, psychoactive medications, such as benzodiazepines, barbituates, and other sedative-hypnotics, may be used with close monitoring.

TREATING SOME SPECIFIC DISORDERS

Depression

The most common dual diagnosis encountered in the outpatient setting is depression and alcohol abuse or dependence. The depressed substance-abusing patient presents a diagnostic dilemma because of the close association of depressive symptoms and substance use. For example, all alcoholics experience some depression as a result of their drinking. Those who experience a cocaine "crash" are also significantly depressed. The problem for the clinician is to determine if the depression that accompanies the substance use is primary, secondary, or independent of the drug problem. Often, only time can resolve this diagnostic uncertainty because the depressive symptoms from abusing substances normally remit in about a month. If the person is still depressed after a month of sobriety, it is a good indication that an underlying depression exists.

I generally request that depressed patients be abstinent for two to four weeks before I will make a referral to a psychiatrist for medications. Let me give a case example:

Ron, a man in his late fifties, came to see me because he thought his drinking was getting out of control. He reported that in the last six months he had been drinking eight to ten beers every night to relax after work. He had been experiencing significant stress on his job, and he believed he had been drinking more to cope with the problem. Ron had been drinking beer since he was a teenager and usually drank three or four beers a night until this most recent crisis at work. Ron also reported that he was depressed, fatigued, had sleeping difficulties, was lacking motivation, and was becoming socially withdrawn. Initially, we worked on his drinking problem. He said he did not want to abstain altogether from drinking, but did want to cut back. I requested that he keep a log of his drinking behavior, and we discussed in sessions his experience of trying to cut back. After a few weeks, he reported that he had succeeded in cutting back his drinking to two beers each night, but still felt depressed and unmotivated. He asked that he see a psychiatrist for medication. I explained to him that his symptoms of depression may be related to his drinking and proposed that he remain abstinent for about two weeks. I told him that if he still felt depressed, I would then refer him to a psychiatrist for a medication evaluation.

An accurate diagnosis is essential for the effective treatment of the dually diagnosed. If the depressive symptoms are secondary to the substance use, antidepressant medication will be unnecessary and will not help to relieve the symptoms. If there is an underlying depression, which is either primary or an independent disorder, medication can be extremely helpful for symptom relief. The medication can take the edge off the depression so the patient can work more effectively on issues in therapy. Medication in this case is a useful adjunct to, not a replacement for, therapy. However, if the underlying depression is not treated, the patient is at risk of relapsing into substance use because the drinking and drug use are frequently a means of self-medicating the depressive affects. A case in which I would not wait to refer the patient for a psychiatric evaluation and possible hospitalization is when the depression is severe and the patient is suicidal. At such a time, it is more important to treat the severe psychiatric symptoms aggressively to avoid a life threatening situation.

The antidepressant medications used today have no addictive potential, but have some adverse interactions with alcohol and other drugs. Patients taking antidepressant meds should be warned that any use of alcohol or drugs can reduce the therapeutic effectiveness of the medication and should be avoided. Furthermore, alcohol and other drugs can produce adverse effects if taken with the prescribed antidepressants. In the case of tricyclic antidepressants, the effects of alcohol use are potentiated, increasing its sedating effect and possibly the risk of suicide. Monoamine oxidase inhibitors (MAOI) can produce life-threatening complications if taken with alcohol and should be prescribed with extreme care. The more recent selective serotonin reuptake inhibitors (SSRI), such as Prozac, Zoloft, and Paxil, are much less toxic and should be prescribed more frequently for the dually diagnosed.

Anxiety

Anxiety symptoms and disorders are encountered among the dually diagnosed as frequently as depression. It is important to assess accurately the etiology of the anxiety in order to treat it effectively. However, as with depressive symptoms, the anxiety can be primary, secondary, or independent of the substance use. The precise relationship of the anxiety and the substance use is often difficult to determine. The observed anxiety may be secondary to the substance use. Central Nervous System depressant withdrawal often involves a protracted phase of up to six months which can mimic generalized anxiety and agoraphobia. However, with most patients, these symptoms will spontaneously improve within weeks after abstinence is established. When a person begins a life of sobriety without the drug they were accustomed to using to cope with the stress of life, he may feel overwhelmed and anxious until he learns more effective coping mechanisms. There is accumulating data suggesting that alcohol, stimulants, marijuana, and hallucinogens may provoke the onset of an anxiety disorder, which the patient then self-medicates with his drug of choice.

A primary or independent anxiety disorder may also exist. For example, many Vietnam veterans suffered post traumatic stress in the war and continued drug use afterwards in an effort to self-medicate. In such cases, treatment of the underlying anxiety disorder is essential for the individual to maintain sobriety. A final diagnostic consideration is the patient's use of caffeine, nicotine, and over-the-counter diet pills, which are stimulants that can aggravate an anxious condition.

A careful assessment for an anxiety disorder is particularly important because the currently employed pharmacotherapeutic strategy of using benzodiazepines for treating anxiety disorders can be hazardous with the dually diagnosed. These prescription drugs have an addictive potential and produce symptoms of physiologic dependence. They also demonstrate cross-tolerance with alcohol, barbiturates, and other antianxiolitics. Furthermore, their use with the dually diagnosed can reinforce a psychological dependence on drugs and lead to a relapse.

For these reasons, a careful clinical strategy must be employed in utilizing the benzodiazepines with this population. Benzodiazepines, such as Librium, Valium, and Ativan, are the most commonly used drugs for detoxification from alcohol and the sedative-hypnotics. These agents help moderate withdrawal symptoms and prevent dangerous conditions, such as delirium tremens and seizures. They are also used in the treatment of acute psychotic symptoms caused by schizophrenia, mania, and cocaine intoxication. However, these drugs should be used only to manage these acute conditions for a brief period of time until the patient is stabilized. Regarding anxiety disorders, the first line of treatment should be nonpharmacological, using some form of psychotherapy. If the anxiety symptoms persist, treatment with antidepressants or buspirone (BuSpar), a nonbenzodiazepine anti-anxiety agent, has been effective with many patients. If these strategies fail and severe anxiety symptoms persist, the physician may consider prescribing one of the slow onset and longer acting benzodiazepines, such as clonazepam (Klonapin). Although many physicians, particularly those with a strong chemical dependency background, make it a policy never to prescribe these drugs to their substance abusing patients, the severity of the symptoms, which may lead to attempts to self-medicate with drugs, warrant the risk of prescribing longer acting benzodiapines. This should only be done if the person has a well-established sobriety. The clinician should give the patient warnings about the effects and abuse potential of the drug and carefully monitor compliance.

Thought Disorders

Patients with psychotic disturbances clearly need to be referred to a psychiatrist for medication. Neuroleptic medications have proven effective in suppressing the positive symptoms of psychosis, such as hallucinations, delusions, and incoherence. As major tranquilizers, they can also have a substantial calming effect on the patient. Since the neuroleptics have no addictive potential, they can be safely prescribed for the psychotic symptoms of the dually diagnosed. However, there is one caution. Antipsychotics can lower the seizure threshold and enhance the seizure potential during withdrawal from alcohol and the sedative-hypnotics.

Frequently, anticholinergic agents are prescribed to alleviate many of the negative side effects of the neuroleptics, such as muscle spasms, restlessness, and involuntary movements. Using anticholinergics to block some of the more distressing side effects of other meds may relieve the patient of the pressure to use alcohol or drugs for that purpose. However, there are reports that these drugs are being abused by some patients to enhance their drug "highs." Therefore, the patient's use of anticholinergic agents should be closely monitored.

In the outpatient setting, the main problem with the mentally ill substance abuser is medication compliance. Antipsychotics can cause many unpleasant side effects which lead the person to discontinue use. Patients may then resort to drugs or alcohol in an attempt to reverse the dysphoria or to self-medicate their psychotic symptoms. Clinicians need to impress upon these patients the importance of consistently taking their medications as prescribed and the dangers of continuing to drink or use drugs while medicated.

Bipolar Disorder

Substance abusing bipolar patients can benefit from medications which help stabilize their moods. Once stabilized, they are more capable of participating in their psychiatric and substance abuse recovery. Lithium and anticonvulsive drugs have effectively been used with this group of patients. There is one danger, however, if the patient continues drinking and takes lithium. Alcohol intoxication and withdrawal disturbs the fluid electrolyte balance in the body, which can lead to lithium toxicity. Consequently, lithium blood levels must be checked regularly to make sure that the medication is maintained at therapeutic levels. As with those using antipsychotic agents, the main problem is with medication compliance because of the negative side effects of the prescribed drugs. These patients also prefer to self-medicate with drugs and alcohol. Therapists can give their patients support in maintaining both their medication regime and their sober life style.

In summary, the following are some strategies for prescribing medication for the dually diagnosed:

1. If the psychiatric condition or withdrawal symptoms are acute and severe, appropriate medications should be prescribed.
2. If the psychiatric condition is mild or moderate, therapy without medication is the preferred and first approach.
3. If the symptoms persist, medications can be prescribed after a period of stable abstinence.
4. Antipsychotic, antidepressant, and antimanic medications can be safely prescribed with close monitoring and warnings about the adverse interactions with alcohol and drugs.
5. Antianxiety medications, which have an addictive potential, should only be prescribed as a last resort and for a limited period of time.

SOME CLINICAL ISSUES

Physician Selection

As discussed in the previous chapter, the therapist should carefully select psychiatrists who are knowledgeable about treating dual diagnosis patients and establish a good working relationship with them. A good working relationship can be fostered if the therapist and psychiatrist have a clear understanding of each other's orientation, expectations, and practices. The clinician also has to be comfortable with the physician's philosophy and prescribing practices. It is imperative that when making a referral to a psychiatrist that the therapist alert him to a substance abuse concern. As the treatment proceeds, ongoing communication about the patient's condition, progress, and compliance with medications is also useful in furthering the achievement of treatment goals.

Ongoing Assessment

Because the symptoms of substance abuse and psychiatric conditions may mask and mimic each other, it is difficult to make an accurate diagnosis of these patients. Even after taking a thorough history, being particularly attentive to the temporal sequence of the disorders and the family history, the clinician may still not be certain of his diagnosis and the relationship of the disorders. The therapist needs to be patient and wait before making a final diagnosis. Only after a period of abstinence, in some cases up to several months, can the symptoms be ruled out as related to the effects of drug use. Only after a significant period of abstinence will the true nature of the psychiatric disorder, if it in fact exists, reveal itself. Furthermore, patients will often not reveal the extent of their drug use until they have come to trust their therapist. That may take time. Therefore, the clinician's assessment of his patient must be ongoing and attentive to the presence and subtle interactions of the disorders.

An accurate diagnosis is critical when prescribing medications. If an underlying psychiatric disorder is not recognized and goes untreated, the patient will be at risk of relapse into substance use to self-medicate. In fact, if the person who is serious about recovery from chemical dependency continues to relapse, the therapist might suspect an unrecognized dual diagnosis and make a referral to a psychiatrist for an evaluation. If the substance abuse problem is not recognized and the individual is treated for a psychiatric condition only, there is a risk of prescribing inappropriate medications. Medications with an addictive potential or with dangerous drug interactions with alcohol or drugs may be inadvertently prescribed. The use of alcohol and drugs may also compromise the therapeutic effectiveness of the prescribed medication. Finally, if the true etiology of the symptoms are not recognized, the patient may be prescribed medications that are either useless or harmful. For example, a person may be given an antidepressant for drug-induced depression whose symptoms would remit over time anyway without medication. An individual in a cocaine-induced psychosis may be given antipsychotic drugs and further risk going into seizure.

Medication Compliance

Therapists, who normally spend more time with their patients than the psychiatrist, can play an important role in securing patient compliance with a specific medication regime. Therapists can help in many ways. First of all, they can help patients understand the importance of following exactly the medication regime prescribed by the doctor and maintaining abstinence. I often explain in clear and simple terms what the patient must do for his continuing recovery for both his mental health and substance abuse problems. For example, if the patient is depressed and abuses alcohol, I tell him:

> You can't forget that you have two disorders that need attention for a full recovery. You have a psychiatric disorder called depression and you have a problem with alcohol. For your depression, you will have to take your medication regularly as prescribed, and we will talk about the issues that underlie the depression. You won't be able to drink, or the medication won't work, and you will become more depressed. To help you maintain your sobriety, you will have to go to AA meetings regularly, get a sponsor, and meet with me each week.

Secondly, the clinician can reinforce what the psychiatrist tells the patient about the side effects and dangers of drug interactions of the particular medications. Most people quit taking their medications because of the adverse side effects. The therapist can explain what the anticipated side effects are and help the patient accept them as a trade off for relief of his psychiatric symptoms. Furthermore, he can warn the patient about the dangers of drinking and using drugs while taking prescription medication.

Thirdly, therapists can confront the all or none thinking of their patients regarding mood altering drugs. On the one hand, some drug abusers have become so accustomed to controlling their moods with drugs that they adopt the same attitude with prescription medication and titrate the dosage as they see fit. They may even switch to their drug of choice if the medication prescribed by the doctor does not give them the immediate gratification they formerly experienced. Some patients may even be reluctant to surrender their control over drugs to a physician. The therapist needs to address directly the underlying control issues involved in the patient's resistance to compliance. On the other hand, other patients, aware of the devastation that mood altering drugs have caused in their lives, are reluctant to take any medication. This attitude is often reinforced by members of the twelve step groups in which they participate. The therapist must explain carefully the difference between prescribed and unprescribed drugs and help the patient see how taking medication fits in with his overall recovery from both the psychiatric and substance use disorders.

Finally, therapists need to encourage their patients to take responsibility for their own recovery from both disorders. They must point out clearly the consequences of following or not following the prescribed treatment regimes. One therapist, a recovering alcoholic, described how she encourages patients to become experts in their own treatment:

> The other thing I try to do with patients is help them to understand their disease so that they can become experts in their own treatment. For instance, if you go to a physician and the physician says this drug is not addictive, and the package insert says you may be sleepy from this drug, now what does the patient do? Discuss it with the physician or just take it because the doctor says you can take this cough medicine? I had a physician many years ago who said you can take this one teaspoon of cough medicine and it won't bother you. I knew darn well it would. So I try to teach patients to be responsible for their recovery and to do what they have to do to stay sober. Because if they don't stay sober, nothing is going to work.

The prescription of medications can be an important adjunct to the treatment of the dually diagnosed, if it is done with caution and careful monitoring. The benefits and risks of specific medications should be assessed. Medications are useful for relieving the distress caused by underlying psychiatric conditions that may lead to relapse. However, some medications, particularly those with an addictive potential, may trigger a relapse, produce another addiction, or cause adverse drug interactions when taken with alcohol or other nonprescribed drugs. Therapists and psychiatrists need to develop collaborative relationships for the most effective treatment of their patients.

10 AN ALLIANCE FOR PROGRESS: ENCOURAGING PARTICIPATION IN TWELVE STEP PROGRAMS

The effective treatment of the dually diagnosed requires that both the substance use and psychiatric disorders be addressed in an integrated fashion. In the outpatient setting, psychotherapy has been the usual treatment of choice for those with mental health problems; with more severe illnesses, medications are also used. For substance abuse, ongoing participation in twelve step programs has proven to be the most effective approach for maintaining sobriety. Unfortunately, there has been a long history of antagonism between professionals in the mental health field and members of AA and NA, which has prevented the integration of these two treatment modalities for those suffering comorbid conditions.

Stephanie Brown (1985) and her associates at the Stanford Alcohol Clinic studied the attitudes of eighty abstinent AA members towards psychotherapy. She found that 77% of the AA participants had been involved in some form of psychotherapy, yet nearly a third (30%) believed that it was not helpful. By contrast, 45% had been in therapy after abstinence, and only 3% claimed it was not helpful. The AA research participants viewed therapists as uninformed about and incompetent in treating alcohol issues and criticized them for failing to diagnose their alcohol problems. Many feared that therapy would interfere with their recovery by driving a wedge between them and AA. From the side of the mental health professional, Brown noted that many therapists have a strong prejudice against alcoholics and believe that alcoholism cannot be effectively treated. Many therapists are ignorant of AA and mistrustful of many aspects of the program, such as its spiritual orientation, unscientific basis, and exclusive focus on alcohol problems. Some clinicians also object to what they see as the AA program's fanaticism, cultism, and intolerance of other methods of achieving abstinence. They are concerned that their patient's involvement in the AA group may interfere with the development of a therapeutic alliance with them in the treatment.

Since the dually diagnosed suffer problems because of drug use, therapists should utilize a treatment approach that has proven successful for over six decades in helping drug abusers to achieve and maintain abstinence. They should encourage the participation of their dually diagnosed patients in twelve step programs as much as possible without placing an intolerable burden on those who may be psychologically fragile. Since these patients also experience mental health problems that may make it difficult for them to participate fully in AA or NA, clinicians need to prepare them for and assist their involvement. In some cases, however, clinicians may have to offer some alternative means of support in addressing their substance abuse problems.

Treatment Principle Nine: Participation in twelve step support groups is an effective complement to individual therapy with the dually diagnosed.

BENEFITS AND LIMITS OF INVOLVEMENT

Benefits

There are many benefits above and beyond what can be achieved in individual therapy to be gained by participation in twelve step groups. First of all, for those patients who are reluctant to admit a substance abuse problem, joining the group can help them address their denial effectively. Some people have stereotypes of what an alcoholic or a drug addict is like and cannot identify with that negative image. Their image of an alcoholic as a skid row bum, or a drug addict as a criminal, reinforces their denial. They may rationalize that they have a good job, live in an upscale neighborhood, are respected members of the community, and therefore, could not possibly be alcoholic. When they attend meetings, they meet people just like themselves who happen to have drinking or drug problems. They begin to realize that being an alcoholic does not mean living on skid row and being jobless. Ignorance about the nature of drug addiction can also reinforce denial. Some people think that being an alcoholic means drinking every day, being regularly intoxicated, having a morning "eye opener," and being unable to hold a steady job. Encountering other alcoholics at all stages of addiction and being educated at meetings about the signs and symptoms of the disease in its various stages can help them gain a more accurate picture of addiction. Such information may also help them identify the problem in themselves.

A second benefit for those who recognize their problem and are trying to maintain sobriety is that the group offers a social support system. The group helps them to resocialize themselves into a sober lifestyle. Alcoholics and drug abusers usually develop a way of life centered around alcohol or drugs. Their friends and acquaintances are users, and much of their social life revolves around drinking or drug use. Giving up drugs involves many losses, of drinking friends, a social life, and a way of relaxing, which create a vacuum in the patient's life. The AA or NA program offers a new social network that enables them to identify with a sober group and gives support to them while they build a new life without drugs. The group setting also provides social pressure and accountability to maintain sobriety. The members will firmly confront their neglect of the principles of the program and gently nurse them back to sobriety after a relapse. Furthermore, beyond this group support, a strong relationship with a sponsor provides individual support and guidance, particularly in times of temptation to relapse.

Thirdly, participation in the group facilitates the personal development of the patient. After using drugs for many years, people tend to remain immature in their interpersonal relationships. They are out of touch with their feelings, which have been covered up with their drug of choice. They are often filled with shame and guilt and cannot tolerate frustration. Their relationships remain superficial because of their inability to express their feelings and resolve conflicts. Within the safety of an accepting group, members can learn to communicate their thoughts and feelings and to listen to each other respectfully. Through the discussion of personal issues, they learn to look more deeply into their own lives and confront the obstacles to their personal growth. In the nonjudgmental atmosphere of the group, members begin to overcome feelings of shame and alienation and to build self-esteem. The give and take of group interaction provides many opportunities for its members to learn how to resolve conflicts and deepen relationships. Undertaking a mission to help other members in their recovery also helps individuals maintain sobriety and build self-esteem. Of course, all of these tasks complement the work of therapy.

Fourthly, the group teaches the patient some useful problem-solving strategies. What all the members have in common are problems that have been caused by substance abuse. In talking with others who share their experience, members feel less alone and overwhelmed. At the meetings, people share their experiences with drugs and what they have done to maintain their sobriety. They alert each other to pitfalls and ways of avoiding problems. Once trust is developed, members can confront each other and help interpret danger signals of a potential relapse. The more experienced members also become sponsors and guides for the newer members. The sponsors offer a listening ear, advice when needed, and the assurance of personal support.

Finally, the group provides a life-long support system for maintaining sobriety. One of the limits of a treatment relationship with a professional is that it is time limited, particularly in this age of managed care. However, alcoholism and drug addiction are chronic diseases that require life-long attention. A firmly established relationship with an AA or NA group and with a sponsor is a valuable ally when times of crisis arise in the substance abuser's life. Relapse is a constant danger, more imminent at some times than at others. Having a support network in place during those times when the individual is tempted to use again can help avoid a painful relapse. Recovery from the disease of addiction is also a life-long task. The group provides the necessary support and tools to continue the work of building a new life without drugs.

Limits

As valuable as the twelve step program is in addressing substance abuse problems, there are limits to its utility with the dually diagnosed.

First of all, many of those whom the clinician comes to recognize as dually diagnosed patients refuse to acknowledge they have a substance abuse problem. Typically, they come to mental health professionals because they feel distressed by some emotional or mental problem. The task of the clinician then is to alert the patient to the substance abuse problem and to attempt to engage him in treatment for it. That is often a difficult sell. The patient is particularly resistant to participating in AA or NA because he does not identify himself as an alcoholic or drug addict.

Secondly, some of the dually diagnosed, particularly those with severe mental illness, are psychologically fragile. They may be unable to tolerate the give and take of a group meeting. These patients are very sensitive to rejection and feel like outsiders wherever they go. They find it extremely difficult to engage in group activities. For example, some paranoid patients would be too suspicious and guarded to become involved with a large group of strangers. Members of twelve step groups may also be unaccustomed to and even threatened by some of the behaviors of the mentally ill. The delusions and strident or bizarre behavior of some psychiatric patients can be particularly intimidating.

Thirdly, those in therapy may encounter among AA or NA members a negative attitude regarding the benefits of psychotherapy. One therapist, who gained a reputation among AA members for his sensitivity to alcohol issues and attracted many patients from AA groups, reported how secretive these patients were:

> It seemed to me that the AA people I saw were more likely not to say anything to anybody about being in psychotherapy. The reason seemed to be a little different than what I would have thought. The initial reason, of course, is that people are just uncomfortable acknowledging that there are things going on inside themselves of which they are not fully aware. They perceive that as a certain kind of weakness. But the AA people also thought they would get a lot of flack from their AA colleagues if they said they were in psychotherapy, because from these patients' accounts, traditional therapy was simply not effective. Some felt they would get derided even by their own sponsors. It was fascinating to me to see a number of people from the same AA group, all of whom felt they couldn't tell anybody else about it, but didn't know they were seeing me.

Finally, and most significantly, many AA and NA members are suspicious of anyone using mood altering drugs because of the havoc that alcohol and drugs have unleashed in their lives. Often they do not distinguish between prescribed and nonprescribed drugs and pressure the dually diagnosed to remain abstinent from all mood altering drugs. Alcoholics Anonymous has a clearly stated position on the compatibility of prescribed medication with recovery, which they published in 1984 in a pamphlet entitled, *The AA Member: Medications and Other Drugs.* However, patients may still encounter in groups members who are adamantly opposed to taking any medication and put subtle pressure on patients not to take their meds.

A SPECTRUM OF INSISTENCE

A Range of Opinions

Given these benefits and limits for the dually diagnosed's participation in twelve step programs, how insistent should a therapist be that his patient attend meetings? I asked this question of a group of clinicians who have worked effectively for many years with this population. All of those interviewed stated that they routinely refer their dually diagnosed patients to twelve step support groups. They all viewed participation in therapy and AA as complementary. However, while all recognized the value of the AA program in treating substance abuse, there was a range of how insistent the therapists were in having their patients attend meetings.

There was a spectrum of expectations regarding participation, from being very insistent and making it a requirement for treatment to not being insistent at all and making it simply a recommendation. At the more insistent end of the spectrum, one therapist affimed: "I am as insistent as I can be. I've had a couple of people who haven't attended meetings, and I had trouble with that." Another clinician reported that he views the patient's willingness or reluctance to participate in AA meetings as an indication of his motivation for change:

> If someone's not willing to go to meetings, then I have to question what their motivation for change is. I'm fairly confrontative

about this. One of the things that always happens is I begin to confront someone about whether they really want to make changes or not and point out the inconsistencies in what they say. "If you really want to make changes, and drinking is hurting you, why not stop it? Maybe you really don't want to make changes, and maybe you should think about whether this is a good idea."

He added that he suggests that people try AA for a year:

I say, "Go to AA, take Antabuse, and go to this substance abuse therapist. After one year, you tell me what has been effective and what has not. All I do is ask you to give it a chance. I don't think AA is for everybody. I think everybody who has a problem owes it to themselves to see if that's for them. I just don't think you can make a decision like that after going to one or two meetings. I think if you're really sincere, you'll spend a year of your life exploring these things. Then you can honestly sit down and say this was very helpful to me and this was not."

Another clinician, who engages in short-term cognitive behavioral therapy, reported that he strongly recommends that his patients attend self-help groups and asks them about their attendance every session:

I will ask them to attend self-help groups to start with, just so they can understand the nature of their problem. As an outpatient therapist, I'm really not able to enforce that other than to ask them every week, "Have you been going to meetings? How many meetings are you going to?" I don't have them sign in and get a signature. I can't require attendance similar to a probation or parole officer. All I can do is help them understand why I think it's important now. . . . I don't make it a condition for treatment, but I include that as a strong recommendation. I will ask them about it every session.

Several other therapists maintained positions on the less insistent end of the spectrum and reported that they recommend and encourage their patients to attend AA. One clinician stated: "I'm not insistent at all. I recommend it almost invariably. I see it as a voluntary thing. I don't systematically monitor it. . . . Not everybody needs it. People often have intact families, circles of friends, fellow employee and colleague groups. They enlist those people in that same role. I think it's that kind of personal relating that is key to the usefulness of AA groups, rather than the actual twelve step process." Another therapist commented: "If they can stay sober without meetings, I don't insist that they attend. But if not attending meetings is a symptom of relapse, I insist that they attend meetings. It is generally not a condition of treatment."

All of these experienced therapists, however, were in agreement that they needed to be insistent on AA attendance if the patient's substance abuse problem is severe. For example, one therapist, who is psychodynamic in approach, related how he presses harder for attendance the more severe the drinking problem:

> I would begin to press indirectly when somebody continues to report, even though they're working very well in therapy, some kind of conflict in their life that could be related to alcohol. I point out, "When you were going to AA before it sounded like these kinds of things didn't happen so often. We don't know why. It's not like you have to choose between going with me and being in AA." I already mentioned the criteria for pushing real real hard. If the disruptions are severe and frequent. If anger and hostility are coming out and interfering with their life. Third, if somebody's endangering their job because of alcohol or substance abuse, I tend to push a lot harder right then. I know how devastating it can be to lose a job. The fourth thing would be driving and drinking. I see that as a major problem in their judgment, a potentially fatal problem.

How Insistent?

In my view, the therapist need not insist that every patient with a substance abuse problem participate in a twelve step program. I always recommend AA or NA to every substance abusing patient and point out the benefits of participation. However, unless the problem is severe and debilitating, I try to take a long view regarding the role of AA in the process of recovery and not become too insistent. In her study of eighty recovering alcoholics involved in AA, Brown (1985) discovered that this group estimated that alcohol was a problem for them for an average of 10.5 years before they stopped drinking. Furthermore, an average of nearly 20 months elapsed between their initial contact with AA and their acknowledged membership in it. Another eight months passed before the average respondent achieved abstinence in the program. In other words, almost two years passed between the time an individual recognized enough of a drinking problem to inquire about AA and another eight months after that before the person achieved abstinence.

Particularly with the dually diagnosed, who tend to be more resistant to acknowledging a drug problem than most substance abusers seeking treatment, it is more effective to take a gradual approach in encouraging participation in AA or NA. Their greater psychological fragility also makes some of them more reluctant to become involved in a group activity with strangers whom they fear may judge and reject them. The danger in insisting too strongly that they attend meetings is that it may increase their resistance and result in their abandoning treatment. A strong therapeutic relationship needs to be developed before the therapist can become more demanding. Building such a relationship takes time and requires patience.

If the substance abuse problem is severe and debilitating, I become more insistent that the patient participate in twelve step programs. In such a case, the risk of continuing drug use outweighs the benefits of waiting. In this regard, it is important to assess accurately the severity of the drug problem. For example, a 40-year-old man came to see me because of marital problems that he recognized were caused by his long history of drinking. While in treatment, he was able to maintain abstinence for three months without attending AA. I did not insist on his attending because he was able to remain sober without going to meetings. However, I explained the benefits and importance of AA and made a contract with him that he begin attending meetings if he should resume drinking. In contrast, a 38-year-old man entered treatment with me because of problems caused by his 30-year habit of smoking marijuana. He began smoking at 8 years of age and at the peak of his addiction he smoked 10 to 12 joints daily. He sought treatment because he was arrested for stealing and placed on probation. As a requirement of his probation, he was given a drug screen, and it turned up positive for marijuana. He was informed by his probation officer that he would be sent to jail if he continued to use. Since this man was unable to stop on his own and I judged his problem to be severe, I was insistent that he attend NA meetings. He agreed and was able to remain clean.

How Often and For How Long?

Clinicians frequently ask how often and for how long they should recommend that their patients participate in twelve step programs. AA suggests that members begin by attending 90 meetings in 90 days and continue participating for the rest of their lives because alcoholism is a chronic disease. This recommendation may seem overly rigid and demanding to some people, particularly the dually diagnosed. A more realistic approach for the therapist is to encourage patients to begin by attending a few meetings just to see if they fit. The main problem with many of the dually diagnosed is that they do not recognize that they have a substance abuse problem. Once they come to that realization, the clinician can recommend regular attendance. The more severe the substance abuse problem, the more meetings the patient should be encouraged to attend, until the person establishes a stable sobriety. The first year of sobriety is crucial for establishing an abstinent lifestyle, and the patient should be encouraged to participate regularly for at least a year and have a sponsor. After that, the patient may become motivated enough to set up his own regular schedule of attendance. AA and NA are envisioned as lifelong support groups for recovery. Individuals will inevitably establish a level of involvement with which they are comfortable. However, therapists should encourage them to increase their involvement in times of temptation to drink and after relapses and to call their sponsors for help.

INTEGRATING THERAPY AND AA

Some therapists will not refer a patient to AA or NA even if they recognize a drug or alcohol problem because of misgivings they have about twelve step programs. Other clinicians will readily refer their substance abusing clients to meetings and focus only on the psychiatric problems in sessions. They reason that the people at AA or NA will take care of the substance abuse problem, while they will treat the psychiatric disorders in therapy. A third group of practitioners will simply insist that their substance abusing patients attend AA as a condition for treatment and never discuss the drug problem in sessions. All of these approaches are relatively ineffective because the treatment of the disorders is not integrated. The treatment is fragmented, and the patient often receives contradictory messages from AA and the therapist regarding recovery.

An integrated treatment approach requires that the therapist be knowledgeable about, and facilitate, the participation of his dual diagnosis patients in twelve step programs. This task involves several strategies.

Making the Recommendation

Once a substance abuse problem is diagnosed, the therapist can begin by making a clear recommendation that the patient attend some meetings. The clinician should explain the reason why he believes attendance at meetings would be helpful without labeling the individual an alcoholic or drug addict. Such labels are usually repulsive to patients, who have many stereotypes about what they mean. It is also helpful to discuss the benefits and importance of participating in twelve step groups and answer straightforwardly any questions the patient might have about them. I always ask patients to express their thoughts, feelings, and fantasies about meetings and I try to respond to any concerns. Frequently, the patient is uncertain about his need to become involved in such a program. I say something like the following: "I realize that you don't think you have a problem, but why not attend a meeting just to see if you fit. Then come back and we can talk about the experience." If the person comes back and still has some reservations about it, I will normally ask him to try three different groups because the personality of groups differ so much. A list of times and places of meetings in the area is a useful reference to give the patient. Otherwise, the patient can be invited to call the AA or NA number in the phone book for times and locations of meetings.

Discussing the Experience

The therapist ought not just send the patient to meetings and leave it at that. Instead, he can invite the patient to talk about the experience and what he learns about himself. Such a discussion is beneficial for several reasons. First, it enables the therapist to evaluate the progress the patient is making toward recovery. It is also a way of monitoring attendance. Secondly, the manner in which the patient discusses the experience is revealing of his personal dynamics and issues needing to be addressed in therapy. For example, feelings of shame or concerns about being judged by others may emerge while the patient is at meetings. These are important clues that can help the therapist understand his patient and the underlying issues that may well contribute to his drinking or drugging behavior. Thirdly, it provides an opportunity for the patient to express his misgivings about attending meetings and his diagnosis of substance abuse or dependence. Aware of these resistances, the therapist can then address them directly in sessions. Finally, if the patient accepts his identity as an alcoholic or addict, the sayings and slogans will take on a new meaning for him. The language, concepts, sayings, and slogans can then be incorporated into the therapy and help the patient integrate the two treatment domains.

Addressing Resistances

Therapists often need to prepare their patients for participation in twelve step groups. Good clinical judgment and sensitivity are required for this task, particularly in working with the dually diagnosed. In general, a confrontative and demanding approach will not work with this group. They will either abandon treatment or withdraw emotionally if they feel pushed too hard. Therefore, the clinician must gently explore any reasons the patient is hesitant about attending meetings. If someone says, "I really don't like those AA meetings and can't see myself attending," the therapist needs to understand the reason and not presume that the refusal means the same thing for everybody. Some individuals just do not want to expend the effort, and this can be confronted directly. However, attending meetings may provoke more anxiety than other patients are able to manage. The therapist then needs to explore the issue carefully without provoking too much anxiety and help the patient understand what is difficult for him. The following are some common resistances and problems for patients.

A hallmark of the twelve step program is the admission, "I am an alcoholic" or "I am a drug addict." These are loaded terms for those not yet in recovery. They are reluctant to assume what they view as a negative identity that will reinforce their already low self-esteem. The therapist can explore and correct any inaccurate stereotypes the patient may have regarding alcoholics and substance abusers. He can also assure the patient that he will not be forced to assume a label that he is not comfortable with, since no one has the right to label another person. Request that the individual attend the meeting simply to learn more about addiction, to hear the stories of others, and to see if anything applies in his personal life. What the patient learns about himself and addiction can then be discussed in therapy sessions.

Some patients complain that they are too shy to attend meetings with a group of strangers. Sometimes it will be necessary for the therapist to explore the meanings of this anxiety and work through it with the patient before he will be able to attend meetings. Assuring the individual that he will not be pressured to say or do anything he is not comfortable with can relieve some anxiety. Others may feel more secure if they are accompanied to a meeting by a friend or someone who has been a member for some time and can help break the ice.

For some individuals, the first step represents a major stumbling block for involvement in the group. It requires that they admit their powerlessness over their substance of choice. The difficulty for them is accepting their powerlessness, particularly if they have been physically or sexually abused. They struggle to set boundaries in their lives and are fearful of others violating these boundaries, as in the past. They may be guarded and mistrustful of any group that wants them to admit powerlessness, which is something they are trying to overcome in their lives. It will take much time, sensitivity, and gentleness to work through these feelings with many patients before they will be able to participate fully in the groups. They will need to be assured that the program is respectful of their need to choose their level of involvement, despite the enthusiasm of some of its members. Remind them of the AA slogan, "Take what you need and leave the rest," which respects their right of self-determination.

One experienced therapist, who has worked for many years with women alcoholics who have been sexually abused, commented:

> Because so many of the people I see are women who have been disturbed by incest, I see them for a while before I become insistent that I want them to go to meetings. I know that two things are hard. First, the first step of AA is really a rough one if you have

ever been powerless. Secondly, I work with them on some spirituality issues because turning their life and will over to a higher power
can be pretty rough if your only perception of a higher power is a
male authority figure. If that's who has abused you, how can I ask
you, or how can the progam ask you, to turn your will over to
something you see as a male authority figure? So I work at expand-
ing their concept of spirituality, differentiating between religion
and spirituality.

It is not uncommon for people to object to the spiritual emphasis of the program. Some think they have to be religious, church going,
or Christian to be a member. However, AA literature is explicit that
the program is nondenominational and that a neutral term, such as
Higher Power, was intentionally chosen to avoid identification with
any religious tradition. Therapists can explain to these individuals the
difference between organized religion, which may have many emotional meanings for the person, and spirituality, which is innately
human. They can also assure patients that they are free to define their
Higher Power in any way that suits them. For those who are still reluctant to participate in any program with a religious dimension, non-
spiritual Rational Recovery groups meet in many areas.

Another area of possible resistance is when an individual chooses
to drop out of AA. The therapist needs to explore this decision because
it may portend an unrecognized decision to resume drinking. If the
person has been in AA and stopped going, this decision needs to be
fully explored. The circumstances and results of not attending meetings need to be looked at. What the patient intends to do to work on
recovery in place of attending meetings also needs to be discussed fully.

Encouraging Medication Compliance

Although the official position of AA is that taking prescribed
medications is compatible with recovery, patients may experience
pressure from members to discontinue their psychiatric medication.
The results, especially for those with serious mental illness, are pre-
dictable. It will lead to a relapse in their psychiatric illness and eventually to a relapse into drug or alcohol use. To counteract the patient's
temptation to discontinue his medication, the therapist needs to emphasize the importance of following the doctor's prescriptions and

to anticipate the pressures of negative attitudes that the patient may face at meetings. The therapist may also help the patient find groups that are more amenable to those who are mentally ill or taking medication. In some areas, there are Double Trouble groups that are composed of members with dual diagnoses.

One of the therapists interviewed remarked, "One of the great strengths of the twelve step movement is its resiliency that allows it to adapt despite the rigidity of many of its members." In the early days, the dual diagnosis patients were rebuffed by the alcoholics in AA, just as the nonalcoholic drug addicts were before them. Bill Wilson, the founder, reinforced that attitude. Gradually, the fellowship became more tolerant of the diversity of its members. In the 1970s and 1980s, many of the alcoholics were cross-addicted, and the fellowship adapted. The growth of Narcotics Anonymous indicated the change in attitude and acceptance of the reality of the polydrug abuser, which is so prevalent today. As the number of dually diagnosed is increasing, there are signs that the fellowship is beginning to adjust to their presence. A few Double Trouble groups have sprung up. Although NA groups still tend to be phobic about any mood altering drugs, including prescribed medications, many AA groups are very accepting of the dually diagnosed and do not discourage the taking of appropriate meds.

In summary, it is clear that psychotherapy and participation in twelve step programs are complementary in treating the dually diagnosed. However, it is the task of the therapist to integrate these two treatment modalities to assure that both the psychiatric and substance use disorders are effectively addressed. The clinician will need to be patient and sensitive to the misgivings of these patients to become involved in the program. He will need to prepare and assist patients, especially those who are psychologically vulnerable, to participate actively in AA or NA meetings.

11 A TIME FOR PATIENCE: REQUIRING ABSTINENCE

Divergent views about the requirement for abstinence exist between the substance abuse and mental health treatment communities. On the one hand, the addiction specialist typically requires that his client be abstinent from all drugs as a precondition of treatment. If the person continues to relapse, it is interpreted as a sign that the individual either needs a higher level of care or is unmotivated for treatment. The goal of treatment is clear and unequivocable: complete, total, and lifelong abstinence from all mood-altering drugs. This sobriety model is reinforced by participation in twelve step groups, which is usually a requirement. On the other hand, mental health professionals often view substance abuse as a symptom of an underlying pathology. They may tolerate continued drug use while they address the psychiatric problems of their patients in therapy. At the same time, they may expect a gradual decline in the drinking or drugging behavior as the distress caused by the psychiatric disturbance decreases. As the patient builds a supportive network and develops more adequate coping mechanisms, it is presumed that the need to drink or use drugs diminishes. Typically, the clinician is not insistent on total and lifelong abstinence. The long range goal of treatment may be controlled drinking if the patient demonstrates an ability to function well without relying on his drug of choice.

In treating the dual diagnosis patient, the clinician must address both the substance use and psychiatric disorders from the beginning and throughout treatment. To accomplish this effectively, he needs to find a middle road regarding the requirement of abstinence that falls between that of the addiction specialist and that of the mental health specialist. On the one hand, if he is too demanding too early for complete abstinence, the patient may feel overwhelmed and flee treatment. Frequently, the dual diagnosis patient is unaware of a drug problem, and the therapist must initially address the patient's denial. It may take considerable time before the patient is ready to admit a substance abuse problem. Furthermore, the patient may experience a demand for immediate and total abstinence as an intolerable burden because he has no other way to cope with the stress of life and his psychological difficulties. On the other hand, if the therapist over-looks the substance abuse problem and tolerates uncontrolled drink-ing, the patient will never be capable of addressing his psychiatric problem in the treatment. In his lack of persistence in focusing on the drug problem, the therapist would also contribute to the patient's enabling system which prolongs the downward spiral of the addiction. Therefore, it is important that the therapist be realistic and patient in requiring abstinence of his patients. Clinical sensitivity and appropri-ate timing to gauge the readiness of the patient are needed in demand-ing sobriety.

Treatment Principle Ten: Immediate and total abstinence should not be re-quired for the dually diagnosed patient to participate in treatment. As a short-term goal, the clinician may expect a reduction and gradual control of the drug using behavior.

THE INTOXICATED PATIENT

One situation in which the therapist ought to demand abstinence is during therapy sessions. There are several good reasons why the clinician needs to make this requirement. First of all, the intoxicated patient is too cognitively impaired to derive any benefit from the meeting. The next day the person may not even be able to remember what was discussed. Meeting with the individual would be a waste of time, leading to frustration and resentment on the part of the thera-pist. Secondly, if the therapist agrees to meet with the intoxicated patient, he communicates to him that it is acceptable for him to act in that way. The clinician then becomes an inadvertent participant in the patient's enabling system that maintains the drinking or drugging behavior. It leads the individual to believe that the consequences of that behavior are not so serious as to interfere with the treatment. Finally, allowing such acting out behavior to enter the treatment violates the boundaries of therapy. If the patient is allowed to act out in the treatment, there is little motivation to talk about what is going on. Seeing the patient while he is intoxicated will encourage the continuation of that disruptive behavior and eventually undermine the treatment.

Treatment Principle Eleven: It is useless and counterproductive to the treatment to meet with an intoxicated patient to explore issues.

If someone comes to a session under the influence, the therapist should inform the patient that he will not meet with him because nothing of value therapeutically can be accomplished while in such a state. He can simply say, "I cannot work with you productively if you have been drinking or using." Some therapists will attempt to evaluate the level of impairment of the patient before deciding whether or not to continue the session. If I detect any impairment due to substance use, I prefer to end the session in order not to give the patient a mixed message about the acceptability of using before sessions. If the person has driven himself to the office while under the influence, the clinician should insist that the patient not drive again while intoxicated and make arrangements for the family or a taxi to take him home. In the next session, the therapist should talk about the incident to understand the reasons for the loss of sobriety.

One experienced therapist described her approach and rationale for not seeing the intoxicated patient:

> I never see somebody if they show up for a therapy session intoxicated. I tell them that I will not see them if they are intoxicated. And I bill them for the session. I think one of the hard things in working with chemically dependent people is to avoid being caught up in their enabling system. By seeing them when they show up intoxicated, by accepting phone calls from them when they are intoxicated, it is making it all right for them to be that way as part

of the therapeutic process. At the same time, I don't want to be judgmental nor do I want to be rescuing. I want to make it clear that I don't think they are bad people because they are alcoholic. It's always balancing not rescuing and not enabling.

She proceeded to give an example of how she handled a case of a woman who was drunk and suicidal and called regularly:

> I had one woman who would be intoxicated and call and tell me how depressed she was and didn't know why she was living. She was actively suicidal. I was accepting these calls at 11:00 and 12:00 when the answering service would call me. I said, "Why am I doing this? I don't need to do this. I'm saying it's OK to get drunk and maudlin and call me, and it's not OK." So I told her I would no longer accept those calls, and if she felt that bad, she should take herself to the nearest emergency room. Afterwards, she got involved in AA. I'm not saying I caused her to be sober, but I think that as long as I was taking those phone calls, I was part of her enabling system.

In the next session, it is useful to talk about the incident and make it an educational experience. Together the patient and therapist can explore the circumstances and reasons for the drinking or drug use and discuss how to avoid its recurrence in the future. During this discussion, it might come to light what issues, thoughts, and feelings the patient was attempting to avoid by his drug use. These insights can be valuable for revealing the vulnerabilities of the patient and furthering the work of the therapy. At times, such acting out behavior may be an expression of some hostility toward the therapist that emerges in the transference. The therapist can gain some important insights into the dynamics of his patient and address this at the appropriate time when the patient is able to utilize the insight. At any rate, the incident is not a disaster for the treatment. It may demonstrate vividly for the therapist how the family experiences the patient on a regular basis. It can thus become a learning experience for both therapist and patient.

In some cases, particularly with the personality disordered, the discussion of the incident might be an opportunity to question the level of commitment of the patient and invite him to rededicate himself to the work of recovery. One experienced therapist, who treats many resistant court-ordered clients, advocated a more direct approach with this type of intoxicated patient:

> I ask him to leave. I tell him, "There's no point in talking. That's a waste of our efforts if you're going to be here intoxicated." Again, I would ask him the same question, "What does that mean about your commitment level here that you would walk in intoxicated? That's just not an allowable thing. If you want to drink, what's the point in being here? This is an explicit contract to improve your life. We've come to the conclusion that drinking affects you negatively. Then you show me you don't have a commitment to change. So let's talk about what you're doing here. If you want to go out and drink yourself to death, that's your choice. But if you come here, I expect you to work. I expect you to make changes." I try to always make demands for adult behavior on people's part.

The only exception to this general guideline of not meeting with an intoxicated patient is when the individual comes to the initial session under the influence. In that case, I evaluate the level of impairment. If the patient seems capable of an intelligible discussion, I will proceed with the session. To send the person away at that point before a therapeutic alliance is established will guarantee that he will not come back for treatment. One therapist reported an experience of an initial session with an intoxicated woman: "One lady came intoxicated for the first session and told me all the gory details of her sexual abuse by her father when she was a child. She also had an alcoholic daughter in recovery. I suppose it was only while drunk she could have the courage to talk about the painful things that happened to her. I had repeated appointments and phone conversations with her, but unfortunately, she never came back."

SHORT-TERM GOAL

In working with the dually diagnosed, it is important to distinguish a short-term and a long-term treatment strategy regarding abstinence. In the short term, experience suggests that a gradual approach to the demand for abstinence is most effective. There are at least two important reasons why the therapist should not be demanding of immediate and total abstinence with the dually diagnosed. First of all, those who come to a mental health professional usually come for a psychiatric problem and are unaware of a substance abuse problem. They tend to minimize or deny their drug use and are often surprised by the therapist's suggestion that they might have a problem. Consequently, the therapist must undertake various strategies to address the patient's denial of a drinking or drug problem. As mentioned previously, if I think substance use may be a significant part of the symptom picture, I ask the patient to undertake an experiment in abstinence and we discuss the experience in sessions. My hope is that the patient will come to recognize his struggle with drinking or drug use and some of the consequences of using in his life. Of course, the danger in confronting the patient's denial of a drug problem too quickly and forcefully is that it will often lead to the person's withdrawing from treatment. Then any chance of helping him address either the substance use or psychiatric issue will be lost. As in working with any individual, it is necessary to take the person where he is and work from there. The therapist cannot go faster than the patient and be effective.

A second reason for a gradual approach to requiring abstinence of the dually diagnosed is that the psychiatric problem often makes them less able to live a life of sobriety. Many of these patients are extremely fragile psychologically. They have learned to rely on their drug of choice to cope with the stress of life and their own painful affects. Therefore, the therapist must take time to develop a supportive therapeutic relationship with the patient. The clinician can also help the person develop social skills and more effective coping strategies so he will not have to rely so much on drugs. The establishment of a supportive network of family, friends, and twelve step members will also help the person sustain a life of sobriety. As one therapist put it bluntly, "You don't ram a diagnosis down their throat until there's a positive way for them to accept that diagnosis."

In the beginning of treatment, the realistic goal is to keep a focus on the patient's substance use and include it in the treatment plan. One therapist, who is psychodynamic in orientation, described his approach regarding abstinence:

> I take a kind of soft approach to the demand for abstinence early
> in the treatment until we attempt to understand the meaning of

the use of the substance in the context of the full symptom picture. Anybody who comes with a dual diagnosis comes with an array
of symptomotology that's pretty pervasive in their life. It's necessary that the meaning of the consumption of a substance in that
context be explicit, especially in the beginning while you are
attempting to come up with a treatment plan which may take several months to evolve.

In short, the problem took time to evolve and will take time to be
resolved.

A key element in this gradual approach is not to argue with, or
preach at, the patient about his substance use. That will only reinforce his defenses and lead to a withdrawal from treatment. The therapist can help the person accept his limits and recognize his inability
to control his drinking through the various strategies described previously to address denial. Even a program as committed to the sobriety model as AA realistically accepts members who are still uncertain
that they are alcoholic. Practically everybody who starts out in AA is
in denial about their drinking and gradually learns about and accepts
their limits through the gentle guidance of other members. Gradually, without coercion, people develop an internal motivation to change
once they experience the benefits of reduced drinking or sobriety. One
therapist observed: "Interestingly enough, especially once they start
going to groups and getting some self-help, their sobriety becomes
very important to them. I have found that people tend to be able to
weather most mental health crises without breaking their sobriety.
Somehow, their sobriety ends up easier to maintain than whatever
mental health crisis they may be having."

What the therapist can realistically expect is a decrease in drinking or drugging behavior in the initial stage of treatment. In fact, such
a reduction in drug use is a sign of progress, a sign the patient is dealing with issues. This progress should be recognized and praised by
the therapist. For example, one therapist noted how he recognizes
even small steps forward:

> I felt somebody had conquered that first successful hurdle in
> therapy if they were able to come in and say, "Now when I'm drunk
> at the bar I call my wife to get me, or I let my buddies take me
> home." I would consider that a major short-term gain. I would be
> delighted with it and would encourage the patient to be delighted

with it too. "A big, important step, a critical step," I would say. "I won't drink around the kids anymore. I'll drink at work with my buddies, but I won't drink at home because of what happens." These are signs of progress.

There are limits to the clinician's tolerance of continued drinking or drug use, even if there is a decline in using. If the therapist does not continue to address the substance use as at least a potential problem, there is a danger that he will collude with the patient's denial system. In being tolerant of continued substance use, the therapist should be confident that he can break through the patient's denial eventually. One clinician gave a case example:

> A borderline woman I was treating acknowledged that her drinking was a problem. She didn't like the way she used alcohol because it caused her to identify with her father. She wasn't ready to acknowledge that she had to stop drinking totally. She said, "Now that I realize that sometimes I drink too much, I will drink less." Although I consistently told her that was not acceptable and wouldn't work, she needed to try that. I knew that that was part of her recovery, that she needed to fail at doing it. In fact, like many alcoholics, she changed her style of drinking. Rather than drinking all the time and drinking publicly, she became a binge drinker rapidly. But that continued to cause problems for her. I thought that ultimately we would break through the denial, and we did.

There are circumstances in which the therapist needs to demand abstinence from the beginning of treatment. One situation is where the drinking or drug use is causing severe and frequent disruptions in the patient's life. For example, the person is becoming intoxicated and physically abusive of his family; his job is threatened by his continued drug use; or his health is failing because of his drinking. The therapist needs to demand complete abstinence at these times. If the patient is unable to remain sober, he may need to be referred for more intensive treatment.

A second situation in which the therapist may be insistent on abstinence from the beginning is if the patient is clearly a primary substance abuser. The hope is that the experience of sobriety will motivate the person to make changes in his life. One therapist, who frequently does forensic work, related his approach: "Most people that come for a primary substance abuse problem do not come voluntarily. . . . What you have to do is impose treatment on them in some way with the hope that after they have been sober for a long period of time, the fear motivation will switch to positive motivation. . . . So it seems to me, you have to impose abstinence on someone with the hope that they begin to see the positive aspects over time."

LONG-TERM GOAL

A Controversy: Abstinence or Controlled Drinking?

There has been a controversy among substance abuse specialists since the 1960s regarding whether total abstinence or controlled drinking ought to be the long range goal of treatment (Peele 1985). A key moment in that controversy was the publication of the Rand Report in 1976. The Rand investigators evaluated the results of the treatment programs of the National Institute on Alcohol Abuse and Alcoholism. In this study, 2339 alcoholics were evaluated 6 months after participating in a program, and 597 after 18 months. The researchers discovered that after 18 months, 24 percent of the treated alcoholics were still abstinent, while 22 percent were drinking normally. The more serious alcoholics were distinguished from the less serious in this study. It was found that even among the more clearly dependent alcoholics, 25 percent were abstaining, while 16 percent returned to social drinking. The substance abuse treatment community, which espouses an AA sobriety model, challenged the report strenuously and criticized it on several methodological grounds. In response, the Rand group conducted a follow-up study in which the subjects were more carefully checked for their drinking patterns four years after receiving treatment. This time, the researchers found that 40 percent of the subjects had returned to nonproblematic drinking, including a portion of those who were initially most severely alcoholic. Again, the opposition of most practitioners in the field was substantial and often emotional.

My survey of practitioners who treat the dually diagnosed demonstrated a lack of unanimity regarding a long-term goal of abstinence with this population. Some were insistent on total abstinence from all drugs, while others allowed for the possibility of controlled drinking. For example, one therapist insisted on abstinence because of the powerful pharmacological effects of drugs and stated: "It's abstinence. There's no sense in even fussing with the other stuff because the other stuff continues to kick off the syndrome all over again. If you allow people to continue drinking even one drink, it kicks off this old rebound effect so they keep going and going. Because I think there's cross tolerance and cross addiction, I don't think any substance abuser can use anything." Another clinician reported his belief that alcoholics can never drink safely:

> In twenty years of practice, I have never seen anyone who has successfully returned to controlled drinking. People drink for effect. Because of the nature of tolerance, they have to drink until they reach that threshold. Eventually, that will take its toll on their nervous system and the rest of their body. It's not just the X factor. If someone has a toxin in their body, they will be altered. I'm not insistent on abstinence, but I'm persistent in my conviction that individuals will not be able to safely continue to use alcohol without returning to their prior pattern and prior problems.

A third therapist stated that she required a basis of sobriety to treat the secondary diagnosis:

> I don't believe anything can be accomplished in treatment until they are sober. If their drinking is ongoing and they have a secondary diagnosis, I cannot treat that secondary diagnosis until they have dealt with that chemical dependency. They cannot function cognitively that well and deal with some painful material. And I don't want to be part of their alcoholic process. I tell people I'm not going to see them while they're drinking, and as soon as they get treatment for their drinking and start going to AA and stop drinking, I'll see them again.

Another clinician stated his belief that the person must be abstinent before an accurate diagnosis can be made: "You can't really make an accurate diagnosis of the other disorder until you have a significant time where the person is not drinking."

Others of this group of interviewed therapists allowed for the possibility of controlled drinking as their long-term goal of treatment. One clinician stated that total abstinence may be the goal for some of his patients, while a return to social drinking may be possible for others: "You have to make their drinking part of the treatment plan. Abstinence from the substance has to become at least the long-term goal. I'm not quite as obsessed with total abstinence as some in the substance abuse community are because not all of my patients are totally dependent or addicted. I'm not sure that somebody who is abusive cannot become a more normal drinker." Another therapist commented: "I recommend complete abstinence for these people also, though sometime down the road they may be able to drink moderately." A third clinician related that he does not subscribe to the total abstinence model, but sees it as a laudable goal for many of his patients:

> When they start going to AA meetings, they get exposed to a sobriety model. I don't personally subscribe to a total abstinence model for therapeutic reasons. Abstinence is certainly a laudable goal. It's interesting to me that everybody refers to Jellinek. When Jellinek did his original research, he found that there were numerous types of alcoholics, only one of whom had a tendency to drink to satiation. Once they had one drink, they had to drink to satiation. That was only one kind of alcoholic, yet people who quote the Jellinek model seem to assume that that's true of all alcoholics. It isn't. That's one of the reasons why abstinence becomes such an important goal. I don't do anything to dissuade them from maintaining that as a goal. It's still a laudable goal, even if they're not a gamma type alcoholic.

In short, this group of therapists who allow for the possibility of controlled drinking distinguish the severity of the alcohol problem. While those who are more severely addicted may need to be completely abstinent, the less severe problem drinker may eventually return to social drinking.

Abstinence for the Dually Diagnosed

In my view, the particular vulnerabilties of the dually diagnosed patient indicate that a long-term goal of complete abstinence from all substances is the most realistic and practical approach. First of all, even if the patient is not clearly addicted to the substance, the fact that he may have used drugs to self-medicate makes him again vulnerable to use when he experiences disturbing thoughts or affects. For example, if an individual has grown accustomed to drink when he is depressed, then when he again suffers a period of depression, he will again be tempted to drink in order to find relief. It is safer for the person to avoid all substances and learn to develop alternative coping skills. Secondly, those with long histories of substance abuse often suffer cognitive deficits, and their ability to exercise good judgment is compromised. These cognitive limitations can be compounded in someone who has also suffered a long history of emotional problems or mental illness. These individuals may not have the capacity to regulate effectively their drinking. It would be better for them to strive for the clear goal of total abstinence with the help of a supportive group. Thirdly, many of the dually diagnosed take medications. Any drinking or drug use would interfere with the effectiveness of some medications or produce adverse effects with others. Finally, many dual diagnosis patients have developed a low tolerance for mood altering substances. The use of any drugs may quickly lead to intoxication and reduce their capacity to control further drinking or drug use. For those with severe mental illnesses, such as schizophrenia or bipolar disorder, a single use of LSD or marijuana can precipitate a psychotic episode.

The effective treatment of these patients also indicates that they ought to remain abstinent. Initially, the therapist cannot make an accurate diagnosis until the patient is sober for a suitable length of time. Substance abuse can mask and mimic a wide variety of psychiatric symptoms. Furthermore, while the person is still drinking or using drugs, he is not able to work productively on his mental health problems. The drugs cover up feelings that need to be dealt with in therapy and render the person less competent mentally to understand and resolve his problems. In the fragile state of still using, the patient would be too vulnerable to explore sensitive personal issues. It would stir up too much anxiety, which could lead to a relapse in order to cope. Therefore, the patient's sobriety must be well established before the therapist can address in depth sensitive mental health problems.

My personal tactic is to inform patients who have a significant drug problem that abstinence is the ultimate treatment goal. I don't insist on that in the beginning of treatment, but I am persistent in expressing to them my conviction that abstinence is the safest and most realistic goal for them to strive for. I try not to overwhelm them at first with the awesomeness of that requirement, but suggest that they try to be abstinent one day at a time and get the support of a twelve step group.

Let me give a case example.

Bill, a young man of 30, came to see me because he felt overwhelmed and depressed. His fiancée had just left him. As we discussed what led to the breakup, it became clear that excessive drinking played a large role in their arguing. He and his fiancée would frequently get drunk together. In fact, Bill admitted that he had been drinking heavily since his teenage years and that his father was an alcoholic. Bill recognized that drinking had caused severe problems in his relationship, but he did not think he needed to give up drinking altogether. He thought he could learn just to cut back. I explained that because of his drinking history and genetic vulnerability due to his father's alcoholism that abstinence would be a safer goal. Bill insisted that he could control his drinking. So I asked him to keep a journal of his drinking and to try to limit himself to two drinks whenever he went out. My hope was that he would come to realize his inability to control successfully his drinking and eventually embrace a goal of abstinence. After several uncontrolled drinking bouts, he came to realize that abstinence was the only realistic goal for him.

In summary, some strategies regarding the requirement of abstinence are the following:

1. Don't meet with an intoxicated patient. Discuss the incident later.
2. Take a gradual approach in insisting upon abstinence at the beginning of treatment.
3. Expect a decline in drug use as a sign of progress in treatment.

4. Wait until the sobriety is well established before exploring in depth sensitive mental health issues.
5. If the person cannot control his drinking or drug use, he may need to be referred for more intensive substance abuse treatment.
6. Help the patient work toward achieving complete abstinence from all psychoactive drugs, except prescribed medications, as a long-term goal of treatment.

12

THE ROCKY ROAD TO RECOVERY: RESPONDING TO RELAPSES

It is well known that relapse into drug use is a common occurence among substance abusers. Studies show that a vast majority will eventually relapse after treatment; estimates for rates of relapse vary from 40% to over 80%, depending on the study. Research also demonstrates that the most vulnerable time for returning to drug use is within the first three months of sobriety. About two-thirds of those who use again do so then. Within the first year, about 70% to 75% return to using. Some of the typical patterns of relapse are also well recognized. In his study of cocaine addicts, Washton (1989) noted three recurring patterns. Some recovering addicts experience a single relapse, usually within the first year of abstinence, learn from it, and remain abstinent thereafter. Others experience a series of sporadic relapses between longer and longer periods of abstinence until they are eventually drug free. A third group relapses continuously and repeatedly after brief periods of abstinence and never recovers.

There have been few studies of the relapse rate among the dually diagnosed. However, as expected, the limited research that has been done suggests that the rates of relapse into both drug use and psychiatric problems are significantly high. Woody and colleagues (1983) found that the severity of psychiatric symptoms among treated substance abusers correlated negatively with treatment outcome. Seven months after treatment, the high-severity patients had more drug use, and more employment, drug use, legal, and psychiatric problems than the groups of low-severity and mid-severity patients. They noted that these high-severity patients made little progress with drug counseling alone, but showed more improvement with additional psychotherapy. Bartels and colleagues (1995) assessed the long-term course of substance use among a group of 148 severely mentally ill patients. Seven years after being treated, the prevalence of an active substance use disorder changed little from baseline to follow-up. Alcohol problems were present in 24% of the patients at baseline and in 21% seven years later; drug abuse or dependence was initially present in 20% of this group and in 17% at follow-up. However, these researchers observed that those with a diagnosis of substance abuse tended to improve more than those with a diagnosis of dependence. The severity of the substance use disorder correlated negatively with treatment outcome.

Treatment Principle Twelve: The dual diagnosis patient is particularly vulnerable to relapses into drug use because of the destabilizing effect of the psychiatric disorder; concommitantly, psychiatric problems are exacerbated by drug use and may worsen.

Because of the vulnerability of the dually diagnosed to relapse, therapists need to monitor closely their patients for any signs of an impending return to drug use. They must also develop strategies for helping them prevent and learn from these relapses.

VULNERABILITY TO RELAPSE

As noted, most relapses occur within the first three months of abstinence. However, with the dually diagnosed, relapses may happen with frequency even after sobriety seems well established. The therapist should be alert to this possibility and not presume that the patient is ever beyond danger. Let me give a case example.

I met with Sam, a 30-year-old single man, after he had completed a substance abuse treatment program and had been faithfully attending AA for six months. He sought therapy because he felt there were issues stemming from childhood that he was not able to address at meetings. He feared that if he did not do something about his long standing depression that he would eventually return to drinking. This man had experienced severe neglect as a child and had attempted suicide as a teenager. He came to realize that he had initially used alcohol to self-medicate and eventually became addicted, drinking large amounts of liquor daily. I had worked with this intelligent, sensitive, and insightful man off and on for over a year addressing many of his narcissistic injuries from childhood. He was attending AA and codependent meetings regularly and never mentioned any threats to his sobriety. His sobriety seemed so well established that we rarely talked about his recovery. Then, seemingly without warning, he relapsed for a month. That occurred after two years of sobriety. He and I were both caught by surprise. Together we attempted to understand what was happening in his life that may have influenced his return to drinking and how to avoid it in the future. We discovered that his relapse was not as unpredictable as we had initially thought. I also learned personally about the need for constant vigilance.

Precipitants

G. Alan Marlatt (1985) has undertaken a thorough study of the nature and process of relapse and developed a popularly used model for relapse prevention. In his research, he identified three high-risk situations that were associated with almost three-quarters of the relapse incidents they studied. In 35% of the cases, the relapse was precipitated by negative emotional states, that is, situations in which the person experienced feelings such as frustration, anger, depression, anxiety, or boredom. The second most common situation, 20% of the cases, was when the person was in a situation in which he felt social pressure from an individual or group to drink or use drugs. Finally, in 16% of the cases, the individuals experienced interpersonal conflict, such as arguing or fighting, with significant people in their lives.

The dually diagnosed display particular vulnerabilities in these three areas because of the destabilizing effect of their psychiatric disorder. They frequently experience dysphoric affects, such as anxiety or depression, as symptoms of their psychiatric problems. Additionally, some of the more seriously mentally ill may experience disturbing thoughts and hallucinations. As is commonly recognized, these individuals often resort to alcohol or drugs in an effort to self-medicate. Secondly, this group frequently experiences interpersonal conflicts with those who are close to them. Their internal turmoil is projected outward and lived out in their relationships. Because they experience so many conflicts within themselves, their relationships are also marked by intense conflict. Many of the signs and symptoms of psychiatric problems are interpersonal in nature and contribute to the unhappiness the dually diagnosed experience. Finally, because of weaknesses in their ego functioning, they may be especially susceptible to influence from others. They may lack the social skills to resist suggestions from others. The more severely ill may have such impairments in judgment and perception of reality that they cannot make proper decisions about whether or not to use drugs or alcohol. They seem oblivious to the negative consequences of using.

A further issue for therapists working with the dually diagnosed is the recognition that addressing sensitive issues in therapy before the person is strong enough to do so may lead to a relapse. While insights in treatment may be helpful, they may also be painful and arouse more anxiety than the patient can tolerate. If the person has used drugs to cope with problems and disturbing affects and has not developed other means of coping, exploratory therapy can be dangerous and harmful. Therefore, the therapist always needs to be sensitive to the readiness of the patient to address painful issues and wait until his sobriety is well established. He should also be conscious that any issue in therapy may unexpectedly trigger a relapse and monitor continuously for relapse symptoms. Furthermore, it is important that the patient be involved in a supportive network for recovery, such as AA or NA, to address temptations to relapse.

A third vulnerability for the dually diagnosed is regarding medication compliance. Any single-diagnosis patient can refuse to take his medication, and often his symptoms will reappear, resulting in a relapse into his illness. In the case of the dually diagnosed, however, the problem is complicated if medications are stopped. A return of the psychiatric symptoms will often lead to a return to alcohol or drug use as a way of self-medicating. A relapse in the psychiatric disorder will lead to a relapse in the substance use disorder, leading to a rapid deterioration of the patient's condition. Therefore, the therapist needs to impress upon the patient the importance of following closely the medication regimen prescribed by the psychiatrist. He also should address any pressures the patient may experience from the recovery community to stop taking meds.

Finally, a relapse into substance use may precipitate an exacerbation of the psychiatric symptoms. Margaret Bean-Bayog (1988) postulates that alcoholism itself is a traumatic experience that may cause psychopathology. She observes that repeated, unpredictable episodes of drunkenness produce many traumatic disruptions in a person's life: feelings of being out of control, damaged interpersonal relationships, health problems, life threatening experiences, and damage to personal integrity. The person may feel overwhelmed by these painful alcohol-induced experiences and react with intense anxiety, depression, guilt, and shame. An already fragile personality structure may become overwhelmed and exhibit signs and symptoms of a psychiatric disorder. Or if the person is dually diagnosed, an exacerbation of the underlying psychiatric problem will occur. Consequently, the therapist must be insistent that his patient be involved in an ongoing recovery program for his substance abuse problem to avoid and minimize the impact of relapses.

RESPONDING TO RELAPSES

One of the therapists interviewed made an important distinction between lapsing, relapsing, and collapsing into drug use. These conditions exist on a continuum of severity. Lapsing means a person has slipped, but has not returned to his prior state or pattern of drug use. For example, an individual who has been sober for a year wants to test if he can drink in a controlled fashion. He lapses. He goes to a party and tries a cocktail. Then he has a drink after work with his friends. This experiment with controlled drinking remains a lapse unless the person returns to his previous pattern of drinking.

A relapse occurs when the person returns to his previous drug-use pattern, but not to his previous state. There will often be a slow decay in his drug using behavior as the person starts to drink more and more. Typically, this type of relapse can occur with the person who has not been adequately diagnosed with a dual diagnosis. When the symptoms of the unaddressed depression or anxiety return, the individual begins using the alcohol or drugs pharmacologically to self-medicate. Individuals who are psychologically fragile and uncomfortable with themselves are also vulnerable to relapse. They will use the alcohol to lubricate themselves socially or to cover up dysphoric feelings. Those whose addiction is biologically driven are also in danger of relapse when they experiment with returning to controlled use. Rapidly, they lose control of their drinking or drug use and repeat the previous pattern. These people are especially vulnerable to regressing to the next level, which is a collapse.

Collapsing is a return to both the prior pattern and state where they started. The collapsers are people who often have severe psychopathology and addiction. They have either not been adequately diagnosed or have not followed their treatment plan in taking their medications and becoming involved in a recovery program. They go back to where they started very rapidly. Most collapses occur within the first three months of treatment.

The basic strategy for the therapist is to prepare the patient for the possibilty of relapses and to help him avoid them. If a temporary lapse occurs, his goal is to keep it from progressing to a relapse or to a full-blown collapse into drug use.

Therapist's Attitude

The clinician should treat the relapsing patient with compassion. If the person has been working on his recovery for a while, he may experience intense guilt and shame because of the return to drug use. Most substance abusers have experienced so much shame in their lives because of the disruptions they have caused in their own and their family's lives that they do not need that burden increased by the therapist. In fact, the relapsing person may want the therapist to take a punitive attitude because of the guilt he feels. The clinician should not indulge the patient's wish for punishment because it will not further the work of recovery; it will only weaken the patient for the redoubled effort that will be needed to overcome and learn from the relapse. It may also create more stress, which may prolong the relapsing behavior.

One of the therapists interviewed described her compassionate attitude with relapsing patients and offered a case example:

> What I find is that when people who are in therapy relapse, it is almost always that something painful has happened. There is a man I have been working with for a couple of years. He relapsed during his partner's last months of dying with AIDS. He had been doing so well in coping. I was very compassionate, very understanding about the relapse. He had been taking care of his partner for years, and I think he was just exhausted, frightened, sad, angry, and the feelings got to be too much. He went out one night and drank. I'm not sure it wasn't something he sort of needed to do. Just one night of not thinking, of blocking stuff out. So I tried to make very light of it. He's someone who was actively involved in AA. I knew that what I needed to do was tell him that it's very understandable, that almost anyone would do that. Just keep going to meetings and forget it.

Another clinician described how he tries to be supportive, help the person not bemoan the relapse, and move forward:

> I will help them take it in stride. I will help them understand why they may have relapsed and to start counting their sobriety from that point forward. "So you blew it. So you had three months of sobriety and relapsed. So now you've got two days of sobriety and have to start counting over again. That's all." But I think the point that is important for them is to understand they were doing real well for a while. They slipped and had a relapse. The important thing for them is not to bemoan the fact they had a relapse, but to move from this point forward, rather than to belabor the past. They've done plenty of that over the course of their lives.

Another helpful attitude for the therapist to assume is to be matter of fact, objective, and curious. Such an approach enables the patient to keep from blaming himself, and to be less defensive and more receptive to learning something about himself through the experience. One therapist described this attitiude:

> I get intellectual with them about their relapses. We sit and look at it like scientists. We see what we can learn from it. We look at

environmental situations, what was going on internally, the cognitive aspect, the old thinking, their belief systems. Rather than slapping hands and saying, "you can never drink safely," we become investigators about it. Scolding does not work. If you get them to become co-investigators with you and conduct a research project, they often can use the data. They also can admit that they are having problems.

A Learning Experience

Examining the relapse episode carefully can provide useful information for both patient and therapist. A relapse never occurs without a prior warning. If the clinician and patient can learn to recognize the warning signs, they are in a better position to take appropriate action to avoid future relapses. Furthermore, the episode of drinking or drug use is the end point of a process. If the therapist and patient can examine together what led up to the relapse, they can learn much about the patient's unique vulnerabilities and become more aware of the warning signs. Washton (1989) describes the typical progressive chain of behaviors, attitudes, and events that is initiated before the individual begins using drugs again:

1. A buildup of stress caused by either negative or positive life events;
2. Stimulation of overly negative or positive thoughts, moods, or feelings;
3. Overreaction or total failure to take action in response to the situation of stress;
4. Denial of the existence or seriousness of the problem and failure to seek support;
5. The original problem "snowballs" and creates other problems;
6. The person perceives the situation as beyond his control and finds drug use appealing;
7. The person increasingly finds himself in high-risk situations for drug use;
8. Stress increases and the person further isolates himself from his support system;
9. Irresistible cravings and urges lead the individual to obtain and use drugs.

The clinician's compassionate and understanding attitude is a step in making the relapse a learning experience for the patient. Together the therapist and patient need to examine carefully what led up to the seemingly unexpected return to drinking or drug use. By coming to appreciate why they relapsed, patients can be better prepared in the future to avoid making the same mistakes. They can understand their vulnerabilities and anticipate making more adequate responses in the future. Relapse typically occurs as a crisis. The first step in making it a learning experience is to examine it retrospectively in the session and try to understand its antecedents.

One of the therapists interviewed gave an illuminating case example of a man who relapsed after attending the funeral of a child and how he responded:

> He came in with a hang-dog look that looked like trouble. He described having gone to a funeral of a child who was a friend of one of his own children. He immediately left the funeral and went on a bender, got arrested, and spent a night in jail. Now he had his professional work threatened. He wound up talking about the affects that were stirred up by the funeral, which had been intolerable to him. He never mentioned the funeral was coming and never called me to talk about it between appointments. It became a learning experience for him to recognize the fact that he doesn't go off on a toot at random moments out of the blue. There's a definite context. There are definite triggers, definite meanings. There are ways in which he is resourceless to deal with his own internal life without substances. You fold it back into the treatment in terms of what we learn from this. In some respects, relapses are even helpful because they convince your patient they've got a problem, if they have any doubts about it. You take apart those instances. You talk about the particular affects, context, circumstances, what it felt like, what made it seem intolerable. You talk about at what point they started feeling better, where they lost track of control. You talk about the whole process, and it becomes an education.

Individuals develop their own unique relapse strategies. There are particular circumstances, stresses, affects, and warning signs that are precursors to the patient returning to drinking or drug use. A second educational task for the therapist is to alert the patient to his own particular warning signs and develop alternative ways of responding. One interviewed therapist elaborated his approach:

> I also point out the relapse strategy. "You cut down on your AA meetings. You stopped taking Antabuse." You try to get people to understand in the service of growth so that the next time they will recognize they're doing this. What I try to explain to people is that when their patterns of behavior or feelings change, it is a precursor to certain things. They need to know their patterns. If they are going to AA meetings four times a week and then stop going for three weeks, I point out to them that that's a signal. They may not be conscious of what's going on, but they're getting prepared to do something. That's what they have to recognize in their lives. In terms of relapse, my job therapeutically is to help that person learn something about himself through the relapse.

In sessions, the therapist needs to be attentive to the warning signs of relapse and teach the patient to be an objective self-observer who can effectively monitor his own behavior. If the therapist can pick up the signals, he can alert the patient to the dangers of a particular situation. Another clinician described how he points out to his patients how they might be setting themselves up for a relapse:

> In a lot of cases, unconsciously they have been setting themselves up for a relapse for several days, maybe even a couple of weeks. They know a family function is coming. They know their dad has liquor in the cabinet. They know there is going to be a lot of alcohol. They know that if they keep taking their Antabuse, they will get violently sick if they drink at the party. So they come in and say they don't need Antabuse anymore, "I'm doing fine and nothing's happening. I stopped taking it last week." I know that Christmas is coming up, and I know it's a crazy family. I know that if a person stops taking Antabuse the week before, even if they don't know it, that they are setting themselves up. So you can deal with it pretty directly when it comes up. Sometimes you can hear it. You point it out.

The therapist can also help his patients anticipate potentially dangerous situations and initiate a discussion about it before it occurs.

Together they can talk about the pressures to drink and how to respond. One clinician said:

> When they are approaching a situation that is potentially dangerous, I will generally talk with them about it. Sometimes it works; sometimes it doesn't work. I had one patient who I knew was going to a wedding. He had been sober for several months. I told him, "You will be out of town and in unfamiliar circumstances. There will be a lot of people doing a lot of social drinking. That's a real good time for you to relapse." We talked about it for about two weeks. Sure enough, he relapsed when he went to the wedding, despite my best attempts to forewarn him that this might be a problem.

A relapse episode can also be an opportunity for the therapist to learn something about his patient and make the treatment more effective. The patient's particular vulnerabilities become obvious when he finds it necessary to resort to drugs again in order to cope. The therapist, like the patient, learns what specific circumstances, affects, and thoughts are intolerable to the individual and can assess his resources for responding. The therapist also has an opportunity to assess his patient's motivation for change. Does the person simply excuse it or redouble his efforts to maintain sobriety? Is he so impatient with himself that he wants to give up the treatment? Does the relapse encourage him to look more closely at his life and increase his efforts to change?

If a patient relapses frequently even though he is motivated for treatment, the therapist ought to suspect that something is missing in his treatment plan. The therapist needs to inquire more deeply into the reasons for the relapsing. There may be an underlying psychiatric disorder that is not recognized and is not being treated. Perhaps the patient needs medication. Perhaps the person needs to be hospitalized because he is incapable of controlling his behavior. Perhaps the therapist is exploring sensitive issues before the patient is ready and arousing too much anxiety. The person may need to be encouraged to get more support for his recovery and attend AA or NA meetings more frequently or keep closer contact with his sponsor. Frequent relapsing is an invitation for the therapist to reevaluate the treatment plan.

In responding to relapses, therapists should employ several strategies:

1. Assume a compassionate and curious attitude. Avoid shaming the patient.
2. Examine each episode carefully and make it a learning experience.
3. Explore the antecedents of the relapse.
4. Discuss what the patient might do differently in the future to avoid relapsing.
5. Alert the patient to his unique relapse strategy.
6. Anticipate potentially dangerous situations and discuss ways of responding.
7. Encourage continued participation in a recovery program.
8. Reevaluate the treatment plan for the patient.

DRUG SCREENS

The ultimate goal of treatment is to teach the patient to monitor his own behavior. In some settings, where the patients have demonstrated an unwillingness or inability to monitor their own behavior, outside measures such as drug screens are used. Drug screens are frequently used in specialized substance abuse treatment programs and in inpatient dual diagnosis units. Screens are also appropriately used within the legal setting for those who are on probation or parole. However, in the outpatient mental health setting, the regular use of drug screens does not seem called for and can actually interfere with the treatment.

There are several reasons why I prefer not to use drug screens. First of all, there are practical problems in requiring patients in the typical office setting to have a urine or blood test. Most offices do not have the proper facilities. One woman therapist told me she was not prepared to monitor her male patient's giving a urine sample. Secondly, drug screens are not particularly reliable. People have become sophisticated enough to find ways of masking the presence of drugs in their bodies. One of my patients, who was on probation, was required to have urine drug screens. He had been using marijuana for thirty years, since he was 8-years-old. He told me that he would drink a certain herbal tea before each screening and that he passed the test every time. Thirdly, patients need to assume responsibility for their own behavior. If the therapist begins checking up on the patient, he takes over that responsibility and gives the patient a confusing message. As mentioned previously, the outpatient setting works effectively only for those who are motivated and able to function in the world. The therapist needs to encourage his patients to internalize their motivation for change and assume responsibility for their own lives. Finally, and most importantly, the clinician needs to develop a trusting relationship with his patient in order to work with him effectively. Demanding external checks will only communicate a lack of trust in the patient and compromise the therapeutic alliance. Usually, drug screens are not necessary. If a person is using, it becomes obvious sooner or later. Besides, I have found that most patients are fairly honest about their drug use, particularly if a trusting relationship has been established.

13 | THE CONTEXT OF CHANGE: INVOLVING THE FAMILY

In recent years there is a growing recognition of the impact of substance abuse on the family to the extent that in some circles it is called a family, rather than an individual, disease. For example, in their often quoted study of the alcoholic family, Steinglass and colleagues (1987) observe that families with an alcoholic member frequently achieve a stable sense of identity as an alcoholic family. While alcoholism may have devastatingly visible effects on some families, other families adapt to the presence of the alcoholic member and remain structurally intact and stable. These families, however, are profoundly affected, but the damage is more subtle and less visible. As alcoholic problems worsen, family members' attention and energy shift from their own needs, interests, and concerns to those of the alcoholic. The fundamental aspects of family life—the daily routines, family rituals, family problem-solving strategies—are profoundly altered to accommodate the behavior of the drinker. Increasingly, and most often without the awareness of the family members, alcohol becomes the organizing principle of family life that provides a sort of unhealthy stability.

Sharon Wegscheider (1981) observes how family members adapt to the erratic behavior of the chemically dependent person and attempt to preserve a sense of security and stability in the family. They hide their true feelings behind artificial behavior patterns, which Wegscheider identifies as five distinct roles played by family members in the alcoholic drama. The alcoholic is a dependent person, who, as he gradually loses power over his own life, paradoxically wields increasing control over the family. In adapting to the alcoholic, one family member may become an "enabler" who feels powerless and angry, but compensates by assuming the responsibility of protecting the dependent person from the destructive consequences of his behavior. Another, often the oldest child, becomes a "hero." In this role, the individual provides a sense of self-worth for the family by his compulsive quest for achievements. Another may assume the role of "scapegoat," the reverse image of the hero. The scapegoat expresses the hurt and anger of the family by acting out in delinquent ways. In so doing, he gains negative attention and distracts the family from the troubling behavior of the dependent person. A family member may also become a "lost child" who isolates himself socially, creates a lonely fantasy world for himself, and withdraws from the confusion created by the alcoholic. Finally, the role of "mascot" may be assumed by another person, often the youngest child. This individual becomes hyperactive and immature. He clowns around to gain attention and provides a distraction for the overwhelmed family.

Psychopathology can also be conceptualized from a family perspective. For example, Minuchin and colleagues (1967) propose that the psychopathology of an individual is maintained by the interpersonal dynamics of the family. Healthy families have clearly defined, yet flexible, boundaries between their various subsystems. Psychiatric problems thrive in troubled families, of which Minuchin distinguishes two major types. The first is the disengaged family, which has excessively rigid boundaries and rules of interacting. In the disengaged family, there is little or no emotional contact between the members and a relative absence of structure, order, or authority. The second type of troubled family is the enmeshed family that has diffuse and weak boundaries. The members are overly involved in each other's lives, and there is considerable resistance to change within each member. From this perspective, the sick individual is only the identified patient who manifests the dysfunction within the family system.

An adaptation occurs in families with an emotionally or mentally ill member, analogous to that within alcoholic families. Increasingly, the family members refocus their attention and alter their routines to accommodate and care for the sick member. In so doing, they achieve a measure of harmony and stability, and even an identity as a mentally ill family, if the psychiatric illness is severe. Family members also assume a variety of roles to make up for the deficits and care for the identified patient. The more severe and chronic the illness, the greater is the pressure exerted on the family system to adapt to and compensate for the sick member. For example, family members will make sure the patient takes his medicine as prescribed and does not harm himself or others. They will take over the responsibilities around the house that would normally belong to the patient. In short, they assume a caretaking role.

With the heightened realization of the impact of both substance abuse and mental illness on the family, the question inevitably arises: should the focus of treatment be on the sick individual or the sick family? In the case of the dually diagnosed patient encountered in the outpatient setting, I believe that the treatment efforts should be aimed primarily at the individual, with an awareness of the family dynamics that maintain the illness. However, family members can be involved to help support the recovery of the patient. They can also be offered assistance through a referral to another therapist and participation in self-help groups.

There are several reasons for recommending that the individual patient ought to be the primary focus of treatment. First of all, most of the dually diagnosed come because of personal distress and problems caused by their psychiatric and substance use disorders. If the individual seeks help for himself, the therapist should address the presenting complaint and not presume a desire for treatment on the part of other family members. Of course, the case is different if the patient requests marital or family therapy; the couple or family then are engaged in treatment. Secondly, the establishment of a therapeutic alliance and a trusting relationship are essential for effective treatment and must be the initial focus for the clinician in beginning therapy. To include other family members too readily in the treatment may compromise the relationship between therapist and patient and violate trust. The therapist can always make a referral of family members to another therapist to help them address their own issues. Finally, most of the dually diagnosed encountered in the outpatient setting do not suffer from an incapacitatingly severe mental disorder or addiction. They are generally functional in the world and motivated for treatment. These individuals are capable of addressing their problems without the immediate presence of family. However, in the more severe cases, the involvement of the family is essential to offer support, structure, and guidance because of the patient's deficits in ego functioning.

Treatment Principle Thirteen: While the therapist focuses the treatment efforts on the dual diagnosis patient, the family can be involved to help support his recovery.

INVOLVING THE FAMILY

Confidentiality

The therapist's first concern is always for the patient who comes for help. In order to be of assistance to the patient, the therapist needs to develop a trusting relationship with him and maintain confidentiality. Just because the person has a substance abuse problem, the therapist is not justified in compromising the boundaries of the treatment by talking with his family, friends, or others about the patient's issues. Occasionally, family members may call the therapist to inform him of concerns about the patient. The therapist can listen and gather information, but should avoid giving advice about what the family member should do to handle various situations. At times, the clinician may need to consult with the individual's previous therapist or medical doctor to make a well-informed diagnosis and treatment plan. In such a case, care must be taken that the patient understands clearly the therapist's need to consult with outside people for the patient's benefit and signs the appropriate releases of information.

Aware of the impact of the family on the person's recovery, the therapist can instruct the patient on the value of relying on family support for recovery and offer his services as a consultant to the family. One therapist described how he assumes this role and gives an example of its therapeutic usefulness:

> I set myself up as a consultant to the family. I try to get an agreement that any family member may call me for any reason. The content of what they tell me will be confidential, but the phone

call will be announced. It's obvious if the wife calls and the husband has been drinking. All I have to say is, "Your wife called, and she's very concerned about you. What do you make of it?" "Oh, she's just too worried and makes a big deal about everything. We were at a wedding, and I had one drink, and that's all I had." I then tell him, "It's of enough concern to her that I think she needs to come in so we can work this through so she feels better. It sounds like it's more about her than about you. Maybe we can help her." That cuts the game playing on the addicted person's part and addresses the family issue.

Assessment and Confronting Denial

There are a few purposes for involving family members in treatment on a collateral basis. The first purpose is to clarify the diagnosis. Those with substance abuse problems are often pressured into treatment by their spouses, who may be threatening divorce if the person does not give up drinking or using drugs. Interestingly, it occasionally happens that the spouse brings the identified patient to the initial session. He or she has grown accustomed to assuming responsibility for the abusing person and wants to make sure the individual comes to treatment and the therapist understands the problem accurately. Family dynamics become evident in such cases. The therapist may meet for a few sessions with the couple to gather data, assess the situation, and determine the most effective treatment approach.

One clinician, who works frequently as a family therapist, described how he involves the family in order to help him assess and confront the patient's denial:

With a patient who couldn't really tell me much about what was happening intrapsychically, if I brought the family in as part of the treatment, stuff started getting stirred up. I could then see what was going on. The wife would come in and destroy the bland picture the guy was painting about how things were the same every day after work. They would just be together and go to bed, according to him. I would hear things from the wife that he wasn't telling me about. I would then be able to work with them. I didn't know that back then when I first started. After a few sessions, if we were stuck at the same point, I would wait for images in the

material about conflict between husband and wife, between parent and kid, then ask if we should consider having her come too.
That works.

In working with couples, this therapist also related how he confronts the patient's denial by pointing out the discrepancies between
the patient's and his spouse's accounts of events:

> The best way to confront denial is if a couple is coming together.
> You talk to them about their problems. You get a history talking
> with them together or separately. I get the picture that alcohol is
> perceived by one patient as not there, by the other that it is a re-
> curring problem. I just point out the disparity of their perspec-
> tives. "You say that he has a drinking problem, while he says that
> he does not. What should we do?" Sometimes the person just gets
> mad and won't participate anymore and won't come back. We just
> keep talking. I bring them back in and talk with them together
> and deal with the issues that come up. When the drinking comes
> up, I talk about it again. "You said you had three fights this week
> and each of them was around drinking issues."

Education and Support

It is helpful on occasion, with the permission of the patient, to
invite family members in for sessions to educate them about the dynamics of addiction and recovery. Family members often inadvertently
engage in enabling behavior when they try to control and manage the
drinking or drug using of the substance abuser. For example, they
may try to hide or pour out the alcoholic's supply of liquor. Because
of their own sense of shame or embarrassment, they may minimize
or deny that their loved one has a drug problem, making excuses for
him at work and even lying to friends. Family members feel out of
control when confronted with the erratic and unpredictable moods
and behaviors of the substance abuser. To compensate, they attempt
to control the use of drugs by cajoling, threatening, or bribing the
addicted person. They attempt to manage his uncontrollable behavior and take over his household responsibilities, like paying bills or
doing his chores. To protect themselves and the addicted person from
impending crises, they make excuses, cover up, and rescue him from
trouble.

Such enabling behavior seems natural on the part of family members who see the substance abuser as in desperate need of help. After all, they are only trying to save their loved ones from permanent damage or some catastrophe. In their eyes, love calls for such self-sacrifice for the good of this person in need. However, their good intentions prove misguided and ultimately harmful because they are attempting to control what is uncontrollable, in part to relieve their own sense of anxiety and helplessness. They are inadvertently protecting the substance abuser from the negative consequences of his behavior and prolonging his illusion that he can drink or use drugs with impunity. If someone is always there to worry about his well-being and save him from the destructive consequences of his behavior, why should he worry? Why should he give up something he enjoys so much if there is no price to pay for using? The substance abuser never has to face the dreadful consequences of his behavior and assume responsibility for his life as long as other people are watching over him. His infantile sense of invulnerability, which is fostered by drug use, can continue.

Such enabling behavior on the part of family members can become entrenched over time and develop into a syndrome that has been labeled "codependency." Someone who suffers from codependency becomes obsessively and compulsively involved in the problems of the substance abuser to the point that this behavior seriously damages his life. He becomes dependent on the alcoholic as the alcoholic is dependent on the booze. The codependent person focuses all his attention and energy on the problems of the drug user to the neglect of himself. Such compulsive behavior is often motivated by a sense of low self-esteem and a desperate attempt to avoid facing personal problems. The codependent person attempts to build his own self-esteem by rescuing the substance abuser, who is seen as needy and incompetent. But in the process, this helping person experiences frustration, a sense of failure, and a further reduction in self-esteem. Failure is inevitable because the codependent person is trying to control what is beyond his control. Only an alcoholic can decide to stop drinking and take responsibility for his life when he is ready. No one can do that for him.

Timmen Cermak (1986) proposes that codependency be included in the *Diagnostic and Statistical Manual* as a diagnosable personality disorder. He observes that codependency is a syndrome with a consistent pattern of traits and behaviors that cause dysfunction in a person's life. He proceeds to identify the criteria for this diagnosis:

1. Continued investment of self-esteem in the ability to control both oneself and others in the face of serious adverse consequences.
2. Assumption of responsibility for meeting others' needs to the exclusion of acknowledging one's own.
3. Anxiety and boundary distortions around intimacy and separation.
4. Enmeshment in relationships with personality disordered, chemically dependent, other codependent, and/or impulse disordered individuals.
5. Three or more of the following: Excessive reliance on denial, constriction of emotions, depression, hypervigilance, compulsions, anxiety, substance abuse, has been (or is) the victim of recurrent physical or sexual abuse, has remained in a primary relationship with a substance abuser without seeking outside help. [p. 11]

At opportune times when the therapist becomes aware of the overinvolvement of a particular family member in the patient's continued drug use, he can suggest to the patient that that family member come for a collateral session. The therapist can discuss any specific enabling behaviors in which he is engaged and point out how what he thinks is helpful might really be harmful to the recovery of the patient. The therapist can educate both the patient and his family member about the family dynamics of addiction, enabling behavior, and codependency. These family members are also suffering terribly as a result of the problems of the patient and need ongoing support themselves. The therapist can recommend that they engage in therapy and make an appropriate referral. They can also recommend that they participate in twelve step programs, such as Al Anon or Alateen, to learn more about their involvement in the addiction process. In these support groups, family members learn that they are not alone in coping with such problems and learn many helpful strategies for living a healthy life with a chemically dependent person. If the codependency or other problems are significant, the therapist can make a referral to another therapist for the family member.

If the patient has a severe mental illness along with his addiction, the family members are even more consumed by the problems of the identified patient and in need of help. On occasion, therapists can meet with the family member to discuss ways of coping with the mental illness and setting appropriate boundaries. They can also provide them with information about the particular mental illness of their loved one. Support groups for family members, such as the Alliance for the Mentally Ill, are also available and can be recommended for ongoing support. Those who live with mentally ill substance abusers can feel particularly overwhelmed and might benefit from attending both twelve step groups and support groups for the families of the mentally ill. Individual therapy can also be beneficial for them.

Living with a dually diagnosed individual can be especially trying for the family. Family members face a similar dilemma in establishing appropriate boundaries to that of the therapist who treats the individual. On the one hand, to avoid enabling behavior for the substance abuse, the family must learn to disengage from the drug seeking and erratic behavior of the patient. On the other hand, because of the psychological fragility and impairments caused by the psychiatric disorder, family members must offer structure and support for the patient and compensate for his inability to care for himself. How involved or disengaged should the family be if one of their members has both a substance use and a psychiatric disorder? Where does their responsibility end and the patient's begin? To what degree should they protect him from his self-defeating or destructive behavior? For example, if the person wants to drink, the common Al Anon wisdom suggests not interfering. However, if the individual is suicidal, the family must take steps to protect the patient. These difficult problems require an integration of approaches from both the substance abuse and mental health fields.

Severe Cases

With the increasing restrictions placed on insurance authorizations for inpatient treatment and the reduction of the number of days of hospitalization, more severely disabled dual diagnosis patients are being encountered in the outpatient setting. The need for family involvement in treatment is heightened when either the psychiatric or substance use disorder is severe and out of control. The family can provide the ongoing support, structure, guidance that the patient needs and the therapist cannot supply. However, the therapist can elicit the support of the family and form a treatment alliance with them for the good of the patient. The more underdeveloped and impaired the ego functioning of the patient, the more the family needs to be called upon. For example, effective work with children, who are immature and unable to care for themselves, requires parental involvement. The care of the mentally retarded and developmentally disabled calls for the active involvement of their caretakers. In the same way, the effective treatment of those who are acutely psychotic or severely addicted requires the ongoing support of their families.

A therapist reported a case example.

> She met with an unmarried 29-year-old man who had just been released from the hospital. He had been diagnosed with paranoid schizophrenia and had a long drinking history. Recently, he had suicidal thoughts and had been hospitalized. The therapist met with him shortly after discharge from the hospital. It became evident that he had been released from the hospital too soon because he arrived at the appointment extremely paranoid. In fact, he had stopped taking his meds and had resumed drinking. During the session, he became agitated and left. The therapist immediately called the family and expressed to them her concerns that he was out of control, and given his history of suicidal thoughts, considered him a danger to himself. She suggested that he might need to be taken back to the hospital. The family responded by having the patient rehospitalized.

As a routine measure, the therapist should get the patient's permission to contact the family in these cases where the psychiatric and addiction problems are severe. The therapist can explain to the patient how important the support of the family is to him for his ongoing recovery from both disorders. The therapist's sharing responsibility with the family provides an invaluable service to the patient. The family can alert the therapist to any change in the patient's condition and head off any full-blown relapses into either the mental illness or the substance abuse. The therapist can alert the family to the risks of treating this person in the outpatient setting and warn them when he senses the patient is becoming out of control and a danger to himself or others. If hospitalization is needed, the family can share in making the decision and follow through with watching over the patient and taking him to the hospital. Such shared responsibility is helpful to the patient and also helps protect the therapist from legal liability.

In summary, the following are some strategies for involving the family in the treatment of the dually diagnosed:

1. The first priority must be to establish a treatment alliance with the patient.
2. The therapist ought to obtain the patient's permission to contact the family, especially in the more severe cases.
3. The family can help in diagnosing and confronting the denial regarding substance abuse.
4. The therapist should educate the family regarding the family dynamics of substance abuse, their enabling behavior, and codependency.
5. The therapist can encourage family members to get help for themselves with therapy and participation in Al Anon and in the Alliance for the Mentally Ill.
5. The therapist can elicit support from the family for the ongoing recovery of the patient.
6. The therapist can share responsibility with the family in the treatment of the more severely disabled patient.

14

A MOMENT IN THE CONTINUUM OF CARE: INITIATING TERMINATION

An important and difficult clinical decision concerns whether, when, and how to initiate a termination with an uncooperative patient. For those working in the mental health field, this is a rare occurence. Patients with psychiatric disorders are viewed as fragile and in need of support, encouragement, and patience in treatment. Therapists tend to avoid confrontations and be more tolerant of patients' difficulties in assuming responsibility for their lives. If the therapist were to initiate a termination, he might feel as though he were abandoning a person in need. In contrast, specialists in the substance abuse field more readily and directly challenge their clients to take responsibility for their lives and recovery. They demand from their clients a commitment to abstinence and participation in a program of recovery. If their clients demonstate a lack of motivation to participate in treatment, these therapists will typically initiate a termination until the individual is ready to invest himself in recovery.

How is the clinician to respond to the uncooperative patient who suffers both a substance use and a psychiatric disorder? How demanding should the therapist be that the patient demonstrate a commitment to recovery? Can a therapist ever present the patient with an ultimatum that unless he follows the treatment plan, the therapy will be ended? These are difficult questions. An effective therapeutic response requires an integration of approaches from both the mental health and substance abuse treatment communities. In my opinion, it also requires an openness to the possibility of initiating a termination of treatment for therapeutic reasons under certain circumstances. This chapter will address the criteria and rationale for terminating treatment and the process by which this is accomplished.

Treatment Principle Fourteen: There are occasions when the therapist must initiate a termination of treatment for therapeutic reasons because uncontrolled drug use will eventually disrupt the treatment if allowed to continue.

Most often, however, premature terminations with dual diagnosis patients occur early in treatment, usually within the first couple of sessions. The patient decides to drop out on his own. It typically occurs while the therapist is in the process of evaluating the patient and formulating a treatment plan and before a treatment contract is really made. As mentioned previously, individuals come to mental health specialists because of mental health problems. During the assessment process, the clinician discovers a second diagnosis of a substance abuse problem, which the patient frequently does not recognize or admit. When the therapist alerts the patient to his substance abuse problem and the need to address it in treatment, the patient may resist the diagnosis and withdraw from therapy.

Let me give a case example.

Pete, a 28-year-old man, came to see me because of his distress over his wife's leaving him. He reported that he had become so distraught that he could not concentrate at work, and his employer requested that he seek treatment. Inquiry into the reasons for the separation showed that drinking played a large role in their disputes. He admitted that he had been drinking more heavily since the separation, about six to nine beers a night. He also related that he came from an alcoholic family and had problems with drinking when he was a teenager. I suggested that his drinking may be contributing more than he realized to his marital problems and requested that he try to remain abstinent during treatment. We would discuss in the sessions what it was like for him to be without alcohol. Pete came for three sessions and dropped out of treatment when he was able to reconcile with his wife.

Apparently, the external pressure for him to cut back his drinking abated.

CRITERIA FOR TERMINATING

Uncontrolled Drug Use

There are several reasons why a therapist might decide to initiate a termination with a patient. The first circumstance is when the patient's drug use remains uncontrolled. It is the consistent experience of therapists who work with the dually diagnosed that unabated drug use will eventually undermine the treatment. As elaborated in an earlier chapter, the use of alcohol or drugs covers up the feelings that are addressed in therapy, and psychiatric problems cannot be effectively treated until abstinence is well established. The individual's cognitive abilities are impaired to the extent that he is not able to participate fully in the treatment and resolve his problems. Furthermore, an accurate diagnosis of the psychiatric disorder remains problematic as long as the drug use continues. In short, the potential effectiveness of treatment is seriously compromised while the patient continues drinking or using drugs and will eventually lead to frustration on the part of both therapist and patient if the therapy is allowed to continue.

One experienced therapist related how she confronts her patients if the treatment reaches a standstill because of their continued drinking:

> I warn them first. "Either stop drinking and go to meetings or there is no sense in continuing. You are wasting your money or the insurance company's money. You are wasting my time. When you're ready, come on back." I warn them if they don't get it together by this date we will have to terminate. It is a therapeutic termination. Sometimes it's necessary. You cannot treat a practicing alcoholic. It just will not work. There's too much cognitive stuff going on or lack of emotional stuff.
>
> I had one woman who kept drinking all the time and wouldn't go to meetings. She just wouldn't do it. She just kept blaming it on her husband, blaming it on this, blaming it on that. So I just gave her six weeks. If she didn't get it together by six weeks, and

this was after we had gone through a long period of trying to figure out what was going on, then I was afraid that I would have to
terminate. I said, "I'm sorry, this is the last session," and I referred
her someplace. You don't leave people high and dry. You can't do
that. It's called abandonment. So you give them three names.

Level of Denial

A second reason for initiating a therapeutic termination is that
the therapist has decided that he cannot break through the patient's
denial. Typically, patients come to see a mental health professional
for their psychiatric problems and are not seeking treatment for a substance abuse problem. Patients may be resistant to admitting their
problem with drinking or drug use. If their denial remains adamant,
the therapist may choose to initiate a termination to help make the
patient aware of the consequences of his continued denial and drug
use. At some point, to continue treatment in the face of this denial
would support the alcoholic process, communicating to the patient
that continuing drug use is not problematic. An excessive tolerance
on the part of the therapist may even reinforce the patient's denial
and continued drug use.

One of the therapists interviewed reflected that the termination
may even be beneficial because it allows life experience to break
through the denial:

> I will not continue to treat them if they continue to use over and
> over again. The level of denial can be broken. However, I'm not
> going to spend my time trying to break through it when I know
> life experiences will break through it sooner, such as getting a Driv-
> ing Under the Influence (DUI) or getting a divorce. Those experi-
> ences seem to raise the level of the denial, raise the bottom, much
> more acutely, more dynamically, with more thrust, than what I could
> do with all my intellectual confrontations. So I won't work with
> them that long. If they don't want help and they continue to abuse
> substances, then I tell them to come back when they are ready.

She proceeded to give a case example:

> I'm seeing one man for marital problems. I told him and his wife
> that his alcoholism was a major problem and that as long as he

was drinking I could not help them with their marital problems. I recommended that he go to AA and she go to Al Anon. She started going to Al Anon, but he didn't go to AA and kept drinking. I said I would continue to see him for a month to talk about his alcoholism and continue to see her to talk about her codependency, but I would not see them for marital therapy as long as he was drinking. He stood up, called me some names, walked out, and went on a binge. I continued to see her.

She reflected further on her reason for refusing to see them for marital therapy: "This man was so adamant that I felt that he would interpret my continuing to see him as supportive of his denial. Somehow he would see it as my problem and not his. Furthermore, I could not allow his wife to think that therapy would make a difference in their marriage if he still drank. What he might agree to or recognize in a marital session he would not think about or recognize while drinking."

Failure to Work on Issues

People always enter treatment with ambivalent feelings. They want relief from the distress caused by their psychiatric or substance abuse problems, yet they are reluctant to give up an accustomed way of life. Slowly, the therapist leads the patient to a realization that relief will come only with personal change. However, especially with problems of chemical dependency, people can manifest a particular resistance to change. They will refuse to participate in the program of recovery requested by the therapist. They will not attend AA meetings, avoid places and people that trigger drug use, or consistently attend therapy sessions. In such a case, the therapist needs to confront the patient's lack of motivation. The hope is that warning the patient of an impending termination may stimulate him to work more seriously on his issues.

One of the therapists interviewed related how he confronts his patients regarding their self-destructive behaviors and lack of motivation to work on issues:

I think it's more intuitive than anything else. There's a point at which it seems to be painfully obvious that something has to be done. There are repetitive instances of problems where you have to say, "Look, it's real obvious that whatever we do in here is being negated by the drinking." I certainly don't have a frequency count, after two or three times. It depends on the person and what else he's doing. It's not just with substance abuse you have to confront when their behavior is self-destructive, negating what they're doing in here. Are they willing to make changes in other ways? I really believe if people are not going to do what's beneficial for themselves, then at some point you're going to have to confront: "What are you doing here? This is a contract to do something helpful and beneficial for yourself. If you're not doing that, what's the point?"

In his presentation of a model of psychotherapy with the dually diagnosed, Edward Kaufman (1989) states that he terminates treatment if the patient or his family do not follow the treatment contract and the patient continues to abuse substances. He lists several elements in his treatment contract with the patient:

1. Agreement on a method of detoxification,
2. Commitment to abstinence,
3. Commitment to a comprehensive method for maintaining abstinence, such as participating in twelve step meetings, educational meetings, group therapy sessions, and having drug screens,
4. Commitment by family members to a program of recovery for themselves, such as Al Anon,
5. If there is a major mental illness, an agreement to take the medication as prescribed. [p. 12]

In evaluating the effectiveness of treatment with the dually diagnosed, the therapist needs to ask also about other aspects of the patient's life than his substance abuse recovery efforts. One of the therapists interviewed related how he monitors his patients' progress and asks about many areas of their lives:

Since I'm not going to be judgmental with them, for the most part they seem to be fairly truthful. If they are making good progress, they will tell me that. . . . I will also use as criteria for termination whether or not they're working, how they're getting along on the job, what they're doing regarding job seeking behavior and job seeking skills if they're unemployed, how they're interacting with family members and with people around them, how they're spending their spare time, what they are doing with themselves.

In short, the therapist needs to evaluate the overall quality of the person's life and gauge the impact of the treatment on his daily living.

Clinicians continually monitor the progress of their patients and the effectiveness of their treatment. If the treatment has reached a standstill or if the patient's condition deteriorates, the therapist needs to ask himself what is missing in his treatment plan. If the patient is not benefitting from his interventions, he needs to inquire into the reasons why and ask the patient directly about it. If the patient is not following his treatment recommendations, the therapist should address the resistance. Proposing a termination of treatment may be the occasion for the patient to reevaluate his motivation for therapy and to address his problems honestly. The therapist-patient match may not be right, and the lack of progress may be an indication that a change in therapist is needed. One of the therapists interviewed suggested accepting honestly the limitations of therapy for improving the patient's life: "If it looks like they're doing things that are not designed to help themselves, then I will tell them there's no point in us continuing together. I realize that I only see them for an hour, and 167 hours pass when they are not with me before I see them again. In the one hour out of 168 in a week, the impact I could have with them tends to be relatively small. There's a lot they have to do for themselves."

Lying

A final circumstance in which a termination may be necessary is when the patient is not truthful or sincere about his involvement in treatment. For example, the patient may be using the therapy because his lawyer told him that it would look good to the judge if he were in treatment. Or an individual comes to avoid a divorce and has no intention of becoming engaged in the treatment process. Or an individual comes to therapy only to keep his job. One of the therapists interviewed reported that he will terminate with patients who are dishonest and lie to him:

Failures of that kind tend to be with patients who are sufficiently advanced in the addiction process that their acting out is wildly out of control, such that there's a lot of dishonesty and lying going on. In such a case, there's no handle for a therapeutic alliance with them. You can't make a therapeutic alliance with a patient who lies to you. That's what it boils down to in my view. Sometimes that even goes so far to involve criminal behavior on the part of some of the patients. You have to make a decision as to whether or not you can have a treatment with somebody who is lying to you or acting out in ways that are not coming into the treatment, that you can tell are going on and know they are denying. There are sometimes bizarre contradictions that come up and people confront you with. Unless you are dealing with somebody with dissociative defenses and they don't know they are lying, there's no point. You simply say, "I can't help you." Then tell them why.

Clearly, therapy will not be of benefit for these people, and the therapist may propose a termination until they are ready to address issues honestly.

In summary, there are several situations in which a therapeutic termination may be warranted:

1. When the drug use continues and is uncontrolled,
2. When the patient's denial of his drug problem is adamant,
3. When the patient does not work on his issues and refuses to become involved in a program of recovery for his substance abuse, and/or
4. When the patient is dishonest about his involvement in treatment and regularly lies to the therapist.

PROCESS OF TERMINATING

Taking Time

In initiating a therapeutic termination, the clinician attempts to integrate insights gained from both mental health and addictions specialists. From the substance abuse specialist, he learns the need to insist that the patient be responsible for his own recovery and be held accountable for his actions. From the mental health professional, he learns the value of patience and sensitivity to the individual needs of the patient. It is my opinion that therapists need to pursue a gradual, yet persistent, approach in making demands on the dually diagnosed. If after a certain length of time the patient continues with his uncontrolled drug use and refusal to participate in a recovery program, the therapist should initiate a termination of treatment.

As elaborated previously, if the patient is initially resistant to admitting a drug problem, the therapist can begin a process of persuasion to address the denial. He can invite the patient to make an experiment with abstinence, keep a journal of his drinking behavior, attend several AA meetings. However, there should be a limit to the therapist's tolerance for the patient's unwillingness to follow the treatment contract. The length of time before initiating a termination may vary according to the clinical judgment of the therapist. One therapist related that he uses a three month rule:

> If they are using the therapy in some avoidant way and we have given it a good three months, I will terminate. I will gently say to them we are not making progress, and it's likely that I am ineffective with them. I take on the ownership. I then provide them with a referral. Often that's enough to ignite them. I use a three month rule. If I have agreed with them to try controlled drinking and they are charting and journaling and we are making progress discussing that, I would continue beyond the three months. If it is so obvious that they are using the therapy as a means to continue drinking, I will say that we are apparently in disagreement. I think it would be irresponsible on my part to continue to participate in their choice to continue using alcohol. I can't in good conscience continue.

There is a three step process in terminating. Once the therapist has thoroughly assessed the patient and made the decision that a therapeutic termination is necessary, he should first warn the patient of an impending termination and explain the reasons. Such a warning may motivate the patient to reevaluate his commitment to recovery. Secondly, at the last session, some appropriate referrals to another therapist or a substance abuse program should be made. It is a good idea to give the person several names from which to choose. Finally, the therapist should extend an invitation to the person to return to treatment when he feels ready to address his problems. The therapist wants to communicate his interest in the well-being of the person and his availability to help.

A Measure of Caution

Careful consideration and caution must be exercised before initiating a termination. The therapist must honestly consider if a countertransferential reaction is motivating the termination. As mentioned previously, the dually diagnosed are difficult patients because of their hostility, noncompliance, manipulating, and acting out behaviors. Therapists can easily become frustrated with them, feel helpless, and become unconsciously punitive in their desire to terminate. Therapists need to examine if they have in any way contributed to the resistance and lack of cooperation of the patient by their own unrecognized hostile or rescuing behavior. Furthermore, if the treatment is at a standstill, the clinician must look for the underlying reason. Perhaps he has missed something in the treatment plan and not accurately assessed for a second diagnosis. Perhaps the patient needs medication or a more intensive level of care.

One therapist described her cautious attitude in initiating a termination:

> I don't think you can judge that in terms of weeks or months. Once again, we have to look at the underlying reason for not being able to get it together. I really don't think we know why some people can get it and other people can't. I don't think we've figured that out yet. Once we do, we may bottle it and sell it. I think motivation is important, and dual diagnosis is important. If you have a dual diagnosis in terms of slipping, I'm not going to terminate until we get that taken care of. For example, if you've got an obsessive compulsive person, because of the obsessiveness, the intruding thoughts, or the hand washing, then he might attempt to drink or take drugs to control life. Once you get him on a regimen of correct medication and some cognitive therapy, then he might be able to get it together. I certainly would not terminate that kind of patient.

Whether and when to terminate can be a very difficult decision. One therapist recommended seeking consultation before making the decision:

I'm a helping professional, and I see someone who needs help. There's a certain sadness, disappointment, that they can't accept the help at that time. There is for me the question, "Have I done it right? Did I make a mistake? Should I have done something different to break down the denial?" So I guess there is some personal competency questions that I would always ask myself. Before I terminate, I need to feel pretty comfortable that I did the best that could be done. I will frequently consult with someone on the case. "What do you think? How would you handle it?" So it's not ever a decision that I make lightly.

A Recognition of Limits

Those who pursue a career in a helping profession may be reluctant to admit limitations in their ability to help their patients and cure their illnesses. Many prefer not to treat substance abusing patients, who are often noncompliant, resistant to recovery, and frequently relapse. These therapists may feel incompetent when treatment fails. Those who treat the dually diagnosed need to realize the difficulty in treating this population and honestly admit their limitations in promoting recovery. Otherwise, they are at risk of becoming extremely frustrated and of experiencing burn-out. One therapist, who has worked for many years with the dually diagnosed, described the realistic attitude he espouses:

> If the problem is extremely severe, it may be that there's nothing we can do to help them with the problem. That's an unfortunate reality that we just have to acknowledge. We may not like it. There are some people we really can't get through to, and there's nothing we can do to break the cycle. We can't live their lives for them. We can point out some pitfalls. We can help them get in touch with support groups. We can provide them with medication. We can point out some of the things they need to be aware of. But what we can't do is solve the problem for them.

Especially in this era of managed care when most of the outpatient treatments are of brief duration, it is essential to keep a realistic perspective on the place that therapy has in the overall recovery of the person. A therapeutic termination is just one moment in the continuum of care for the patient. The brief crisis that the therapist may cause the patient by initiating a termination may provoke changes at a future date and prepare the person for a later engagement in treatment. One therapist perceptively and insightfully referred to the need for clinicians to respond to the *kairos*, or opportune moment, when he can have an impact on the illness of the patient:

> If it's only brief therapy, I see myself as part of a continuum of care because the person will relapse again. My word for this is *kairos*. It is biblical time, the moment of truth. The Greek physicians used it to describe that point in time when an illness comes to crisis. Either their fever breaks or they die. There's nothing they can do about that until it happens. Let's face it. An addictive disorder is a mental illness. The resistance is part of the illness. We have the time on our hands, and there will be a moment of truth when something so bad happens that they realize the truth. Did I have anything to do with that? Only that I try to educate them about their disorder. Every crisis is an opportunity. Maybe in a single session of brief therapy I can open up the crack in the armor. I may have called the family, refused to write a letter, insisted on going to AA. At some point, when they are ready, they may remember that.

15 A LONG-TERM PERSPECTIVE: MEASURING SUCCESS

There is a notable lack of treatment outcome literature with the dually diagnosed. This is not surprising for several reasons. First of all, the dually diagnosed have not been identified as a group until quite recently. Secondly, substance use disorders and many psychiatric disorders are relapsing and chronic illnesses. To measure accurately and reliably the treatment outcome of these disorders requires significant time and a longitudinal perspective. Progress can be observed and measured most meaningfully after years, rather than months. For example, if someone is abstinent for six months, it cannot be presumed that he is cured because the relapse rate for substance abusers is particularly high for at least a year. Thirdly, those with a dual diagnosis have also shown themselves to be a heterogeneous population with a wide variety and combination of diagnoses. In the literature, there are no agreed upon definitions about what constitutes a dual diagnosis patient because of the range and differing levels of severity of the coexisting psychiatric and substance use disorders. Finally, even if a group of the dually diagnosed is identified for study, these patients are notoriously noncompliant with treatment and research, and their retention rate is low. Indeed, the researcher faces a bewildering maze of problems in attempting to study this group.

Jerrell and Ridgely (1995) have attempted to outline a minimal set of outcome indicators to assess the effects of specialized treatment for patients with severe mental illness and substance use disorders.

They applied the criteria they developed in assessing the effectiveness of treatment for 147 dually diagnosed patients. These researchers devised their outcome indicators from a review of the literature about the primary problems that need to be addressed in interventions for those with dual disorders. According to these researchers, several areas of functioning over a significant length of time need to be evaluated to determine the effectiveness of treatment for this population. First, both the psychiatric and substance abuse symptoms must be measured. Secondly, various measures of psychosocial functioning by means of self-report and interviewer rating are important. Functioning at home, at work, and in relationships, along with personal reports of life satisfaction, need to be assessed. The use of mental health and support services also should be considered: for example, the number of inpatient care days, outpatient care visits, and emergency room visits. The wide range of indicators selected suggests the extent of the impact of coexisting disorders on an individual's life.

Treatment Principle Fifteen: Successful treatment is measured by a decrease or elimination of symptoms of both the psychiatric and substance use disorders.

The experience of anyone who works with the dually diagnosed testifies that a relapse in one disorder will lead eventually to a relapse in the other. Consequently, therapists need to establish treatment goals that address realistically both the substance use and psychiatric problems. Genuine progress cannot be assured until the symptoms of both disorders have remitted.

RATES OF SUCCESS

The few outcome studies that have been done have focused on the severely mentally ill substance abusers. The criteria that have been developed, such as those of the study quoted above, are also more appropriate for these severely disabled patients. No studies that I am aware of are concerned with the treatment outcomes of the dually diagnosed encountered in the typical outpatient mental health or private office setting. While some of the patients treated in the outpatient setting have chronic mental illnesses, most have psychiatric problems with low to moderate degrees of severity. The majority suffer depression or anxiety with a coexisting alcohol abuse or dependence disorder.

In the absence of rigorous scientific studies, I did a personal survey of nine fully licensed psychologists who have worked in the outpatient setting with the dually diagnosed for an average of over fifteen years. Their reports of success and failure in treating this population are instructive.

One therapist, who has sixteen years experience working in both the mental health and substance abuse fields, noted: "If anything characterizes the dually diagnosed typically, it's treatment failures in any situation, in any setting, whether it's substance abuse treatment centers, or psychiatric hospitals, or psychotherapies." Yet all the interviewed therapists reported a high degree of success in treating their dual diagnosis patients, estimated in the 80 percent range for those who remain in treatment. They acknowledge, though, that a high percentage of those who come with a dual diagnosis drop out of treatment early because, in general, they are not ready to admit or address their substance abuse problem. Some of these therapists commented:

"My success rate has been very high."

"I think I've been very successful."

"I consider my success rate quite high, remembering that most of the people I see are people who come to me early in recovery and know that they have to do something else, that something else is going on. So their motivation is high."

"If I forced myself to choose, yes or no, for these sixteen patients [I am now seeing], it looks to me that 75 to 80 percent have done well. I suppose it's probably as good as any other group of patients."

"Ninety-five percent of the people who start with me finish with me. When we finish, about 75 percent of those have completed their treatment plans."

Another therapist remarked that he has been very successful, but acknowledged that this is a biased sample of motivated patients he is treating:

You're talking to a biased sample. My primary emphasis is not substance abuse. My primary emphasis is on psychotherapy. Some of the people I see have substance abuse problems. I think I've been very successful. . . . The ones I treat do very well. There are specific criteria for treating them. They are motivated to make changes. They are open to the fact during the initial evaluation and can acknowledge the fact that substance abuse is playing a part in preventing their growth and hampering their life in some way. For those people, I have been very successful. I would say I have a very high cure rate, probably 80 percent or so.

According to this group of therapists, most treatment failures are with primary substance abusers and those who abuse cocaine or heroin. In these cases, a referral to a specialized substance abuse program is usually required. One therapist commented: "I think I've been very successful. It's much harder when you are dealing with a person who is a primary substance abuser, who gets sent to you because he has to be there. That's where the real therapeutic failures are." Another therapist spoke frankly about his frustration in treating some substance abusing patients:

> The failures I have to admit have been strictly substance abuse cases where I didn't know what to do with them. After five, ten, twenty sessions, they still kept coming in, sitting passively, just looking at me, and answering the questions I ask them with one word responses. They were not able to associate at all. I found myself forced into either tugging with questions or trying to lecture them about things. I've had to fill in the blanks in that way or sit in an awkward silence and stare at each other. It didn't happen a lot. But it was a specific substance–abusing personality with whom I would feel helpless and could not really do anything that would be helpful to them.

These therapists admitted their limitations and lack of success in treating those addicted to cocaine or heroin. One clinician reported: "In terms of true addiction, where I saw someone long enough to know it's there, there have only been three cocaine addicts. All of them lied to me about their use. . . . My success rate with cocaine is zero. Where it's been a major problem, I've never had a successful treatment. . . . I had one or two heroin users, but they didn't keep coming." A second therapist who has been working for nineteen years with the dually diagnosed stated: "I've not been able to work successfully with those addicted to cocaine in an outpatient setting. Day treatment or residential programs are alternatives." Another therapist also commented on the necessity of referring these patients to specialized programs: "I have not had much success in dealing with dual diagnosis when crack or cocaine are involved. I have to send them to a specialized program dealing with chemical dependency." Regarding heroin addicts, she said: "You have to send them to an inpatient setting or methadone setting where the addiction is controlled."

CRITERIA FOR SUCCESS
The Substance Abuse Problem

The therapists interviewed elaborated their criteria for success. Regarding the substance abuse problem, they look for the maintenance of sobriety in their patients, or at least a return to controlled drinking. One therapist stated: "I measure success by the number of people who remain sober, by the number of people I see out there that still write to me and say they have been sober so many years." Another clinician reported that she also uses sobriety as a measure of success: "Certainly, sobriety is a measure. If they can't stay sober, then I don't feel I have been successful in dealing with either diagnosis. So that's the bottom line." A third therapist related that he measures success by placing abstinence in the context of a general life enhancement: "I use general life enhancement more than just abstinence as a criterion for success. Again, for many of these people, because they are chronic alcoholics, abstinence is part of it because they can't drink socially." A fourth therapist related that sobriety is a criterion for him, but he does not discount the possibility of relapses:

> I do see maintaining sobriety as a criterion of success, but I don't see the relapse into drinking behavior as a failure of the treatment exactly. What I think I've really learned from the people being in AA is that a relapse means that they need AA and shouldn't stop those meetings. I don't take the responsibility for them being cured, anyway. I've seen other people who do well for a while, stop going to AA, then have a relapse and come back to me. They seem to do better when they see me and go to meetings once a week.

Several of the other therapists interviewed believe in the possibility of controlled drinking for some problem drinkers. While they may generally advocate sobriety for their patients, they recognize that some people may be able to reduce their drinking and improve the quality of their lives without embracing a commitment to lifelong abstinence. One clinician related that he looks for an arrest of the deterioration of life caused by the substance abuse: "Treatment success implies an arrest, at the very least, of the deterioration of life because of the addictive process. In virtually every case, even my non-successes would probably qualify for that degree of success, except for that group that leaves early on. Ideally, you want not just to arrest the deterioration, but to help people construct alternative forms of managing affects and seeking gratification." A second therapist, who also accepts controlled drinking as a goal of treatment, noted the difficulty of using abstinence as a measure of success:

> If you talk with people who go to AA about long-term goals, they say, "My goal is not to get drunk today. I take it one day at a time. I don't know if I'll stay sober tomorrow." How the heck do you measure outcome when their outcome criterion is one day at a time? They may have been doing it one day at a time and been sober for ten years and still doing it one day at a time. I understand that it's an important part of their philosophy, even though it does make it very difficult to measure outcome.

The Psychiatric Problem

In measuring success, these experienced clinicians are not satisfied solely with helping their patients achieve sobriety. They also look for an improvement in the overall quality of the person's life. They described this improvement in various ways, which reflect their theoretical orientations and views of human wholeness. One practitioner, who seeks a "general life enhancement" for his patients, noted that sobriety merely opens the door for change:

> In general, I look for more than just someone stopping drinking. If someone just wants to stop drinking, I tell him, "What are you seeing me for? There are more effective ways than coming to therapy. Therapy makes you want to explore your life and make significant changes." This is a common problem you see with a lot of substance abusers. They stop drinking and say, "My life is still lousy. I'm sober now, but I still don't get along with my wife

or like my job." You have to explain to them that the alcohol cessation opens up the door for changes. All it does is make change possible.

Another clinician remarked that for her the lack of serious impairment is an indication of success: "Beyond sobriety, I think success is when neither the patient nor I see serious impairment in any aspect of their lives. They generally feel pretty good about themselves. I'm reluctant to use the word *happy*, because for some people, their lives are such that there is not much happiness." A third therapist commented that success entails a quelling of anxiety: "With the dual diagnosis, success is reached, like one of my professors used to say, 'When the lion at the door has become a kitten.' The emotional stuff is not as important as it was, the anxiety is quelled, and life goes on. We're not going to make people perfect by any means." A fourth practitioner stated that for him successful treatment results in "the stability of the structure of their life, typically, in terms of their capacity to be self-sustaining and independent, their ability to maintain some gratifying relationships with other people, and to report a general satisfaction with the quality of their life." A fifth therapist reported that he looks at the global functioning of the patient: "Their global assessment scale functioning would be 80 to 85 when they leave. They're abstinent. Their family and work lives are stable. They are generally still on medication. Less than one percent come back because they are having problems. I attribute the success to the one-on-one work." A sixth clinician related that he uses qualitative issues regarding how a person is doing, rather than an improvement in their situation, as measures of success:

> My measure of outcome is not only their sobriety, but also the qualitative issues in their family relationships and on the job, recognizing that they can't control the behavior of others around them. Sometimes, if things are not going well in general, that's not necessarily a measure of failure. For example, I explain to a lot of women that if they come in and say they have a bad marriage now, that as they grow and become more independent, things in their marriage may become worse. I have to base my outcome criteria on how they are doing, rather than on how their situation is. Sometimes, the situation may in fact seem worse because the individual is doing better.

There are many different definitions of success, not only according to the theoretical orientation of the therapist, but also according to the depths of the goals of treatment. Of course, in the end, success is measured in terms of what the patient thinks he has accomplished: his specific goals, ongoing mood, coping skills in responding to crises and day-to-day situations. However, different levels of treatment goals can be distinguished. The first level is the elimination of the immediate symptoms, which can typically be accomplished in a few sessions. For example, an individual feels overwhelmed because of a breakup of a relationship. Through therapy, he comes to accept the loss of the relationship, to learn how he may have contributed to its ending, and to begin relating again to others. Such immediate, specific, and short-term goals are consistent with the brief therapies promoted in today's managed care environment. A second level is the restoration of a more satisfactory level of functioning after its loss through a gradual erosion. For example, a person has become increasingly depressed as he struggles to cope with the alcoholism of his spouse. Therapy might help him become more aware of his enabling role in their marriage, learn to set boundaries with his spouse, and focus more on his own needs and interests. A third level of treatment involves altering the individual's personality structure, which includes working through childhood traumas and their relationship with present functioning. Such personality change through therapy may take considerable time.

Treatment can be considered successful if the goals at any of these levels are accomplished to the satisfaction of the patient, even though the therapist may be aware that underlying problems still exist and may emerge at a later date. Every therapy reaches plateaus where the immediate symptoms recede and the immediate goals have been achieved. From this goal-centered perspective, even a single therapy session can be successful if the person gains something of value for his life.

LENGTH OF TREATMENT

The therapists interviewed reflected on the length of treatment required with their dual diagnosis patients. All agree that the treatment takes longer than with single diagnosis patients because both the substance use and psychiatric disorders must be addressed. Most of these clincians generally follow a long-term approach with their patients. Some are psychodynamic in orientation, willingly explore any issues that arise, and place no time limits on their treatment. For them, treating the dual diagnosis patient is not a great deal different than treating any other patient, unless the substance abuse is severe enough to interfere with therapy. In that case, treatment is postponed, and thus lengthened, until the substance use is controlled. Other therapists explicitly state the necessity of following a two part strategy in the treatment of the dually diagnosed patient, which also suggests a lengthening of the treatment. One clinician stated: "I look at it in terms of stages for most people. The first stage may be abstinence from cocaine or alcohol. The second stage may be to work on these underlying problems that make their lives unhappy or interfere with things." He recommended six months to a year of sobriety before working on other issues. One practitioner, a brief therapist, admitted that treatment is lengthened because two issues have to be addressed: "Because you're dealing with two issues, it takes longer to address. Plus, people who have substance abuse issues need a somewhat longer time in terms of follow-up to insure that they are using the tools they have learned to deal with the various problems that arise."

Several factors contribute to the lengthening of the treatment for the dually diagnosed. First of all, the assessment phase is complicated and prolonged because the signs and symptoms of both disorders can mask and mimic each other. It takes time and a period of abstinence before an accurate diagnosis can be made. Secondly, many of those seeking treatment are in denial regarding their substance abuse problem. They must first be persuaded of the necessity of addressing that issue before they can be actively engaged in treatment. Thirdly, patients should be abstinent from the use of substances for a period of six to twelve months before sensitive psychological issues can be addressed. The first part of treatment will inevitably focus on the substance-abuse problem and on establishing a drug-free lifestyle. Even after the sobriety is well established, the therapist needs to proceed slowly in exploring issues in order not to arouse too much anxiety, which may lead to a relapse. Fourthly, medications should be prescribed more cautiously to avoid adverse drug interactions and potential abuse. Such caution may also prolong the treatment. Fifthly, substance abuse is a chronic, relapsing disorder that requires a lengthy follow-up care. Finally, many of the psychiatric illnesses of the dually diagnosed are also chronic, relapsing disorders that will require long-term care.

The effective treatment of the dually diagnosed requires continuous care, sometimes lasting for years, particularly with those suffering a severe mental illness. In the present managed care environment, which restricts the length of treatment for cost-saving purposes, there is an obvious difficulty for the therapist who is seeking clinical effectiveness with his patients. The realistic clinician must learn to adjust his treatment approach to balance what is ideal with what is possible, given the limited resources at his disposal. For example, the therapist should liberally make referrals of his patients to twelve step support groups that address a variety of problems, such as substance abuse, agoraphobia, and sexual abuse. There are also other support groups in the community for the mentally ill and their families. The modern-day clinician needs to be well acquainted with the resources in his community to help those with emotional and mental problems. If long-term and intensive care is needed, the therapist can refer the patient to the community mental health system which has greater resources for their ongoing treatment. Furthermore, the therapist needs to budget well the use of therapy sessions. If a patient has a restriction on the number of sessions his insurance will pay for in a given year, the clinician can plan wisely the utilization of these sessions. He can schedule appointments more frequently when the problems are acute and space them out when the illnesses are under control. Patients may be willing and able to pay out-of-pocket to extend their coverage, and the therapist can propose this to them. Finally, the therapist needs to develop a realistic perspective in treating these patients and acknowledge his limits. The treatment he offers is just a moment in the patient's continuum of care. Ultimately, recovery is a lifelong process that is accomplished in the day-to-day living of the person. The clinician must merely respond as best he can to the *kairos*, the opportune moment when the individual is ready to address his problems and benefit from the therapist's interventions.

INPATIENT TREATMENT

III

16 BUILDING BRIDGES FOR ONGOING RECOVERY: THE INPATIENT SETTING

There is an increasing amount of literature on the treatment of the mentally ill substance abuser. Those dually diagnosed patients with severe mental illness present the clinician with the most complex treatment problems and require intensive and ongoing care in a variety of settings. When their psychiatric or substance abuse symptoms become acute and severe, they require treatment in an inpatient setting.

In the literature, two inpatient models are described. The first, the more common, is the separate dual diagnosis unit in a psychiatric hospital. Generally, the unit's program is a new creation through the integration of psychiatric and substance abuse treatment protocols. For example, Mowbray and colleagues (1995) describe in detail the dual diagnosis program at Northville Regional Psychiatric Hospital, a state-run facility located near Detroit, Michigan. The program provides specialized, coeducational treatment on two 30-bed wards. One ward is for briefer stays of about two weeks, while the other accommodates patients for longer periods. The program philosophy endorses the belief that both mental illness and substance abuse are biopsychosocial illnesses that require simultaneous treatment. Both disorders are addressed in an integrated fashion by a staff specifically trained to treat them. The program goals include the stabilization and preparation of the patients to achieve a lifelong recovery from both psychiatric and substance use problems. The well-structured and intensive program incorporates comprehensive treatment modalities to address a wide range of problems. Each patient has a primary therapist who provides individual therapy and monitors progress. A psychiatrist monitors detoxification and prescribes psychotropic medication when necessary. Group psychotherapy is provided daily along with a series of forty didactic lectures on a variety of topics associated with addiction and mental illness. Family education sessions and therapy are offered as needed. Two AA and NA meetings are scheduled each week. Daily activity therapy to help patients achieve a balanced lifestyle is also included in the schedule.

The second model is one in which an outside agency provides specialized substance abuse treatment on an already existing psychiatric unit. An example of this model is the consultation-liaison service at McLean Hospital, a 180-bed private teaching hospital at Harvard Medical School. Greenfield and colleagues (1995) describe the substance abuse consultation service offered to all the psychiatric inpatient units. An individual with expertise in substance abuse is assigned to each hospital unit to assess for addiction problems among the psychiatric patients, help with detoxification, and aid in determining the most appropriate aftercare program for the dually diagnosed patient. The consultant also leads inpatient dual diagnosis groups twice a week on each unit and provides educational material for both patients and staff. Since engagement in continuing treatment has been recognized as a critical problem with this population, the consultant establishes a bridge for the patient's involvement in the hospital's outpatient substance abuse program upon discharge.

Since the literature is replete with examples of inpatient programs for the dually diagnosed, this chapter will not offer another detailed program description. Instead, I will suggest some critical components for an effective inpatient program and some strategies for facilitating the transition of the dual diagnosis patient to the outpatient setting.

THE INPATIENT SETTING

The Dual Diagnosis Patient

There have been many studies of the type of dual diagnosis patient encountered on the inpatient setting, distinguishing him from the patient with a single psychiatric diagnosis. Kay and colleagues (1989) studied the diagnostic and behavioral characteristics of psychiatric patients who abuse substances. These researchers contrasted and compared two groups of patients from the Bronx Psychiatric Center, a 600 bed state psychiatric hospital in New York: a substance-abusing group and a nonsubstance-abusing group. There were 167 subjects in this study. Regarding behavioral characteristics, the researchers found that the substance-abusing psychiatric patients tended to be more suicidal, homicidal, destructive, and irresponsible, while their nonsubstance-abusing peers were significantly more bizarre, socially withdrawn, and functionally impaired. From a demographic and diagnostic perspective, the substance-abusing psychiatric patients were distinguished from their peers in that they were younger, hospitalized for briefer periods, more likely to be diagnosed with personality disorders, and less likely to be classified as schizophrenic.

In a larger, more recent study, Lehman and colleagues (1993) examined the characteristics of 314 patients from two inner city hospitals and a residential substance abuse treatment facility to determine the interactive effects of mental illness and substance abuse on the lives of hospitalized individuals. They divided this sample of patients into four groups for comparison. The first two groups were dually diagnosed with either 1) a primary Axis I mental disorder and a comorbid substance use disorder, or 2) a substance use disorder and substance–related mental disorder without a primary Axis I mental disorder. The other two groups had a single diagnosis, either 3) a primary mental disorder, but no lifetime substance use disorder, or 4) a current substance use disorder without a lifetime primary Axis I mental disorder. As expected, the results confirmed that the dually diagnosed patients have more adverse life circumstances than patients with single diagnoses. The dually diagnosed group with a primary mental disorder also had a higher percentage of men, a higher rate of anxiety disorders, and a higher overall rate of personality disorders than the group of single disordered patients with only a primary mental disorder. A comparison of the two groups of dual diagnosis patients showed that the first group with a primary mental illness were more likely to have schizophrenic and anxiety syndromes, less likely to have major depressive disorders, and more likely to be using marijuana. The second group with a substance-related mental disorder tended to be using opiates, cocaine, and polysubstances. Both groups had high rates of personality disorders. These authors suggest that different treatment strategies are required for patients with these different classifications of diagnoses.

There is an obvious difference in the type of dual diagnosis patient encountered in the inpatient and the outpatient settings. While those with substance abuse and dependence problems are found in both settings, those with a coexisting severe mental illness, particularly in phases of acute exacerbation, are treated within more intensive and restrictive environments, such as the inpatient, partial, and residential programs. As mentioned previously, those who are met and effectively treated in the outpatient or office setting are generally motivated and not suffering severe functional impairments. However, the line between the inpatient and outpatient settings should not be drawn too sharply because many of the severely impaired, once stabilized, can become engaged and treated effectively in the outpatient setting.

It is useful, though, to distinguish in a general way between two groups of the dually diagnosed who are most frequently encountered in different treatment settings. Director (1995) suggests distinguishing the groups according to whether or not the patient is psychotic. One group, composed of the mentally ill substance abuser (MISA), suffers from a psychotic mental disorder, principally schizophrenia, but also schizoaffective disorder or major affective disorder with psychotic features. These patients are encountered frequently on the inpatient services and generally require intensive and ongoing care in partial and residential programs. The second group of the dually diagnosed, in addition to substance abuse problems, suffers from nonpsychotic mental disorders, including depression, bipolar disorder, anxiety disorders, or personality disorders. Because these patients are usually less seriously impaired, they can be effectively treated on an outpatient basis. It should be noted that those with severe personality disorders are also encountered on the inpatient services, as the above studies indicate, particularly when they become suicidal or violent.

In summary, the dually diagnosed can be divided into four groups according to whether the patient is psychotic or not and whether he has a second diagnosis of substance abuse or dependence. A four-by-four matrix is formed in which the patient can be classified as 1) psychotic with substance dependence, 2) psychotic with substance abuse,

3) nonpsychotic with substance dependence, or 4) nonpsychotic with substance abuse.

Those who are psychotic with acute episodes of their mental illnesses are typically encountered in the inpatient setting. Their second diagnosis may be one of either substance abuse or dependence. In the outpatient setting, the dually diagnosed typically are not psychotic and have coexisting diagnoses of either substance abuse or dependence. In other words, the severity of the psychiatric problem, not the substance abuse problem, determines the patient's placement in the mental health setting, although it is generally recognized that psychiatric symptoms can be significantly exacerbated by the use of substances.

Treatment Goals

Individuals are admitted to the inpatient services when they are a danger to themselves or others or show signs of mental illness rendering them incapable of caring for themselves. Many of those who enter the hospital today are suicidal and require 24-hour care in a protective environment. It is commonly recognized that persons with substance abuse problems tend to be depressed, impulsive, and at high risk of succeeding with suicide. The literature also shows that the dually diagnosed tend to act out in destructive, threatening, and even violent ways and require a restricted environment for their safety and the safety of others. However, as the number of psychiatric hospital beds decreases around the country and the number of prison cells increases proportionately, research is showing that the prison system is being flooded with the dually diagnosed who are unable to control their acting out behaviors.

TABLE 16–1   Groups of Patients According to the Diagnoses of the Disorders

		Substance Use Disorder	
		Dependence	Abuse
	Psychotic	1	2
Psychiatric Disorder			
	Nonpsychotic	3	4

Many of the dually diagnosed are so impaired by their illnesses that they are unable to care for themselves. They may have few social and economic supports. Often their families are unable to care for them or have abandoned them altogether. Because of their disabilities and lack of interpersonal skills, they have few, if any, friends. They also lack the psychological stability to maintain employment and support themselves. A growing body of research is showing that a large number of the most severely impaired dually diagnosed are homeless and jobless. Some of these individuals are immersed in the drug culture and find a home there. They are caught up into a web of addiction that they cannot break alone. The hospital provides a safe place for these individuals where their basic needs are met, their disorders can be stabilized with medications, and they can be taught some social and drug-free coping skills. Finally, many of the dually diagnosed suffer from severe health problems from their substance abuse. The hospital provides medical care as needed, particularly detox from drugs.

In short, the first goal of inpatient treatment is to stabilize the severe exacerbations of the symptoms of both the psychiatric and substance use disorders. This entails a careful assessment for both disorders, detoxification, the initiation of an effective medication regimen, the maintenance of an initial period of sobriety, increased self-awareness regarding both disorders, a reduction in denial regarding the disorders, improvement in social skills, and development of drug-free coping skills.

One of the main disadvantages of the inpatient program is that it necessarily creates an artificial environment, which protects extremely vulnerable people, but which cannot be continued indefinitely. What is learned in the hospital needs to be tested and lived out in the real world. It is the experience of those who work in this setting that many patients relapse within hours after discharge. Therefore, an essential goal of inpatient treatment is to motivate and prepare patients for continuing recovery after discharge and help them make the transition to community life. One therapist, who has worked for many years with the dually diagnosed and helped create a dual diagnosis unit, stated:

> The inpatient is for those whose problems are more severe and extensive. Outpatient treatment is more important for long-term success and recovery. Sometimes, there is the expectation that if

the patient participates in an inpatient program that the problem will be solved. Sometimes, the best we can do in an inpatient setting is get the person motivated and prepared for long-term outpatient treatment. Inpatient keeps them alive and stabilized for work in the outpatient. Philosophically, you have to get people to assume personal responsibility for behavior changes.

Treatment Principle Sixteen: Once the dually diagnosed patient has been stabilized, the goal of inpatient treatment is to motivate and prepare him for the continuing recovery from both disorders in the outpatient setting.

PROGRAM COMPONENTS

Engagement

Those working with the mentally ill substance abusing population have identified four phases of treatment: engagement, persuasion, active treatment, and relapse prevention (Minkoff 1989). Since many of these severely impaired individuals do not recognize their need for treatment, clinicians, as an initial step, must develop strategies for engaging them in the treatment process. Next, because these patients are frequently unmotivated to commit themselves to a life of sobriety, the therapist needs to address the denial and persuade the person to work on recovery. Once the patient has admitted a substance abuse problem, the phase of active treatment can begin. Finally, once the patient has become committed to a life of sobriety, the clinician can focus on teaching the person relapse prevention strategies.

Mowbray and colleagues (1995) have observed that while this stage theory is useful conceptually, it has little clear applicability on an inpatient setting. For any given patient, the stages are not absolute, and there is great variability among patients in how they progress through the stages. Some skip stages; others shift between stages; still others revert back to issues from previous stages. The variability among patients in passing through these stages makes it impractical to design a program around such a deceptively clear-cut stage theory.

Nevertheless, the inpatient environment presents many occasions for engaging the resistant patient. First of all, some patients are hospitalized on an involuntary basis. Because they may be a danger to themselves or others, coercion into treatment becomes necessary and even life saving. In this case, the individual is forcibly engaged in treatment. The clinicians can help the patient transform his motivation and recognize his need for help once the immediate crisis has passed. Secondly, through respect, patience, and understanding, those who work with the patients can develop a trusting therapeutic relationship that can help motivate them to work on issues. In this regard, it is critical that those who work with the dually diagnosed honestly face their own countertransference issues and remain nonjudgmental. Finally, it is generally recognized that emotional confrontations with the dually diagnosed are ineffective and even harmful. In the inpatient setting, patients can be educated about their illnesses in a nonthreatening way that may gently lead them to embrace the help offered.

A Dual Focus

As in the outpatient setting, it is necessary to address both the psychiatric and substance use disorders from the beginning and throughout treatment. Typically, patients are admitted into the hospital because of an acute and severe exacerbation of one or both of the disorders. Of course, the more threatening problem must be the focus of therapeutic attention, and sometimes, both disorders must be treated aggressively at the same time. If the individual's withdrawal is causing a medical emergency, that must be addressed immediately. If a person is profoundly depressed and suicidal, antidepressant medication should not be withheld. If there are floridly psychotic symptoms, medication can be given to stabilize the patient while observation continues in order to determine the precise etiology of the psychotic symptoms.

Throughout the hospital stay, the staff should maintain attention on both the substance use and psychiatric disorders. They should also present to the patient in clear, simple, and concrete terms the nature of his problem and what he needs to do about it. Many of these patients are so cognitively impaired from their illnesses that they must be addressed in clear and simple language, and important information must be repeated often. One therapist, who works with the severely impaired dually diagnosed in a public hospital, stated:

My model was always this, and I would repeat it time after time: "You suffer from two disorders. You have a diagnosis that fits each disorder. That's why you're here: not just for one, but for both. If you see yourself as mentally ill and not drug addicted, you won't make it. If you see yourself as alcohol dependent and not mentally ill, you won't make it either." I do it rigidly, authoritatively, after I'm convinced it's true that they have a dual diagnosis, in order to convince them it's true. I make it as clear and simple as possible. I know it's hard for them to accept the diagnosis.

The clinician must then explain precisely what the patient needs to do to address both disorders.

Assessment

In the inpatient setting, there is the same need as in the outpatient setting to assess fully for both substance use and psychiatric disorders from the beginning and throughout treatment. In many ways, the whole assessment process is easier in the hospital setting and can be more thorough. First of all, there is more time to observe and interact with the patient in an environment free from external influences. Since the patient is kept in an abstinent state on the unit, the clinician can observe the emerging symptoms without the complicating influence of drugs. As noted previously, symptoms of intoxication and withdrawal can mask and mimic many psychiatric disorders; conversely, many psychiatric symptoms can disguise an underlying substance abuse problem. For example, someone high on cocaine may appear to be suffering from a paranoid psychosis; the paranoia may not remit for several hours after use. Often an accurate diagnosis cannot be made until the person has been abstinent for a period of time. However, it should be kept in mind that in many instances the normally brief hospital stay does not afford sufficient time to make a final diagnosis. For example, those experiencing a protracted alcohol withdrawal syndrome may be anxious and depressed and have mood swings for many months after abstinence and appear to be suffering from an affective disorder.

A second advantage in the inpatient setting for the process of assessment is the availability of the family for collateral sources of information regarding the patient. Most often, the patient is accompanied by a family member to the emergency room or hospital for admission. The clinician has the opportunity to interview the family member and obtain more information about the patient. Frequently, the patient is too distraught or impaired to report accurately what is happening in his life and provide personal information. The family member can offer another valuable perspective, particularly regarding the patient's current drug use, substance abuse history, and family background.

Thirdly, patients being admitted to the hospital often have a previous history of psychiatric treatment. Their records are readily available and can be another valuable source of information. However, one therapist offered a caution in reviewing these records:

> In an inpatient setting, the majority of these patients come with a well-established psychiatric history. It's the new people who are the challenge. The mental illness diagnosis is generally pretty accurate. However, the diagnosis of the addictive disorder may have been missed right along and needs to be assessed more carefully. In contrast, in the substance abuse treatment setting, the substance abuse diagnosis is well established, and the psychiatric diagnosis needs to be carefully assessed.

Two recent studies underline the need for the clinician to make a particularly careful assessment for an addictive disorder. Ananth and colleagues (1989) undertook a study to assess the extent to which the diagnosis of substance abuse was missed in psychiatric patients admitted to a state hospital. Seventy-five patients were interviewed and diagnosed by three groups: the referring university hospitals, the state hospital psychiatrist, and the research team. The research team diagnosed 54 of the 75 patients with a substance use disorder and documented 187 separate diagnoses of drug abuse, ranging from alcohol abuse to cocaine dependence. However, the emergency room personnel made only four diagnoses of substance abuse, while the hospital psychiatrists assessed only 29 substance use disorders in this group of patients. In a more recent study, Milling and colleagues (1994) reviewed the medical records of 200 adult inpatients for their diagnoses and treatments. Forty-three percent of the patients admitted to the hospital were found to have a history of substance abuse, but a third (31.4%) of these had never received a formal diagnosis of a substance use disorder. Only half of those with a substance abuse diagnosis had documented evidence that they received any treatment for their drug problem.

A final advantage for assessment is that the inpatient setting affords the time for psychological testing. A standard battery of psychological tests, such as the MMPI and Rorschach, can be given to clarify personality dynamics. In the case of those who have abused substances for a long period of time, neuropsychological deficits may also be in evidence. One therapist, who is a neuropsychologist and has twenty years experience treating the dually diagnosed, recommended testing: "Because I have more time with them, I might also do some neuropsychological testing. At a minimum, I look at their problem-solving abilities and memory function. I use the Categories Test, Trails B, the Wechsler Memory Scale, and Connor's Continuous Performance Test to measure attention. We are testing for the key areas affected in brain damaged individuals who have experienced toxicity." A clear awareness of the patient's strengths and weaknesses determined through testing can aid in treatment planning.

Addressing Denial

Just as in the outpatient setting, once a substance abuse problem is diagnosed, the staff must begin to address the patient's denial for the treatment to progress. Frequently, the clinician in the inpatient setting needs to undertake a persuasion process that begins with the assessment and may last the entire hospital stay of the patient. Previous hospital records may alert the staff to the presence of a substance use disorder, even though the patient may minimize his drug use. The clinician may confront the patient with this discrepancy and begin educating the individual regarding the signs, symptoms, and progression of addiction. As soon as he is convinced of the accuracy of his diagnosis, the therapist should present to the patient in clear and simple terms the findings of his assessment and what the patient needs to do to address this problem. Of course, the patient may be resistant to the diagnosis, and the therapist should avoid arguing or taking a confrontative approach to the patient's denial. A gentle, objective, and educative approach works best. One experienced therapist observed: "If you do hard, direct confrontation in an outpatient setting, the patient just doesn't come back. If you do it on an inpatient setting, they don't come back either. They are there physically, but you lose them emotionally and mentally."

In order to treat effectively the substance abuse problems of the patient, the staff needs to address their own denial and counter-transferential issues. The staff, who are usually better trained to treat psychiatric disorders, may overlook substance abuse problems and perceive them as secondary to the seemingly more severe psychiatric problems, especially such a serious illness as schizophrenia. They may even develop a nonchalant attitude towards the drinking of the patient because they are so focused on treating the psychiatric disorder.

One notable difference between inpatient and outpatient treatment is that individuals with severe mental illness frequently deny their psychiatric problems, and their denial of their mental illness also needs to be addressed through educational efforts. There is a great social stigma surrounding mental illness, and individuals may be frightened to admit that they are "crazy." One therapist, who has worked for many years on a dual diagnosis unit, noted: "Many patients would love to be mentally ill, because if they are not an addict, they can continue drinking and drugging. Others would rather be an addict, because that's the source of their whole problem. All they have to do is stop using, and they won't be crazy and different from other people. So we have to have our patients accept both disorders, and that's hard to do."

Addressing denial is much easier in an inpatient setting than an outpatient setting. It takes longer in an office setting. One of the problems is that if the patient feels at all threatened, he can skip appointments or withdraw from treatment altogether. If he is using or bingeing, he will not come to sessions, particularly if he knows the therapist will confront the issue. However, in an inpatient setting, the patient cannot physically withdraw from treatment, and his denial can be addressed in a more intensive manner.

There are three treatment components for addressing denial intensively in the inpatient setting. First of all, in individual therapy sessions the clinician can help the patient see the relationship between his substance use and problems in living. They can also explore the relationship between the substance abuse and the psychiatric disorder as it plays itself out in the person's life. The patient's resistance about admitting being addicted or mentally ill can also be addressed. Secondly, the dynamics of group therapy and twelve step meetings are powerful forces in breaking down denial in a supportive context. Some patients are reluctant to speak honestly about their drug use within groups of nonusers for fear of being judged or penalized. However, in a group of fellow addicts, they may feel freer to speak, and those who have accepted their addiction are particularly adept at spotting and confronting the denial of their fellow users. The most effective groups are those in which the therapist assumes the role of facilitator of the group, encouraging interaction among all the members. If patients interact with each other, the interventions will be much more powerful than if made by the therapist. Thirdly, intensive educational sessions about both disorders and their interaction are effective means of addressing the denial. A variety of instructional modalities, such as video presentations, live lectures, and group discussions, helps keep the patients interested and involved in the learning process that gradually leads to the acceptance of the need for treatment.

Medications

Caution and clinical sensitivity need to be exercised in prescribing medications. While the severity of the psychiatric problems calls for aggressive pharmacological treatment, the risk of dangerous drug interactions and of encouraging other addictions necessitates a restrained approach. One therapist described the balanced approach to prescribing medications employed on his dual diagnosis unit:

> We provide a modified drug-free environment. That's different from the typical psychiatric or substance abuse setting. Substance abuse settings are usually totally drug free. Most have the philosophy that if you use meds, you are not in recovery. So we educate them about their problems and why they are on medication. We do use some medications that are traditionally used in psychiatric treatment, like antipsychotics, antidepressants, and mood stabilizers. We do not use, if at all possible, the anxiolitics, the benzodiazepines, for either sleep or anxiety reduction. That means we may have a more agitated kind of patient. The exception is that we might use a benzodiazepine with an acutely psychotic or acutely agitated patient to calm him down. We would be careful about the rein-

forcing effects of those minor tranquilizers. Patients may act up just to get an injection. We have to monitor that carefully. We would use this medication only briefly. We do not use addictive narcotic drugs, pain killers. If they require pain medication, they will be on the medical unit. We would like to have all patients drug free if possible, or at least have them on the lowest dose possible. We tend to undermedicate patients compared to other psychiatric facilities. That means we may keep patients there longer.

One of the greatest problems with the dually diagnosed, which persists in aftercare, is medication compliance. The inpatient staff needs to develop strategies that will encourage compliance upon discharge. One clinician described how the staff makes contracts with patients to facilitate compliance:

> Because we are a public mental health facility and don't have to deal with insurances, we can keep patients longer and make deals with them. If a patient is resistant to taking medication because he is not sure of his mental illness, we can make a contract with him. "OK, we'll make a deal and see how you do over the next two weeks. If you are still depressed and suicidal after that time, then we'll begin meds." So they have some control over their own treatment and may have to stay longer. Or we will have a patient who has been on a neuroleptic medication because he has shown signs of psychosis. Now he is on the medication and doesn't like it and wants to stop taking it. We'll try to reduce his medication or take him off it with the agreement that if he decompensates, then he will go back on the medication. We get better compliance this way. We also try to educate them about medication.

Twelve Step Groups

An essential component of a dual diagnosis program is the inclusion of twelve step groups. Such groups have proven over time to be one of the most effective tools for addressing denial and maintaining abstinence for substance abusers. However, as mentioned previously, those with a dual diagnosis often have difficulty becoming engaged in these groups. The dually diagnosed frequently have difficulty interacting in social settings and are extremely sensitive to rejection. Members of twelve step groups may not understand mental illness and be intolerant of the erratic and sometimes bizarre behavior of the dually diagnosed. They may also discourage these patients from taking their psychotropic medications because of their belief that recovery entails abstinence from all mood-altering drugs.

Since participation in twelve step groups will be important for the ongoing recovery of the dually diagnosed after discharge from the hospital, the staff should prepare the patients for involvement in these groups. Several strategies can aid in building bridges for the utilization of AA or NA meetings. One approach towards familiarizing the dually diagnosed with AA and adapting the program to suit their needs is to conduct "panel meetings" on the ward. One therapist described the evolution of this type of meeting:

> The panel meetings evolved when those in NA discovered that they could not use their traditional approach with psychiatric patients. Rather than letting everybody talk or have a single speaker, they brought in a panel of speakers. Instead of one person talking for 45 minutes, you have three people talking for ten or fifteen minutes each. There might also be a discussion of issues with the audience. You won't find the term "panel meeting" in the literature, but that is what people unofficially are calling it. It's not an open meeting, but it's more directed and seems to work with the more severely impaired dual diagnosis patient.

A second strategy is to invite people who are more advanced in recovery to speak to the patients on the ward about their experience. One clinician explained how he uses recent program graduates as speakers: "At the hospital, we invited one of our successful graduates who was able to use AA to come back to the unit every Friday morning and talk about his experience with AA. It was part of our educational series, 'Introduction to Self-Help.' This person was able to come in and identify with the patients and help to build bridges."

A third approach to encouraging and preparing for twelve step involvement is through making referrals to carefully selected groups in the community. Some AA or NA groups have shown themselves to be more amenable than others in welcoming the dually diagnosed and respecting their treatment plans, including the use of medication. One therapist stated:

> Some groups were ready and others not for dual diagnosis patients. Some are quite tolerant of psychotic people. The major issue from the beginning was medication. Patients would be told to get off their medication, stop taking their meds, and then relapse into their

psychosis. Then they would relapse into their addiction and be back where they started. Certain groups were accepting. In the network, we tended to know where those groups were. The recovering staff and the patients would get around and know where they would be accepted. More recently, there have been Double Trouble groups exclusively for dual diagnosis patients. However, there are not enough of them.

Abstinence

The treatment goal for the mentally ill substance abuser is complete abstinence from all nonprescription drug use. However, the clinician cannot expect these patients to abstain totally until they have a network in place to support that abstinence: the family, twelve step groups, and individual and group therapy. Controlled drinking does not appear to be a realistic goal for this population for several reasons. Many of these patients will have to take psychotropic medication for the rest of their lives. Drinking or drug use can interfere with the effectiveness of these meds and may even cause dangerous interactions. These patients often have a low tolerance level and do not have to drink much to get intoxicated and into trouble. The temptation is always great to choose their drug of choice rather than their prescribed medication to cope with the dysphoria of their psychiatric conditions. Finally, these patients have demonstrated limited insight and impaired judgment. It may be extremely difficult for them to titrate their drug use without causing problems for themselves.

The staff should make it clear to patients from the beginning that the goal of treatment is complete abstinence. The dangers of attempts at controlled drinking should also be explained. Kofoed (1993) employs a useful image in explaining to his patients the need for sobriety. He distinguishes between reliable control and complete loss of control. Many substance abusers believe that they have at least some control over their drinking. However, an honest look at their experience shows that their control is unreliable, that at unexpected times they drink more than they intend and suffer adverse consequences. In speaking with his patients, Kofoed compares attempts at controlled drug use to throwing matches on a pile of rags in the attic. Any given match may not ignite the rags, but using a single match is a risk because it may ignite the rags and burn down the house.

An advantage of inpatient care is that abstinence is enforced, and the patient is given an experience of sobriety. Because of the instability of these patients, it is important that abstinence be closely monitored with regular drug screens. One clinician described the routine of using screens on his dual diagnosis unit:

> We do random drug screens on a daily basis. One patient is screened each day by lottery, so everyone has the chance of being screened at least once during their stay. We screen everyone at admission. If we find contraband, we may screen everyone, or just that hallway, or just that room. That's decided by the team. If someone goes on a leave and is not escorted by staff, he is screened when he returns. If it's dirty, he has to start the program over. If someone elopes, he is automatically screened when he is brought back.

Family Involvement

Family involvement is crucial for sustaining the recovery of the patient upon discharge from the inpatient setting. The more genuinely supportive the family is of the patient, the better the prognosis. If some family members are relatively healthy themselves, they can provide the structure, support, and guidance needed by these patients who are so fragile and unstable. However, it is often difficult to engage family members on behalf of the patient because of the problems the patient has caused in their lives. The patients may have stolen from family members to support their drug habit, or their behavior may have been so erratic and threatening that their relatives have withdrawn from them. Furthermore, these patients often come from dysfunctional families in which substance abuse and mental illness are rampant. Since research demonstrates such a strong genetic association of both mental illness and substance abuse, it is not surprising to find many sick family members among the dually diagnosed. One clinician commented: "Sometimes we have had the families come up on a Saturday and discovered that the patient was right. Their mother was crazy, and not them. We've even had security take family members away and have them petitioned because they were so disruptive."

Nevertheless, any connections that the staff can create between patient and family will help to build bridges for ongoing recovery. In the inpatient setting, there is more opportunity for family involvement because the patient is captured and a structured program is in place. Staff can facilitate family involvement in several ways. First of all, family members should be interviewed when the patient is admitted to provide additional information. Frequently, the patient is unable to give an accurate history, and the family members can fill in the blanks. Such an interview will also make it clear how much the patient's illness reflects a family pathology that reaches back many generations.

Secondly, family members can be invited to the hospital for educational sessions to learn more about mental illness and substance abuse and how they have been personally affected by the patient's problems. The family can also learn how they may have inadvertently contributed to the patient's problems by their enabling behavior. It is admittedly difficult to get family members to attend Al Anon meetings to aid in their own recovery because they often fail to recognize the substance abuse diagnosis and tend to think of the problems as belonging only to the patient.

Thirdly, therapy sessions can be conducted with the patients and their families. These family meetings provide excellent opportunities for creating supportive networks for the patient and for aftercare planning. One therapist related his experience of family meetings in the hospital lobby:

> When the family comes, it is a big boost for the patient. Sometimes there would be a large group of people, and it would be like a family outing. Because children were not allowed on the ward, we would have sessions in the lobby so everyone could be there. Sometimes a brother of the patient would be the major support and show up, especially in the African-American community. This brother is bonded and would allow the patient to come live in his house. Then we would set up conditions and rules that the patient would agree to and even sign.

Relapse Prevention

While some of the dually diagnosed are unable to recognize their addiction problems, others have been in treatment before for substance abuse, admit their problem with drugs, and continue struggling to maintain sobriety. These patients do not need to be persuaded that they have a drug problem. Instead, they need to be taught skills to help them keep from relapsing. For these patients, it is beneficial to include group relapse prevention training. In such groups, people can discuss openly what thoughts, feelings, and circumstances led to their return to substance use. Through interaction with other group members who share their experiences, patients become more aware of their individual vulnerabilities and of the external events that trigger relapses. A trained professional should lead the group and facilitate the interaction of the participants. The leader can offer educational material on the relapse chain described previously. He can also teach the participants skills to manage distressing affects, to respond to cravings, and to counter social pressures to drink or use drugs. In short, this group is a problem-solving group for those in recovery.

Success

Not surprisingly, the success rate of treatment among the mentally ill substance abusers encountered in the inpatient setting is significantly lower than of those treated solely in the outpatient setting. One clinician, who works in a large public mental health facility, reported:

> The success rate with the dual diagnosis population in that setting is not real high. We tend to be dealing with chronic patients who have lost a lot of their support. We also did not have good contacts with outpatient programs. Generally, we just see the failures when they come back. You don't know who is making it. Are they dead or clean and sober? It's a good sign if they stay away. You don't get that feedback. If they come back, they tell you they have not relapsed in two years. The only other feedback is out of the twelve step community. The report comes back that this person is clean and sober, coming to meetings, and active in the network. I would estimate the success rate at 10 to 20 percent.

It is extremely difficult to measure accurately the success rate with this population. These patients are often noncompliant with both treatment and research and difficult to track down for followup study. Most are chronic patients who never fully recover, although some attempts have been made to measure improvements in the quality of their lives. For example, as noted previously, Jerrell and Ridgely (1995) have developed a comprehensive set of outcome criteria for this population. Two concrete and practical measures of success with this population that can be used for research are the number of, and length of time between, hospitalizations. These patients can be followed up fairly easily if they continue to live in the same catchment area and are served by the same public facility.

Experience shows that the success rate even with the chronic patients increases if the continuity of care is maintained in the outpatient setting. The more the program can facilitate the transition to the community from the inpatient setting, the greater will be the success rate. If patients can be engaged with outpatient therapists, twelve step groups, drug-free housing, and other step-down programs, their recoveries will have a greater chance of continuing. In the long run, comprehensive and consistent treatment will guarantee the highest recovery rate.

In summary, there are several ways that inpatient programs can build bridges for the ongoing recovery of the dually diagnosed:

1. By engaging the patient in the treatment process,
2. By effectively addressing the patients' denial and persuading them of the need for continuing treatment,
3. Through educational efforts regarding both disorders and the necessary steps in treating them,
4. By preparing patients to participate in twelve step programs,
5. Through involving the family in treatment,
6. By teaching relapse prevention and stress management strategies.

AFTERCARE PLANNING

Individual Therapy

There are several approaches for continuing the treatment of the mentally ill substance abuser after discharge from the hospital. Involvement in an ongoing recovery program is crucial for these chronic patients to remain stable and relatively functional. The first approach, through individual therapy, has been elaborated in the previous chapters. With this more severely impaired population, sessions may have to be scheduled more frequently than once a week, particularly in times of stress when their sobriety and emotional stability are tested. Because these patients are so impaired mentally and emotionally, therapists will need to be even more supportive, directive, and educational than with their more functional clients. Both the substance use and psychiatric disorders will need to be addressed in therapy with a particular emphasis on the importance of medication compliance. The extent to which the patient will be able to participate in twelve step programs will have to be evaluated by the clinician on an individual basis.

Engaging the dually diagnosed in outpatient treatment is particularly difficult. Inpatient programs can facilitate the involvement of the patient in outpatient therapy by having the therapist meet the patient before discharge and take the first step toward establishing a therapeutic alliance. In some programs, clinicians split their time between the inpatient and outpatient services. In that case, patients can continue to meet with the same therapist after discharge. The advantage in this arrangement is that a therapeutic relationship is already established, which facilitates the continuity of treatment.

Group Therapy

A second approach is with group therapy, which is the most common treatment modality in intensive outpatient and day hospital programs. Kofoed and colleagues (1986) evaluated the treatment outcomes of thirty-two mentally ill substance abusers who participated in an outpatient pilot program designed for the dually diagnosed that used group therapy. The patients began treatment in weekly assessment groups where they learned about dual disorders and their management and the requirements and benefits of the ongoing recovery program. The initial focus was on symptom control, medication compliance, and the need for abstinence. After this phase of initiation and persuasion, patients attended special hour-and-a-half weekly support groups which addressed both disorders. They were also encouraged to participate in twelve step programs. Abstinence was monitored by random drug screens, and Antabuse was routinely used. The success of this innovative program with these difficult patients was modest, but significant, suggesting that some of these severely impaired patients can be engaged effectively in ongoing treatment. While two-thirds (21) of the patients dropped out within two months, a third (11) remained for three months or more; of these, seven remained for one year or more. Treatment retention was associated with reduced hospital utilization.

The inpatient use of groups that are sensitive to the unique needs of the dually diagnosed can facilitate the transition to outpatient groups. Nigam and colleagues (1992) describe some essential ingredients for a successful relapse prevention group approach with the dually diagnosed. They suggest that the therapist assume an active stance with the group and begin with a small number of patients, about three or four. Abstinence is a goal, rather than a requirement for admission, although attending the group intoxicated is clearly forbidden. Good communication with the patients' primary therapists and case managers is fostered in an effort to coordinate treatment. Group members are encouraged to discuss openly any lapses to substance abuse and to participate in twelve step programs. The emphasis during the meetings is on psychoeducation regarding both disorders and skill-building to avoid relapses.

Case Management

A third followup approach is for case managers to help patients utilize the programs and supports within the community that they need to continue their recovery (Kline et al. 1992). In this model, case managers assertively link patients to existing substance abuse and mental health programs. Their role is also to expedite referrals through advocacy and careful client tracking and to establish and maintain collaborative relationships with these various service programs. Frequently, case managers have to educate various organizations about the specific needs of the dually diagnosed.

Unfortunately, the work of the case managers is complicated by the lack of available resources for the integrated treatment of the dually diagnosed. Mowbray and colleagues (1995) enumerate some of the problems. Besides the lack of dual diagnosis programs, both mental health and substance abuse programs are frequently overcrowded and unable to accommodate new patients on a timely basis. Discharged patients may have to wait several weeks to get an appointment at some agencies. Patients can become discouraged and revert to previous substance abuse patterns before the initial appointment. Specialized medical services to treat the frequent complications of prolonged drug use are scarce. There is also a lack of suitable housing for the dually diagnosed. Some residential programs for the mentally ill exclude those with substance abuse problems, while others take no steps to support the abstinence of their clients. Some residential programs for substance abusers discourage their clients from taking medications, even if they are prescribed by a physician. Programs providing employment and vocational rehabilitation services for the dually diagnosed are also needed, but many patients end up receiving disability income, are forgotten, and never participate in these programs.

Intensive Outpatient/Day Treatment

Intensive outpatient and day treatment are transitional programs between inpatient and outpatient services. These programs contain many of the elements of inpatient treatment in a less intensive form. Individual therapy, group therapy, and didactic sessions are provided. Furthermore, patients live at home and commute to the facility, providing a link between everyday life and treatment. Connor and colleagues (1995) describe a partial hospitalization program for mentally ill chemically abusing patients developed at the University of Rochester Medical Center-Strong Memorial Hospital. Patients attend the program four-and-a-half hours a day, five days a week, for nearly two months. Most treatment is delivered in a group format, although weekly individual therapy is also provided. Abstinence is a goal, not a prerequisite, for the program, and is monitored through random drug screens. Didactic groups focus on issues regarding addiction, depression, anxiety, medications, and physical health. Patients are also taught social skills, relapse prevention strategies, and stress management techniques in various groups. AA or NA attendance is strongly encouraged, but not required; reasons for not attending are explored individually and in groups to help motivate participation. Families are involved in the treatment process through weekly multifamily groups. Finally, as patients progress through the program, aftercare plans are regularly discussed, and appropriate referrals are made.

Residential Settings

Research shows that a large proportion of the most severely impaired dually diagnosed are homeless. A psychologist who works on a dual diagnosis unit perceptively described the rootless situation of many of these patients:

> Frequently, when people come out of a psychiatric hospital setting, they do not have a place to go; they're homeless. They might just go to a rented room in a drug-ridden environment. Or their home environment is not supportive of recovery from psychosis. Or they may go into CMH settings that are not drug free. Sometimes pushers come into the building, and the staff is part of the business. I've had patients who even before they were settled in their beds were met by a pusher. They were using even before they got to a meeting.

Therefore, a crucial need for many of these patients upon discharge is for suitable housing that will support their ongoing recovery.

Unfortunately, suitable housing for the dually diagnosed is in short supply. On the one hand, some chemical dependency halfway houses are so adamant about abstinence from all mood-altering drugs that they either expressly forbid the use of prescribed medications or subtly discourage such use. On the other hand, many halfway houses or group homes for the mentally ill offer little support for maintaining the abstinence of the residents and even have explicit policies banning the acceptance of substance-abusing clients. Patients who have a history of suicidal and violent behavior are often shunned in both of these settings because of the responsibility they place on the facilities that accept them.

Some attempts are being made to provide suitable housing for the dually diagnosed. For example, McLaughlin and Pepper (1992) describe a residential dual diagnosis program that was developed by incorporating mental health services into a traditional addiction setting at Harbor House in the Bronx, New York. Harbor House is a forty-five bed facility that was originally created for homeless drug abusers with a major mental illness. A mental health treatment team works with the drug abuse counselors in providing services for the clients. The mental health staff prescribe and monitor psychiatric medications and provide individual therapy as needed. They also sit in on the group counseling sessions conducted by the substance abuse counselors. The therapeutic approach is much less confrontative than in typical addiction settings. However, residents are expected to remain alcohol and drug free during their entire stay. Compliance is monitored by regular urine testing. A positive test or a refusal to be tested is grounds for immediate discharge. In short, the program is designed to support the patient's recovery from both disorders.

In summary, many approaches are being developed for the ongoing treatment of the mentally ill substance abuser:

1. Individual therapy that focuses on both disorders;
2. Group therapy that is psychoeducational and supportive in nature;
3. Case managers that can assertively link patients with substance abuse and mental health programs within the community;
4. Comprehensive day hospital programs that provide support and structure;
5. Residential settings that respect and support the patient's need for abstinence from drugs and compliance with medications.

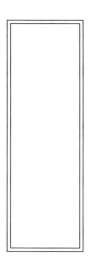

EPILOGUE: BUILDING BLOCKS FOR A TREATMENT MODEL

SIXTEEN TREATMENT PRINCIPLES

Several authors propose principles of treatment for dually diagnosed patients. They have formulated these principles primarily from their experience of working with the severely mentally ill substance abuser in inpatient settings (Drake et al. 1993, Minkoff 1989, 1992, Osher and Kofoed 1989, Ridgely et al. 1987, Zimberg 1993). From my personal experience of working with the dually diagnosed, my discussions with therapists experienced in treating this population, and from my reading of the literature, I have arrived at sixteen treatment principles for the treatment of the dually diagnosed in the outpatient setting. These principles, elaborated fully in the previous chapters and summarized here, can serve as building blocks for an integrated treatment model for the dually diagnosed.

Treatment Principle One: The effective treatment of most dual diagnosis patients requires some modification of techniques and an integration of treatment approaches from both the mental health and substance abuse fields.

Because of the substance abuse problem, therapists need to learn from substance abuse professionals strategies for addressing that issue and become more active and directive, more supportive, and more educationally oriented. Furthermore, they need to employ twelve step groups and use medications differently. Because of the presence of the coexisting psychiatric disorder, however, clinicians cannot incorporate without modification the approaches of the addictions specialist. They need to avoid being too rigid and confrontational in working with these patients. They must also allow for the use of appropriate medications and employ protected environments as needed. If they are too demanding and confrontative, they may raise anxiety in the patient and precipitate either a return to drug use or a premature termination on the part of the patient. Therapists need to tailor their approach according to the individual needs of the patient, cognizant of the patient's personality dynamics and fragility because of their psychopathology.

Treatment Principle Two: It is necessary to address both the psychiatric and substance use disorders from the beginning and throughout treatment.

If the substance abuse problem is ignored or overlooked, the effective treatment of the psychiatric disorder will be compromised because of the cognitive, emotional, and functional impairment caused by continued drug use. If the psychiatric problem is not addressed, there is an increased risk that the patients will continue using drugs or relapse in order to cope with their unresolved problems.

Treatment Principle Three: While maintaining attention on both the substance use and psychiatric disorders, the therapeutic focus ought to shift to address the more severe or threatening disorder.

The therapist must remain flexible in shifting his therapeutic focus according to the individual needs of his patient. This requires an ongoing and sensitive assessment of both disorders. If the substance abuse problem is recognized as severe, it is necessary to focus therapeutic attention on stabilizing the patient and helping him achieve abstinence before work can begin on the mental health problem. Acute withdrawal can cause a medical emergency and must be taken care of immediately. A life threatening situation could occur if the person is not detoxed. There are several reasons to focus first on a severe drug problem. Uncontrolled drug use interferes with the patient's capacity to participate competently in the treatment process. Treating the psychiatric problem before sobriety is well established may raise anxieties that can lead to an increase in substance use. Furthermore, the therapist's allowing the continued drug use may also contribute to the patient's enabling system. If the drug problem is severe, more structure and support than is offered in an outpatient setting may be required. The clinician may have to refer the patient to a physician for detoxification and/or to an inpatient or intensive outpatient substance abuse program.

If the psychiatric problem is more severe than the substance abuse, it should be addressed first. Patients who are actively psychotic, suicidal, or homicidal need immediate attention and may have to be hospitalized until their condition is stabilized before treatment can begin on their substance abuse problem. They may also need medication for the ongoing management of their psychiatric disorder. If both the addiction and psychiatric problem are severe, they will both need to be treated aggressively, most likely in an inpatient setting, until the conditions are stabilized.

Treatment Principle Four: It is necessary to assess fully for both substance use and psychiatric disorders with every patient from the beginning and throughout treatment.

This principle emphasizes taking a full psychiatric and substance abuse history and being particularly sensitive to the patterns of drug use which patients tend to deny or minimize. Since most psychologists have limited training in substance abuse treatment, it is imperative that they learn to discern the signs and symptoms of abuse. Because of the prevalence of patients with coexisting conditions, they should maintain a high index of suspicion regarding the possibility of a drug problem with every patient and inquire directly about their drug use.

Treatment Principle Five: The assessment process must be ongoing because an accurate diagnosis for both disorders may take time.

Because substance abuse masks and mimics many psychiatric disorders, it may be difficult to diagnose accurately the true nature of

the psychiatric disorder. It will be unclear whether the observed symptoms are primary or secondary to the substance use. A period of abstinence, ranging from a few weeks to a year, may be necessary to arrive
at a final diagnosis. Diagnosing the substance abuse disorder may be
difficult because of the patient's tendency to resist admitting a drinking or drug problem. It may take time for the therapist to build a
therapeutic relationship with the patient before the patient will trust
him enough to reveal the extent of his drug use.

Treatment Principle Six: Once a substance abuse problem is diagnosed, the
therapist must begin to address the patient's denial for treatment to
progress.

The process of breaking down denial begins at assessment with
informing the patient clearly of the substance abuse diagnosis and
attempting to include the cessation or curtailing of drug use in the
treatment plan. Normally, an addicted person does not make his own
insightful diagnosis at the beginning of treatment. The clinician will
need to undertake a process of persuasion to convince the patient of
the validity of his diagnosis. If the therapist does not help the patient
see the negative consequences of his drug use, it is not likely that the
person will admit the problem and begin the recovery process. If the
substance abuse problem is not addressed and the individual does not
achieve a measure of sobriety, the treatment of the psychiatric disorder will not progress to a successful conclusion.

It should be noted that the dually diagnosed who suffer from
severe mental illness may deny their psychiatric problem because of
the stigma associated with it. Their denial of their mental illness needs
to be addressed through education.

Treatment Principle Seven: Therapists must assess the suitability of treating
the dual diagnosis patient in the outpatient setting, and if necessary,
make an appropriate referral.

An implicit self-selection process occurs for the patient who comes
to outpatient therapy. The outpatient setting works well with those
people who are motivated to change and able to control their acting
out behaviors. Individuals who cannot tolerate the relatively unstruc-

tured nature of the outpatient setting or the pressure to explore and discuss anxiety-provoking issues and make personal changes generally withdraw from therapy. Therefore, clinicians need to evaluate the stability and motivation of their patients. If their patient's psychiatric disorder is so severe that he cannot contain his acting out behavior, a referral to a psychiatrist for medication or to a psychiatric hospital may be necessary. If their patient's substance abuse problem is primary or so severe that he cannot control his drug use, a referral to a substance abuse specialist, inpatient program, or to a physician for medical clearance and detox may be called for.

Treatment Principle Eight: Care must be exercised in prescribing medication for the dually diagnosed; the benefits and risks need to be evaluated for every case.

If the patient continues abusing substances, there are significant risks in prescribing medications. The therapeutic effectiveness of these medications may be reduced, and adverse drug interactions may result. Particular care must be exercised in prescribing medications with an addictive potential so that another addiction does not develop or a "pill-taking" mentality be reinforced. Before prescribing medications, the patient should be abstinent and involved in a recovery program for his drinking or drug use problem. Contrary to the view of some substance abuse specialists, it may be helpful and necessary to prescribe medications for patients with thought disorders and serious affective disorders. The therapist should consult only physicians and psychiatrists who are knowledgeable about addiction medicine.

Treatment Principle Nine: Participation in twelve step support groups is an effective complement to individual therapy with the dually diagnosed.

There has been a long-standing antagonism between Alcoholics Anonymous and traditional therapy. AA members have accused therapists of ignoring drug problems and colluding with the denial of their substance-abusing patients. Therapists have accused AA of reducing all the drinker's problems to alcohol abuse. However, the effective treatment of the dual disorders may require both participation in twelve step groups, which have shown themselves to be effective means of resocializing alcoholic and drug abusing individuals into a sober lifestyle, and involvement in therapy to address the psychiatric disorders that coexist with or underlie the drug problem. Since the dually diagnosed may be psychologically fragile or resistant to participating in a group, the therapist may have to prepare them for involvement in AA/NA or offer some alternative means of support in addressing their substance abuse problems. If patients receive confusing messages from AA or NA regarding the treatment of their psychiatric disorders, the therapist needs to clarify any misunderstandings and integrate the treatment of the disorders.

Treatment Principle Ten: Immediate and total abstinence should not be required for the dually diagnosed patient to participate in treatment. As a short-term goal, the clinician may expect a reduction and gradual control of the drug using behavior.

Typically, individuals come to a therapist in the mental health setting because of the pain caused by their psychiatric disorders and are not seeking help for a problem with drinking or drugs. The clinician needs to discover that there is a substance abuse problem. Usually, the individual is resistant to recognizing a drug problem, and the therapist must begin a persuasion process in addressing the denial. If the therapist were to demand abstinence immediately, in all likelihood the patient would withdraw from treatment. Furthermore, these patients may be using the substance to cope with intolerable pain caused by their psychopathology. A lessening of the anxiety through the therapeutic relationship may be necessary before the patient is ready to admit and work toward giving up this coping mechanism. In cases where the abuse of substances is severe, the clinician may need to be more directive and insist on abstinence before the treatment can proceed effectively. As a short-term goal and as a condition for treatment to continue, the clinician may expect a reduction and gradual control of the drug-using behavior. Nevertheless, the therapist should state clearly the need for complete abstinence as a long-term goal.

Treatment Principle Eleven: It is useless and counterproductive to the treatment to meet with an intoxicated patient to explore issues.

In a state of intoxication, the individual is incapable of participating actively and productively in therapy. If the patient comes to a session intoxicated, it is necessary that the therapist point out the inappropriateness of the behavior and terminate the session. To continue the session would acknowledge in action the acceptability of the substance abusing behavior and reinforce the patient's enabling system. At a later date, it is helpful to explore with the patient the circumstances and reasons for the drug use.

Treatment Principle Twelve: The dual diagnosis patient is particularly vulnerable to relapses into drug use because of the destabilizing effect of the psychiatric disorder; concommitantly, psychiatric problems are exacerbated by drug use and may worsen.

The dually diagnosed are always at risk of relapsing into substance abuse when the symptoms of their mental health condition worsens. In the case of the mentally ill substance abuser, they are also vulnerable to relapse in their psychiatric condition if they return to drug use. Consequently, the therapist must always be monitoring the patient for relapse symptoms and recognize that relapses are a frequent occurence in the recovery process. If a relapse occurs, the clinician should attempt to prevent the isolated episode of drinking or drug use from developing into a full-blown relapse. To accomplish that, the clinician should treat the patient with compassion and understanding when relapses happen because of the heavy burden of shame the person already bears. Relapses can become learning experiences for the patient if the therapist helps him explore the thoughts, feelings, behaviors, and circumstances surrounding his return to drug use. The therapist can also help the patient become aware of his symptoms of impending relapse in order to avoid a future return to substance use. Continued and frequent relapses may alert the therapist to the possibility of a dual diagnosis that is not being adequately addressed or to the patient's need for a more intensive level of care.

Treatment Principle Thirteen: While the therapist focuses the treatment efforts on the dual diagnosis patient, the family can be involved to help support his recovery.

Both substance abuse and mental illness, in addition to being individual pathologies, are family illnesses. The family is profoundly affected by the problems of the dually diagnosed member, and family members often contribute to maintaining his condition. Therefore, the comprehensive treatment of the dually diagnosed requires the involvement of the family. Even though the clinician forms a therapeutic relationship with the dually diagnosed patient, he can invite the family to assist in providing information for an accurate diagnosis and in supporting the ongoing recovery of the patient. The more severe the condition of the patient, the more the family will be needed to provide support and structure for his ongoing recovery. Family members will also need assistance from the clinician for their own recovery from the debilitating effects of living with an alcoholic or substance-abusing individual. Without compromising the boundaries of the treatment with the patient, the therapist can provide marital and family sessions as needed, education regarding codependency, and referrals to self-help groups and other therapists.

Treatment Principle Fourteen: There are occasions when the therapist must initiate a termination of treatment for therapeutic reasons because uncontrolled drug use will eventually disrupt the treatment if allowed to continue.

Since continued and excessive drug use causes significant emotional and cognitive impairments, the non-abstinent patient has a compromised ability to participate in the treatment process and explore issues. Consequently, if the patient continues to abuse substances and adamantly refuses to admit a drug problem or do anything to help himself, the therapist may need to initiate a termination of treatment. Warning about the possibility of termination is also a way of confronting the patient's denial, making him aware of the unacceptable consequences of his continued drug use. To continue therapy would be supportive of the patient's denial and ultimately become a frustrating and self-defeating experience for both the therapist and patient.

Treatment Principle Fifteen: Successful treatment is measured by a decrease or elimination of symptoms of both the psychiatric and substance use disorders.

Continued substance abuse will eventually sabotage the gains from the relief of emotional distress accomplished through therapy. It will also interfere with the effectiveness of prescribed medication and lead to a relapse in the psychiatric disorder. Continued emotional distress and disturbing thoughts will eventually precipitate a relapse in drug use in order to self-medicate. Therefore, therapists need to set as goals for treatment both the maintenance of sobriety and the improvement of the overall quality of the person's emotional and mental life.

Treatment Principle Sixteen: Once the dually diagnosed patient has been stabilized, the goal of inpatient treatment is to motivate and prepare him for the continuing recovery from both disorders in the outpatient setting.

Since both substance abuse and mental illness are chronic relapsing diseases, recovery is a lifelong process. Inpatient treatment is a brief moment in the necessary continuity of care when the patient's symptoms are severe and acute. After being stabilized in the hospital, the patient will need to continue the work of recovery in the outpatient setting, often for an extended period of time. Programs in the hospital can serve as valuable bridges for involving the discharged patient in outpatient treatment and in community life. Those in denial of their problems are initiated into a persuasion process regarding their dual diagnosis and offered support. Those who have admitted their problems are prepared for, and put into contact with, community resources that will aid them in the ongoing work of recovery.

CONCLUSION

While the work of developing effective treatment models for the dually diagnosed has begun in earnest, it is still in its infancy. Several authors have suggested an elaborate and comprehensive research agenda that remains for the task of improving the quality of service for this neglected population. For example, in their review of the literature, Ridgely and colleagues (1986) recommend continuing research on three tiers: the population, the patient, and the programs that serve them. They call for longitudinal treatment outcome studies that measure the best "interactive fit" between patient, provider, and the care system. More recently, Nunes and Deliyannides (1993) propose several fruitful areas of research. A more precise elaboration of the possible interactive relationships between various substance use and mental disorders is called for. According to them, more research is also needed to develop diagnostic instruments that will systematically elicit information regarding the onset and relative courses of both disorders. Finally, treatment protocols for the various dual diagnoses need to be developed and measured for their effectiveness.

What will be needed throughout the arduous work of constructing effective treatment models is the continued collaboration of clinicians from both the mental health and addiction treatment fields. Today, there is a new openness and willingness to listen and learn from each other among those in these disciplines. The effective treatment of the dually diagnosed depends on the ongoing dialogue that has been initiated. Clinicians from both fields need to continue meeting and exchanging experiences, information, methods, and strategies for working with this population. They need to work together in developing integrated treatment models in a variety of settings. It is hoped that this book will be at least a modest contribution and stimulus towards continuing the dialogue.

REFERENCES

The AA Member: Medications and Other Drugs. (1984). New York: AA World Services.

Adelman, S. A., Fletcher, K. E., and Bahnassi, A. (1993). Pharmacotherapeutic management strategies for mentally ill substance abusers. *Journal of Substance Abuse Treatment* 10:353–358.

Alcoholics Anonymous: The Big Book. (1976). 3rd ed. New York: AA World Services.

American Psychiatric Association. *Diagnostic and Statistical Manual of Mental Disorders*, 3rd ed. rev. Washington, D.C.: American Psychiatric Association, 1994.

Ananth, J., Vandewater, S., Kamal, M. et al. (1989). Missed diagnosis of substance abuse in psychiatric patients. *Hospital and Community Psychiatry* 40:297–299.

Anthenelli, R. M. (1994). The initial evaluation of the dual diagnosis patient. *Psychiatric Annals* 24:407–411.

Bachrach, L. L. (1982). Young adult chronic patients: an analytic review of the literature. *Hospital and Community Psychiatry* 33:189–197.

Baranckie, K., Crits-Christoph, P., and Kurcias, J. (1992). Therapist techniques used during the cognitive therapy of opiate dependent patients. *Journal of Substance Abuse Treatment* 9:221–228.

Bartels, S. J., Drake, R. E., and Wallach, M. A. (1995). Long-term course of substance use disorders among patients with severe mental illness. *Psychiatric Services* 46:248–251.

Baxter, L. R., Schwartz, J. M., Phelps, M. F. et al. (1988). Localization of neurochemical effects of cocaine and other stimulants in the human brain. *Journal of Clinical Psychiatry* 49:23–26.

Bean-Bayog, M. (1988). Alcoholism as a cause of psychopathology. *Hospital and Community Psychiatry* 39:352–354.

Bell, C. M., and Khantzian, E. J. (1991). Drug use and addiction as self-medication. In *Dual Diagnosis in Substance Abuse*, ed. M. Gold and A. Slaby, pp. 185–204, New York: Marcel Dekker.

Bolo, P. M. (1991). Substance abuse and anxiety disorders. In *Dual Diagnosis in Substance Abuse*, ed. M. Gold and A. Slaby, pp. 45–56, New York: Marcel Dekker.

Brower, K. J., Blow, F. C., and Beresford, T. P. (1989). Treatment implications of chemical dependency models: an integrative approach. *Journal of Substance Abuse Treatment*, 6:147–157.

Brown, S. (1985). *Treating the Alcoholic: A Developmental Model of Recovery.* New York: John Wiley.

Carroll, K. M., Rounsaville, B. J., and Gawin, F. H. (1991). A comparative trial of psychotherapies for ambulatory cocaine abusers: relapse prevention and interpersonal psychotherapy. *American Journal of Drug and Alcohol Abuse* 17:229–247.

Cermak, T. L. (1986). *Diagnosing and Treating Co-Dependence.* Minneapolis: Johnson Institute Books.

Ciolino, C. (1991). Substance abuse and mood disorders. In *Dual Diagnosis in Substance Abuse*, ed. M. Gold and A. Slaby, pp. 105–116. New York: Marcel Dekker.

Cohen, J., and Levy, S. J. (1992). *The Mentally Ill Chemical Abuser: Whose Client?* New York: Lexington Books.

Connor, K. R., Silverstein, S. M., McCullock Melnyk, K. A., and Maxey, J. T. (1995). The development of a partial hospitalization program for mentally ill chemically abusing (MICA) patients. *Journal of Substance Abuse Treatment* 12:311–318.

Corty, E., Lehman, A. F., and Myers, C. P. (1993). Influence of psychoactive substance use on the reliability of psychiatric diagnosis. *Journal of Consulting and Clinical Psychology* 61:165–170.

Dackis, C. A., and Gold, M. S. (1991). Psychopathology resulting from substance abuse. In *Dual Diagnosis in Substance Abuse*, ed. M. Gold and A. Slaby, pp. 205–220. New York: Marcel Dekker.

Daley, D., Moss, H., and Campbell, F. (1987). *Dual Disorders: Counseling Clients with Chemical Dependency and Mental Illness.* Center City, MN: Hazelden.

Director, L. (1995). Dual Diagnosis: outpatient treatment of substance abusers with coexisting psychiatric disorders. In *Psychotherapy and Substance Abuse*, ed. A. M. Washton, pp. 375–393. New York: Guilford.

Drake, R. E., Bartels, S. J., Teague, G. B. et al. (1993). Treatment of substance abuse in severely mentally ill patients. *Journal of Nervous and Mental Disease* 181:606–611.

Drake, R. E., and Wallach, M. A. (1989). Substance abuse among the chronic mentally ill. *Hospital and Community Psychiatry* 40: 1041–1046.

Emrick, C. (1982). Evaluation of alcoholism psychotherapy methods. In *Encyclopedic Handbook of Alcoholism*, ed. E. Pattison and E. Kaufman, pp. 1152–1169. New York: Gardner.

Engel, G. L. (1977). The need for a new medical model: a challenge for biomedicine. *Science* 196:129–136.

Evans, K., and Sullivan, J. M. (1990). *Dual Diagnosis: Counseling the Mentally Ill Substance Abuser.* New York: Guilford.

First, M. B., and Gladis, M. M. (1993). Diagnosis and differential diagnosis of psychiatric and substance use disorders. In *Dual Diagnosis: Evaluation, Treatment, Training, and Program Development*, ed. J. Solomon, S. Zimberg, and E. Shollar, pp. 23–37. New York: Plenum.

Flores, P. J. (1988). *Group Psychotherapy with Addicted Populations.* New York: Haworth.

Freud, S. (1914). On narcissism. *Standard Edition* 14:67–104.

Gawin, F. H., and Kleber, E. H. (1986). Abstinence symptomatology and psychiatric diagnosis in cocaine abusers: clinical observations. *New England Journal of Medicine* 43:107–113.

Giannini, J., and Collins, G. (1991). Substance abuse and thought disorders. In *Dual Diagnosis in Substance Abuse*, ed. M. Gold and A. Slaby, pp.57–74. New York: Marcel Dekker.

Greenfield, S. F., Weiss, R. D., and Tohen, M. (1995). Substance abuse and the chronically mentally ill: a description of dual diagnosis treatment services in a psychiatric hospital. *Community Mental Health Journal* 31:265–276.

Hall, R. C., Popkin, M. K., DeVaul, R., et al. (1977). The effect of unrecognized drug abuse on diagnosis and therapeutic outcome. *American Journal of Drug and Alcohol Abuse* 4:455–465.

Hanson, M., Kramer, T. H., and Gross, W. (1990). Outpatient treatment of adults with coexisting substance use and mental disorders. *Journal of Substance Abuse Treatment* 7:109–116.

Imhoff, J., Hirsch, R., and Terenzi, R. (1984). Countertransferential and attitudinal considerations in the treatment of drug abuse and addiction. *Journal of Substance Abuse Treatment* 1:21–30.

Jellinek, E. M. (1954). Phases of alcohol addiction. *Quarterly Journal of Studies on Alcohol* 13:673–684.

———— (1960). *The Disease Concept of Alcoholism.* New Haven: Hillhouse.

Jerrell, J. M., and Ridgely, S. M. (1995). Evaluating changes in symptoms and functioning of dually diagnosed clients in specialized treatment. *Psychiatric Services* 46:233–238.

Kadden, R. M., and Penta, C. R. (1995). Structured inpatient treatment: a coping-skills training approach. In *Psychotherapy and Substance Abuse*, ed. A. M. Washton, pp. 295–313. New York: Guilford.

Kaufman, E. (1989). The psychotherapy of dually diagnosed patients. *Journal of Substance Abuse Treatment* 6:9–18.

———— (1994). *Psychotherapy of Addicted Persons.* New York: Guilford Press.

Kaufman, E., and McNaul, J. (1992). Recent developments in understanding and treating drug abuse and dependence. *Hospital and Community Psychiatry* 43:223–236.

Kaufman, E., and Reoux, J. (1988). Guidelines for the successful psychotherapy of substance abusers. *American Journal of Alcohol and Drug Abuse* 14:199–209.

Kay, S. R., Kalathara, M., and Meinzer, A. (1989). Diagnostic and behavioral characteristics of psychiatric patients who abuse substances. *Hospital and Community Psychiatry* 40:1062–1064.

Kessler, R., McGonagle, K., Zhao, S. et al. (1994). Lifetime and 12 month prevalence of *DSM-III-R* psychiatric disorders in the United States: results from the National Comorbidity Survey. *Archives of General Psychiatry* 51:8–19.

Khantzian, E. J. (1980). The alcoholic patient: an overview and perspective. *American Journal of Psychotherapy* 34:4–19.

—— (1981). Some treatment implications of the ego and self disturbances in alcoholism. In *Dynamic Approaches to the Understanding and Treatment of Alcoholism*, eds. M. Bean and N. Zinberg, pp. 163–188. New York: Free Press.

—— (1985a). Psychotherapeutic interventions with substance abusers—the clinical context. *Journal of Substance Abuse Treatment* 2:83–88.

—— (1985b). The self-medication hypothesis of addictive disorders: focus on heroin and cocaine dependence. *American Journal of Psychiatry* 142:1259–1264.

—— (1986). A contemporary psychodynamic approach to drug abuse treatment. *American Journal of Drug and Alcohol Abuse* 12:213–222.

Khantzian, E. J., Halliday, K. S., and McAuliffe, W. E. (1990). *Addiction and the Vulnerable Self.* New York: Guilford.

Kline, J., Harris, M., Bebout, R. R., and Drake, R. E. (1992). Contrasting integrated and linkage models of treatment for homeless, dually diagnosed adults. In *Dual Diagnosis of Major Mental Illness and Substance Disorder*, ed. K. Minkoff and R. Drake, pp. 95–106. San Francisco: Jossey-Bass.

Kofoed, L. (1992). Assessment of comorbid psychiatric illness and substance disorders. In *Dual Diagnosis of Major Mental Illness and Substance Disorder*, ed. K. Minkoff and R. Drake, pp. 43–55. San Francisco: Jossey-Bass.

—— (1993). Outpatient vs. inpatient treatment for the chronically mentally ill with substance use disorders. *Journal of Addictive Diseases* 12:123–137.

Kofoed, L, Kania, J., Walsh, T., and Atkinson, R. M. (1986). Outpatient treatment of patients with substance abuse and co-existing psychiatric disorders. *American Journal of Psychiatry* 143:867–872.

Kushner, S. F. (1991). Substance abuse and neurological disorders. In *Dual Diagnosis in Substance Abuse*, ed. M. Gold and A. Slaby, pp. 75–104. New York: Marcel Dekker.

Lehman, A. F., Myers, C. P., and Corty, E. (1989). Assessment and classification of patients with psychiatric and substance abuse syndromes. *Hospital and Community Psychiatry* 40:1019–1025.

Lehman, A. F., Myers, C. P., Thompson, J. W., and Corty, E. (1993). Implications of mental and substance use disorders: a comparison of single and dual diagnosis patients. *Journal of Nervous and Mental Disease* 181:365–370.

Lishman, W. A. (1987). 2nd ed. *Organic Psychiatry: the Psychological Consequences of Cerebral Disorder.* London: Blackwell Science.

Marlatt, G. A. (1985). Relapse prevention: theoretical rationale and overview of the model. In *Relapse Prevention*, ed. G.A. Marlatt and J.E. Gordon, pp. 3–70. New York: Guilford.

McCrady, B. S. (1987). Implications of neuropsychological research findings for the treatment and rehabilitation of alcoholics. In *Neuropsychology of Alcoholism*, ed. O. A. Parsons, Butters, N., and Nathan, P. E. New York: Guilford.

McLaughlin, P., and Pepper, B. (1992). Modifying the therapeutic community for the mentally ill substance abuser. In *Dual Diagnosis of Major Mental Illness and Substance Disorder*, ed. K. Minkoff and R. Drake, pp. 85–93. San Francisco: Jossey-Bass.

Meyer, R. (1986). How to understand the relationship between psychopathology and addictive disorders: another example of the chicken and the egg. In *Psychopathology and Addictive Disorders*, ed. R. Meyer, pp. 3–16. New York: Guilford.

Milling, R. N., Faulkner, L. R., and Craig, J. M. (1994). Problems in the recognition and treatment of patients with dual diagnosis. *Journal of Substance Abuse Treatment* 11:267–271.

Millman, R. B. (1986). Considerations of the psychotherapy of the substance abuser. *Journal of Substance Abuse Treatment* 3:103–109.

Minkoff, K. (1989). An integrated treatment model for dual diagnosis of psychosis and addiction. *Hospital and Community Psychiatry* 40:1031–1036.

——— (1992). Program components of a comprehensive integrated care system for serious mentally ill patients with substance disorders. In *Dual Diagnosis of Major Mental Illness and Substance Disorder*, ed. K. Minkoff and R. Drake, pp. 13–27. San Francisco: Jossey-Bass.

Minuchin, S., Montalvo, B., Guerney, B. et al. (1967). *Families of the Slums.* New York: Basic Books.

Mowbray, C. T., Solomon, M., Ribisl, K. M. et al. (1995). Treatment for mental illness and substance abuse in a public psychiatric hospital. *Journal of Substance Abuse Treatment* 12:129–139.

Newman, M. (1991). Substance abuse and anorexia nervosa and bulimia nervosa. In *Dual Diagnosis in Substance Abuse,* ed. M. Gold and A. Slaby, pp. 117–126. New York: Marcel Dekker.

Nigam, R., Schottenfeld, R., and Kosten, T. R. (1992). Treatment of dual diagnosis patients: a relapse prevention group approach. *Journal of Substance Abuse Treatment* 9:305–309.

Nunes, E. V., and Deliyannides, D. A. (1993). Research issues in dual diagnosis. In *Dual Diagnosis: Evaluation, Treatment, Training, and Program Development,* ed. J. Solomon, S. Zimberg, and E. Shollar, pp. 287–309. New York: Plenum.

Oepen, G., Levy, M., Saemann, R. et al. (1993). A neuropsychological perspective on dual diagnosis. *Journal of Psychoactive Drugs* 25:129–133.

Osher, F. (1989). The dually diagnosed: patient characteristics and treatment strategies. *Community Support Network News* 5:1–11.

Osher, F., and Kofoed, L. (1989). Treatment of patients with psychiatric and psychoactive substance abuse disorders. *Hospital and Community Psychiatry* 40:1025–1030.

Parsons, O. A., and Farr, S. P. (1980). The neuropsychology of alcohol and drug use. In *Handbook of Clinical Neuropsychology,* ed. S. Filskon and T. Boll, pp. 320–365. New York: John Wiley.

Peele, S. (1985). *The Meaning of Addiction.* Lexington, MA: Lexington Books.

Pepper, B., Kirshner, M. C., and Ryglewicz, H. (1981). The young adult chronic patient: overview of a population. *Hospital and Community Psychiatry* 32:463–469.

Rawson, R. (1995). Is psychotherapy effective for substance abusers? In *Psychotherapy and Substance Abuse,* ed. A. M. Washton, pp. 55–75. New York: Guilford.

Regier, D. A., Farmer, M. E., Rae, D. S. et al. (1990). Comorbidity of mental disorders with alcohol and other drug abuse. Results from the Epidemiologic Catchment Area (ECA) Study. *Journal of the American Medical Association* 264: 511–2528.

Resnick, R. B., and Resnick, E. B. (1984). Cocaine abuse and its treatment. *Psychiatric Clinics of North America* 7:713–729.

Richards, H. J. (1993). *Therapy of the Substance Abuse Syndromes.* New Jersey: Jason Aronson.

Ridgely, M. S., Goldman, H. H., and Talbott, J. A. (1986). *Chronic Mentally Ill Young Adults with Substance Abuse Problems: A Review of Relevant Literature and Creation of a Research Agenda.* Baltimore: University of Maryland School of Medicine, Mental Health Policy Studies Center.

Ridgely, M. S., Osher, F. C., and Talbott, J. A. (1987). *Chronic Mentally Ill Young Adults with Substance Abuse Problems: Treatment and Training Issues.* Baltimore: University of Maryland School of Medicine, Mental Health Policy Studies Center.

Ries, R. (1993a). Clinical treatment matching models for dually diagnosed patients. *Psychiatric Clinics of North America* 16:167–175.

——— (1993b). The dually diagnosed patient with psychotic symptoms. *Journal of Addictive Diseases* 12:103–122.

——— (1994). *Assessment and Treatment of Patients with Coexisting Mental Illness and Alcohol and Other Drug Abuse.* Rockville: U.S. Department of Health and Human Services.

Rollnick, S., and Morgan, M. (1995). Motivational interviewing: increasing readiness for change. In *Psychotherapy and Substance Abuse*, ed. A. M. Washton, pp. 179–191. New York: Guilford.

Rounsaville, B. J., Glazer, W., Wilber, C. H. et al. (1983). Short term interpersonal psychotherapy in methadone maintained opiate addicts. *Archives of General Psychiatry* 40:629–636.

Rounsaville, B. J., Spitzer, R., and Williams, J. (1986). Proposed changes in *DSM-III* substance abuse disorders: description and rationale. *American Journal of Psychiatry* 143:463–468.

Schmidt, L. (1991). Specialization in alcoholism and mental health residential treatment: the dual diagnosis problem. *The Journal of Drug Issues* 21:859–874.

Schuckit, M. A. (1986). Genetic and clinical implications of alcoholism and affective disorders. *Journal of American Psychiatry* 143: 140–147.

Steinglass, P., Bennett, L. A., Wolin, S. J., and Reiss, D. (1987). *The Alcoholic Family.* New York: Basic Books.

Wallace, J. (1985). 2nd ed. Working with the preferred defense structure of the recovering alcoholic. In *Practical Approaches to Alcoholism Psychotherapy*, ed. S. Zimberg, J. Wallace, and S. B. Blume. New York: Plenum.

Wallen, M. C., and Weiner, H. D. (1989). Impediments to effective treatment of the dually diagnosed patient. *Journal of Psychoactive Drugs* 21:161–168.

Warner, L. A., Kessler, R. C., et al. (1995). Prevalence and correlates of drug use and dependence in the United States. *Archives of General Psychiatry* 52:219–229.

Washton, A. M. (1989). *Cocaine Addiction: Treatment, Recovery, and Relapse Prevention.* New York: Norton.

Way, B. B., and McCormick, L. L. (1990). *The Mentally Ill Chemical Abusing Population: A Review of the Literature.* Albany: Bureau of Evaluation and Services Research, New York State Office of Mental Health.

Wegscheider, S. (1981). *Another Chance: Hope and Health for the Alcoholic Family.* Palo Alto: Science and Behavior Books.

Woody, G., Luborsky, L., McLellan, A. T. et al. (1983). Psychotherapy for opiate addicts. *Archives of General Psychiatry* 40:639–645.

Woody, G. E., McLellan, A. T., Luborsky, L., et al. (1984). Severity of psychiatric symptoms as a predictor of benefits from psychotherapy: the Veteran Administration–Penn Study. *American Journal of Psychiatry* 141:1172–1177.

Wurmser, L. (1984). More respect for the neurotic process: comments on the problem of narcissism in severe psychopathology, especially the addictions. *Journal of Substance Abuse Treatment* 1:37–45.

——— (1987). Flight from conscience: experiences with the psychoanalytic treatment of compulsive drug abusers. *Journal of Substance Abuse Treatment* 4:157–168.

Zimberg, S. (1985). Principles of alcoholism psychotherapy. In *Practical Approaches to Alcoholism Psychotherapy*, ed. S. Zimberg, J. Wallace, and S. Blum, pp. 3–18. New York: Plenum.

——— (1993). Introduction and general concepts of dual diagnosis. In *Dual Diagnosis: Evaluation, Treatment, Training, and Program Development*, ed. J. Solomon, S. Zimberg, and E. Shollar, pp. 3–21. New York: Plenum.

Zweben, J. E. (1986). Recovery oriented psychotherapy. *Journal of Substance Abuse Treatment* 3:255–262.

INDEX

in dual diagnosis patients, 10–11,
58–60, 249–250
effects of, 39–41, 60–62, 184–187,
223–226
interaction with psychiatric disorders,
37–50, 84, 86, 194, 201
referrals to facilities, 133–144,
238–239
treatments for, 14–15, 56–58,
76–81
Substance abuse therapists. *See*
Addiction therapists
Sugar addiction, 143
Suicidal tendencies, 149, 251
and family involvement, 219, 220
referrals for, 150–151, 158–159
Sullivan, J. M., 105
Support
by families, 33, 200, 213–214,
219–221, 263–264
for families, 219
social, 136, 188
of therapist, 55–56, 113, 121–122,
162, 188, 202–203
through twelve step program,
169–170, 200
and treatment settings, 136, 252,
263–264
Support groups, 71, 244. *See also*
Twelve step programs
Symptoms, 9, 52
interactions of, 7, 28, 34, 74, 78,
101–102, 255
of withdrawal, 41, 102–103, 161

Termination, initiating, 223–234
Testing, 95
neuropsychological, 60–61, 257
Therapeutic alliance, 175
building, 17, 129–130
and disclosure of substance abuse,
84, 96, 97, 100, 163, 209
and families of patients, 213,
219–220
and giving up substance abuse,
121–122

with inpatients, 254, 267
trust in, 228–230
Therapists, 7, 31–32, 183
addressing denial of, 110–112
and primacy of disorders, 43–48,
67–81
recognition of limits, 233–234, 244
responses of, 23–24, 85–86,
201–204
self-examination before termination,
232–234
treatment models of, 8, 51–52
Therapy, 17–19, 155. *See also* Group
therapy
and AA, 167, 171, 176–181
anxiety in, 160, 200
individual, 248, 258–259, 266–267,
269
need for sobriety in, 184–187
for substance abusers, 14–15, 23–
24
and type of drugs, 137–144
Thought disorders, medications for,
149, 161
Transference, 17, 186
Trauma. *See also* Abuse; Post traumatic
stress disorder substance abuse
as, 58–59, 201
Treatment, 33–35, 109, 256. *See also*
Coercion, treatment under
assessment of, 207, 229, 265–266
and beliefs of primacy of disorders,
48–50
integration of, 176–181, 183–184,
230–231, 247–248, 254–255,
268
length of, 242–244
modified techniques in, 52–64
obstacles to, 61–62, 268–269
order of, 48–49, 67–81
shifting focus of, 71–72, 76–81
variables in, 249–250
Treatment models, 14–16, 62–64
for dual diagnosis patients, 8–10,
13–14, 51–52, 247
on order of treatment, 68–77